THE ANIMATED MARX BROTHERS

THE ANIMATED MARX BROTHERS

by Matthew Hahn

BearManor Media

2018

The Animated Marx Brothers

Published in the United States of America by:

Bear Manor Media
P O Box 71426
Albany, GA 31708

BearManorMedia.com

Printed in the United States.

Cover: The Four Marx Brothers in *Bosko's Dog Race* (1932), author's collection.

TheAnimatedMarxBrothers.Tumblr.com

Typesetting and layout by John Teehan

ISBN—978-1-62933-224-6

To my wife, Cheri, who makes my life worth living even though she never understands any of my jokes.

Marxtoon (marks-'tūn) *n.* 1. an animated cartoon featuring the likenesses and/or sounds of one or more of The Marx Brothers; either in human form or as an anthropomorphic animal, plant, or object; 2. BROADLY: a cartoon that references The Marx Brothers.

TABLE OF CONTENTS

ACKNOWLEDGEMENTS

Over thirty years ago, at *The Freedonia Gazette*'s legendary Open House, I saw the Marxtoons *Soda Squirt* (1933), *Bosko's Picture Show* (1933), and *The Brave Tin Soldier* (1934). I wondered, *Were there more of these?*

The editor of *The Freedonia Gazette* is my friend, Paul Wesolowski, and his Marx shrine/research center, The Weseum, is the first stop for every serious Marx Brothers writer. This author is no exception. The video presenter was Robert Bader, who is responsible for many Marx Brothers books and DVD collections. Their groundbreaking Marx scholarship is the basis for everything that came after. Joe Adamson was an early influence, showing me that a Marx Brothers book could actually be funny.

Glenn Mitchell was probably the first to publish a list of Marxtoons, in *The Marx Brothers Encyclopedia*, although he warned, "Examples are discovered with considerable frequency, rendering inadvisable any claim to a complete list."

Antony Mitchell-Waite is the co-author of *Laurel & Hardy's Animated Antics A–Z 3rd Edition*, which not only identified many of the cartoons in this book, but gave me the idea to write it. Further correspondence with Ant has helped identify more. He also eliminated some possibilities, saving me work.

Bill Marx, Son of Harpo and president of Marx Brothers, Inc., was of great assistance. Robert Finklestein, president of Groucho Marx Productions, and his assistant, Matt Schreiber, provided info and encouragement.

Jerry Beck is the guru of all things animation, and he, too, helped me out. Without the videos on his Cartoon Research Garage Sale, I don't know how this book could have been written. Henry Golas and Dave Smith gave me the story that makes up the Epilogue. Brent Seguine of The Stoogeum provided info on Joe Besser and The Three Stooges cartoons. Ron Hutchinson supplied information for this book before I even knew it was going to be a book. He also wrote the Paul Whiteman joke. Steve Stoliar supplied information on his own Marxtoons and a behind-the-scenes look at Groucho's household. Paul F. Etcheverry is the authority on Scrappy, and he took time out to answer my questions. Rick Goldschmidt is the go-to guy for Rankin-Bass cartoon info. Kim Campbell Beasley of Paws, Inc. provided me with a screener of a Marxtoon that is not commercially available. Doug Stone supplied production details of *The Marx Brothers Show* (2000). My beloved niece, Joy Udvig, and her husband, Josh, answered a video game question for me. My other beloved niece, Jillian Hahn, answered an anthropological question for me. My dear cousin, Jennifer Isaacs, provided tech support. Rolf Ronestar's The Marx Brothers Museum at www.marxbrothers.nu is an invaluable font of info. My friends Nick Santa Maria, Ed Polgardy, Chris Neeson, and Gino Dercola reached out to friends of theirs for me for this book. So did the Vlasic Pickle Stork.

A book like this does not write itself, and God knows I tried. I sent out a query for titles and boy, did you come through. There are too many of you to name individually, but thanks to each and every one.

I am fortunate to live in an area of such great libraries and museums. The National Library of Medicine has the ultra-rare *Laughter is Good Medicine* (1981) and they still have VHS players, God bless 'em. The staff at the Smithsonian Institution's National Museum of American History Archives were happy to show me their Groucho and Harpo Marx Collections. From the Smithsonian Institution's National Portrait Gallery, Erin Beasley, Robyn Asleton, and Rachel Tuteur all gave of their time so I could see the Disney caricatures in their collection.

Frank Ferrante gets the next-to-closing slot here. Frank was my first call when I got the contract for this book. He offered to help me in any way he could, and I took full advantage of that. Frank also keeps Groucho Marx alive through his stage shows and voice-overs in Marxtoons, helping assure that there is an audience for this book.

Finally, I would like to take a bow for Groucho, Harpo, Chico, and Zeppo.

FOREWORD
BY JOE ADAMSON

Fans of The Marx Brothers have grown tired of being limited to the small batch of thirteen feature films the brothers actually made—especially since it's generally only about half that batch that any individual fan cares passionately about. While Laurel & Hardy devotees have 94 theatrical features and short comedies to savor, compare, and contrast—not to mention 337 solo ventures produced before and after the comedians teamed—Marxists have found ourselves limited to a narrow œuvre. In his own lifetime, Groucho once remarked, "There are more books on our films than there are films that we made"—something which was never actually true in his lifetime yet has since proved tellingly accurate. Fans have pored endlessly over every word in those books and every gag in those films like a squad of police dogs worrying a drawer full of socks, and puzzling over such questions as, "Who are those five kids up in Canada?" "What the heck is a Calomel?" and "Why would Groucho get in touch with Chic Sale if he wants to live in a telephone booth?" British fan Matthew Coniam has gone to some length reacting to the critical statement that *Duck Soup* (1933) is the "most typical" of The Marx Brothers' films—although I can't say that I'm aware of any such statement actually having been made.

Once we've exhausted this vein, we sometimes branch out into solo roles and cameos in films such as *Double Dynamite* (1951) and *The Story of Mankind* (1957), surviving episodes of *You Bet Your Life* (1950), and other television appearances, and under-chronicled theatrical short subjects such as the Screen Snapshots and Hollywood on Parade series.

When Richard Patterson, Bob Weide, and I featured the lone surviving production still from the Marxes' silent two-reel comedy, *Humor Risk* (1921), in our documentary, *The Marx Brothers in a Nutshell* (1982), a frame enlargement from a videotape of the show made it to the Internet, where it's been probed, examined, picked over, questioned (Is that really Jobyna Ralston?), and otherwise obsessed over. (One fan has found an "obvious attempt to manipulate the image" where there is, in fact, nothing more than the usual distortion resulting from several generations and variations of copying.) One of these days, I fully intend to get around to making a good digital scan of the photographic copy I was originally given, and either put this speculation to rest, or start it all over again in some other direction.

Here, then, is a treasure trove of material for Marxists of all stripes. Fans who've been poring over *Monkey Business* (1931) and *At the Circus* (1939) for any detectable peep out of Harpo's larynx may be surprised to uncover an entire battery of existing films in which he talks and sings without reservation, usually in a voice appropriate to neither the specific actor in question nor the character he generally played—all this apparently written and animated by people with no real awareness that the performer they were caricaturing was a mime.

Aficionados will no doubt be let down by lame, low-budget efforts such as Columbia's *Hollywood Picnic* (1937) (The Three Marx Brothers hit a baseball, then use a motorcycle to round the bases on a diamond mysteriously devoid of infielders or outfielders.) But if they haven't already discovered Disney's *Mother Goose Goes Hollywood* (1938), and the fact that its few seconds of Marx Brothers comedy are funnier frame for frame than *Room Service* (1938), their live-action effort of the same year, they're in for a treat. (The Disney studio doesn't always acknowledge that the Fats Waller footage in this cartoon, which we managed to include in *The Marx Brothers in a Nutshell* (1982), was ever part of the original release version of the film, but it was.) For reasons I could never figure out, animators generally found it most appropriate to depict The Four Marx Brothers merrily pedaling a bicycle built for four—something they never actually did in any one of their films. Simply providing a fleshed-out list of The Marx Brothers references from *The Simpsons* (1989) marks a major first for this volume.

The Marx Brothers' filmography just got a tremendous boost, but there's more to be done. When John McCabe put together his Laurel and

Hardy filmography for his book, *Mr. Laurel and Mr. Hardy,* in 1961, he apologized for covering their early solo films in only the sketchiest terms and for his subjects' memories being "not equal to the task of remembering films that in their own day were regarded by their creators as little more than evanescent cartoons."

Even evanescent cartoons could conceivably come in for their share of attention, as they did when I finally got *Tex Avery: King of Cartoons* published in 1975, raising a lot of eyebrows by referring to Avery's cartoons not necessarily as great films, or even good films, but just films at all, providing the first filmography of his credited (and some of his uncredited) directorial efforts. This was followed by Leonard Maltin (who is really responsible for publishing *Tex Avery: King of Cartoons*) bringing out *Of Mice and Magic* (with Jerry Beck's filmographies of "evanescent cartoons") in 1980, and many other books and filmographies.

Robert Bader (author of *Groucho Marx and Other Short Stories and Tall Tales* and the new *Four of the Three Musketeers*) startled me when he first made the point that any relevant films shot for television, like Harpo's appearance in *Silent Panic* (1960), should be included in any complete filmography, but the Internet Movie Database (IMDb) now makes those a standard part of its listings, as well as live television appearances, retrospectives, and other documentaries—but even the IMDb doesn't include animated cartoon caricatures.

The first book I've seen to perform that trick is James Fisher's *Eddie Cantor: A Bio-Bibliography*, which came out in 1997, listing animated cartoon caricatures of Cantor in cartoons such as *Mickey's Gala Premier* (1933) and *What's Up, Doc?* (1950), and also newsreels, but segregating both into separate appendices, with only features and shorts in its filmography proper.

James Curtis' 2003 book *W.C. Fields: A Biography* contains the only filmography I'm aware of that integrates animated cartoon caricatures of its subject into the listing of live-action films starring or featuring that personality.

Let's face it, in spite of Ten Best Lists appearing every year and Andrew Sarris in *The American Cinema* declaring that "The feature film… is just one kind of cinema, but the one that most people would identify, rightly or wrongly, as the cinema," live-action feature films were never the Alpha and Omega of the film business—actors, writers, directors, animators, and other film personalities appeared in and/or contributed to all kinds of films, including short subjects, television films, newsreels, documentaries, home movies, advertising films, industrial films, and public service announcements—and yes, animated cartoons!

When you get right down to it, every filmography—not excepting the massive Marx Brothers caricature filmography contained in this volume—is probably best regarded as a work in progress. Now if you'll excuse me, I've got to figure out how I'm going to chronicle Tex Avery's commercials in his next filmography.

PROLOGUE

ANIMATED CARTOONS CONTAINING CELEBRITY caricatures are almost as old as film itself. Felix the Cat was the first animated star to interact with caricatures of movie stars in *Felix in Hollywood* (1923). The advent of sound brought a new crop of actors to the screen, most of whom had extensive theatrical backgrounds and were able to handle the demands of dialogue.

This also added a new dimension to the caricatures on screen, the ability to talk. This was handled with widely varying results. The same characters tended to appear over and over again in these shorts. Some are still familiar today (Charlie Chaplin, W. C. Fields, Laurel & Hardy) while others are, shall we say, less known. (Hugh Herbert, anybody? Ned Sparks? No? How about Roscoe Ates?)

"I wonder if it ever crossed the minds of these stars of yesteryear that many would remain alive in the public consciousness through the cartoons they were caricatured in."

Animation expert Michael Barrier says, "It's, I'm sure, hard to grasp how popular celebrity caricatures were in the 1930s. They were everywhere. Magazines and newspapers ran page after page of them. People like Miguel Covarrubias and Al Hirschfeld were very popular then, and, of course, Hirschfeld did that for many years."

Animators, such as Joe Grant and the aptonymous T. Hee, got into the motion picture business and bounced from one studio to another largely on the strength of their caricatures. A lot of the jokes were also carried over from one picture to another, such as Greta Garbo had big feet, Joe E. Brown had a big mouth, and Sinatra was skinny.

Some studios used caricatures of their own in-house stars under contract. Warner Bros. often did this, for example. Of course, they were not limited to picking from their own stables, and Warner Bros. frequently used The Marx Brothers in their cartoons. This in spite of the fact that The Marx Brothers never did a picture for Warner Bros., and in spite, or because of, the fact that Groucho and Jack Warner had a public (and fabricated) feud over the rights to the title of The Marx Brothers movie, *A Night in Casablanca* (1946).

Animation historian Keith Scott says, "Warner Bros. was the cartoon studio, more than any other, that specialized in parodying celebrities. Friz Freleng said that was because most of the people who worked there were show biz buffs themselves. Friz Freleng was an old Vaudeville buff." Columbia, a Poverty Row studio with few stars of its own, also showcased The Marx Brothers often.

Caricatures of The Marx Brothers would have been instantly recognizable to an audience in the 1930s, with their distinctive looks and sounds. They were frequently used as a form of shorthand, to inject zaniness into a scene that isn't really that zany.

As with the team itself, the animated Marx Brothers' heyday was the 1930s. Zeppo left the team after *Duck Soup* (1933), but his cartoon career continued. In the 1940s, appearances tapered off, and by the 1950s, team cameos were rare in cartoons. As a solo act, Groucho became a star all over again with his radio quiz show, *You Bet Your Life* (1947). In 1950, the show moved to TV and ran eleven seasons. Many of these seasons had animated caricatures of Groucho and others driving DeSotos, his long-time sponsor, in the credits. There were also stand-alone animated commercials, with and without Groucho, and different animated credits after he and DeSoto parted ways. Some of the syndicated versions also have animated credits. *You Bet Your Life* (1950), with its duck and Secret Word, has been much parodied in animation, even long after the show was cancelled.

Chico died in 1961 and Harpo in 1964, but Groucho lived long enough to see the beginning of The Marx Brothers revival. The college students of the 1960s, with their antiestablishment stance, saw The Marx Brothers as heroes and role models, and Marx Brothers posters decorated dorm walls. Filmation did a pilot for an animated series, *The New Marx Bros. Show* (1966). In 1970, Groucho himself repeated his Broadway role in an animated version of the "Napoleon's First Waterloo" sketch from *I'll Say She Is* (1924), the only time this skit was committed to film. (Zeppo did not repeat his role.) In 1974, *Animal Crackers* (1930) received a rerelease, and was treated as though it was a new picture. *You Bet Your Life* (1950) reruns went into syndication again.

Groucho died in 1977 and Zeppo in 1979, but it's a measure of The Marx Brothers' popularity and importance that they live on in caricatures in television shows such as *The Simpsons* (1989) and *Family Guy* (1999). Fans on the Internet make their own Marx Brothers avatars and Marx Brothers cartoons. The search goes on today for an animated television pilot or even a feature film with The Marx Brothers.

THEATRICAL MARXTOONS

The Bird Store (January 16, 1932)
Walt Disney Productions. Directed by Wilfred Jackson. Produced by Walt Disney. Animated by David Hand. Animators: Rudy Zamora (Four Marx Birds), Norm Ferguson.

After serving as an ambulance driver in France just after World War I, Walt Disney returned to Kansas City, where he worked as an apprentice artist at the Pesmen-Rubin Commercial Art Studio and met fellow artist Ub Iwerks. Later, he founded Laugh-O-gram Films with Fred Harman, and hired Ub Iwerks, Rudolf Ising, and Fred's brother, Hugh. Disney had a tame mouse at his desk, and Hugh Harman drew some sketches of mice around a photograph of Disney. In 1923, the studio went into bankruptcy, after Disney had moved to Hollywood, where his Alice Comedies ended up being distributed by Charles Mintz.

Disney created the animated character of Oswald the Lucky Rabbit for Mintz, who distributed the character through Universal Studios. In spring 1928, he asked for a budget increase. Although the character was doing well, Mintz insisted Disney take a 20% budget cut, reminding him that Universal owned the character, and informing Disney that Mintz had already signed most of Disney's employees, including Robert McKimson, Hugh Harman, and Rudolf Ising, but not Ub Iwerks to a new contract. Disney produced the shorts he contractually owed Mintz, and vowed to never again create a character to which he did not own the rights.

A Silly Symphony. The Silly Symphonies series started in 1929, was heavy on music and light on plot, and was much-imitated by other studios.

Birds in the store sing. The Four Marx Birds whistle just enough of Chico's theme, "I'm Daffy Over You" (written with Solly Violinsky), to avoid a lawsuit. A hungry cat prowls outside. He gains access through the transom and pounces on a roller canary chick that has left its cage and is eating in a sack of feed. The other caged birds watch helplessly. The chick escapes through a patch in the feed sack and locks himself in a cage, but it falls apart. He gets in another cage which is unlocked, but the cat is able to reach him. Some birds manage to escape their cage, rescue the chick, and imprison the cat in a cage, which is then launched through a skylight, landing in the City Dog Pound.

Apparently the first Marxtoon.

• • • • • • • • •

Hollywood Goes Krazy (February 13, 1932)

Columbia Pictures. Directed by Manny Gould, Ben Harrison. Produced by Charles Mintz. Animated by Jack Carr. Writer: George Herriman (comic strip). Story: Manny Gould. Music: Joe DeNat.

Under Charles Mintz at Columbia, Krazy Kat lost the original George Herriman comic strip setting, supporting characters, and everything that made this sexually ambiguous character unique. He became a Mickey Mouse wannabe, a bland figure with a look-alike girlfriend and a dog. Mintz even changed the design of the character.

Krazy and his girlfriend arrive in Hollywood, where she is preyed upon by a literal Wolf with a casting couch. Krazy hears her cries for help and tries to get past the guard into the studio, disguising himself as Charlie Chaplin and then Groucho Marx. He manages to sneak in when Eddie Cantor shows up. The guard pursues him through the lot. Krazy finally finds her and beats up the Wolf, only to be told by the Director that he has "ruined the scene."

• • • • • • • • •

Bosko's Dog Race (June 25, 1932)

Warner Bros. Directed by Hugh Harman. Produced by Hugh Harman, Rudolf Ising. Animated by Rollin Hamilton, Norman Blackburn. Music: Frank Marsales. Cast: Rochelle Hudson (Honey), Johnny Murray (Bosko).

A Looney Tune, Warner Bros.' answer to Disney's Silly Symphonies, but more plot-based than some of the Merrie Melodies that would follow. Bosko, the first star of the series, was created by Hugh Harman in 1927 to capitalize on the invention of talking pictures (talkies), and originally registered with the US Copyright Office as a "Negro boy" who spoke in dialect, although in later years, Harman denied this. A test cartoon led to a contract with Leon Schlesinger and Warner Bros. for not only Harman and Ising, but also animator Isadore "Friz" Freleng. Freleng was an animator who worked with Harman and Ising at the United Film Ad Service in Kansas City, Missouri. Walt Disney hired him to work on the Oswald the Lucky Rabbit cartoons at Harman's suggestion. Later, Freleng worked for Charles Mintz and Walter Lantz.

Bosko sees a billboard for an upcoming dog race, with a prize of $5000. He tells his dog, Bruno, "You're gonna run in this race, and you're gonna win." Bruno morphs into Joe E. Brown and cries, with his big mouth, "Noooooooooooo!" At the dog race, we see why the dogs are running so fast: they are pursued by dogcatchers, The Four Marx Brothers, who sing, even Harpo. Bruno ends up chased by bees, which drive him across the finish line first. Iris out on Bosko and his girlfriend, Honey.

FUN FACTS: Harpo would play a dogcatcher later that year in *Horse Feathers* (1932).

The Marx Brothers footage was later reused in *Bosko's Picture Show* (1933).

• • • • • • • • •

Seeing Stars (September 12, 1932)

Columbia Pictures. Directed by Manny Gould, Ben Harrison. Produced by Charles Mintz. Written by George Herriman (comic strip). Story: Ben Harrison. Music: Joe DeNat.

Krazy Kat is playing an upright piano at a Hollywood nightclub. The Four Marx Brothers pop up out of the top of the piano, and then ride away on a four-seat tandem bike. Harpo hops off the bike to pursue the cigarette girl into the Ladies Lounge, which he is thrown out of. Krazy shares a plate of spaghetti with Ben Turpin until Jimmy Durante smashes it over Krazy's head. Harpo plays the spaghetti strands and then he is distracted by some pretty women. Krazy tangos with Marie Dressler until Groucho cuts in.

Celebrity Chase, a Krazy Kat Marxtoon of unknown vintage, not seen by this author, is believed to be this cartoon edited for the home film market.

• • • • • • • • •

Scrappy's Party (February 13, 1933)

Columbia Pictures. Directed by Dick Huemer. Produced by Charles Mintz. Animated by Sid Marcus, Art Davis. Music: Joe DeNat.

Dick Huemer created Scrappy, a little boy character, for Charles Mintz in 1931. After Huemer left Mintz's studio in 1933, colleagues Sid Marcus and Art Davis took over the series.

It's Scrappy's birthday, and he and his little brother, Oopy, decide to have a party. He calls to invite Joe E. Brown, Laurel & Hardy, The Four Marx Brothers (who are in the shower), Marie Dressler, Jimmy Durante, Greta Garbo, John D. Rockefeller, Albert Einstein, Mahatma Gandhi, and others. Most guests arrive by bicycle, including The Marx Brothers on a four-seat tandem. Al Capone calls in his regrets, he is in prison. This time, all four Marx Brothers tango with Marie Dressler.

• • • • • • • • •

The Lumber Champ (March 13, 1933)

Walter Lantz Productions. Directed by Walter Lantz, Bill Nolan. Produced by Walter Lantz. Animated by Walter Lantz, Bill Nolan.

Walter Lantz was a newspaper cartoonist, who started animating at various studios in New York City, including Bray Pictures Corporation, where he animated, directed, and appeared in the cartoon series Dinky Doodles. Eventually, he moved to California, where Carl Laemmle, President and founder of Universal Pictures, asked him to set up a cartoon studio on the lot. Lantz did the Oswald series for Universal, and hired Harman, Ising, and Freleng. Pooch was an anthropomorphic dog who appeared in thirteen shorts. Lantz explains how he came up with the character: "The situations were like this: there was a little tramp with a small bundle on his back walking down the railroad track with his dog, Pooch. The stories were like the ones I made for Bray—like Dinky Doodles. I got the idea from those, using similar situations."

Pooch gets hired at a lumber camp, but is sleeping on the job. He only escapes the boss's lash because a squirrel cuts it with a pair of scissors. Pooch goes into the woods to cut trees, and meets his girlfriend, a coonhound, who is painting pictures. They sing "The Cute Little Things You Do" to the accompaniment of an all-tree orchestra. A Harpo Marx tree plays along on a spider web and a Groucho Marx tree sings. A sexy female tree sings, and Harpo tree chases after her.

The boss dognaps Pooch's girlfriend and takes off downriver on a log. Pooch follows on another log, propelled by beavers. The boss ties Pooch's girlfriend to train tracks and runs the train towards her. Pooch bends one track, causing the train and the boss to split in half and saving his girlfriend.

• • • • • • • • •

The Organ Grinder (April 8, 1933)

Warner Bros. Directed by Rudolf Ising. Produced by Hugh Harman, Rudolf Ising. Animated by Rollin Hamilton, Thomas McKimson. Music: Frank Marsales.

A Merrie Melodies cartoon. The early Merrie Melodies were more like Silly Symphonies, music-based. This one uses the title tune, several traditional ditties, and songs from the Warner Bros. catalog. A talented monkey dances, plays as a one-primate band, and imitates celebrities, including Laurel & Hardy and Harpo Marx.

• • • • • • • • •

Bosko's Knight-Mare (April 29, 1933)

Warner Bros. Directed by Hugh Harman. Produced by Hugh Harman, Rudolf Ising. Animated by Robert McKimson, Robert Stokes. Music: Frank Marsales.

A Looney Tune. Bosko falls asleep after reading a book on knighthood and dreams he is back in medieval days. Dressed in shining armor, he arrives at the moat of a castle and calls out, doing a Joe E. Brown imitation. Even Bruno wears armor. The drawbridge lowers, and he meets the Knights of the Round Table, including The Four Marx Brothers, Jimmy Durante, Ed Wynn, Mahatma Gandhi, and Oliver Hardy. Bosko does a Stan Laurel imitation. Everybody dances to the song I love the melody of, "42nd Street."

A villain arrives at the side door of the castle and chews through the lock to get to Honey in the tower. Bosko hears her cries for help and goes to rescue her. The villain leaps out of the tower with Honey onto his horse, and the chase is on.

Bosko pursues them back to the villain's castle, where the villain knocks him out. Honey tries to bring him to. When he wakes up, Bruno is licking him.

• • • • • • • • •

Mickey's Gala Premier (July 1, 1933)

Walt Disney Productions. Directed by Burt Gillett. Produced by Walt Disney. Music by Frank Churchill. Character Design by Joe Grant. Animators: Art Babbitt, Chuck Couch, Joe Grant, Jack King, Ed Love, Dick Lundy, Hamilton Luske, Fred Moore, Charles Philippi, Leonard Sebring, Ben Sharpsteen, Cy Young. Cast: Walt Disney (Mickey Mouse), Marcellite Garner (Minnie Mouse), Jerry Lester (Maurice Chevalier/Ed Wynn/Jimmy Durante/Eddie Cantor).

At his new studio, Walt Disney asked Iwerks to come up with a funny animal character. Iwerks drew a horse and a cow (these later became Horace Horsecollar and Clarabelle Cow), dogs and cats, and a frog (which later became Flip the Frog). The origin of Mickey Mouse is unclear, although it is clear that Ub initially drew them for Walt, perhaps inspired by Harman's sketches from the Laugh-O-gram days. He was first named Mortimer until Disney's wife, Lillian, persuaded Disney to change it. The character made two false starts before making his official debut in *Steamboat Willie* (1928). Walt Disney originally voiced the character. Mickey Mouse spawned a spate of imitators, but none of them ever eclipsed his star power, and few if any are going strong today.

At Grauman's Chinese Theatre, all the stars are out. The Keystone Kops (Ben Turpin, Ford Sterling, Mack Swain, Harry Langdon, and Chester Conklin) sing the title song. Wallace Beery arrives with Marie Dressler. Lionel Barrymore (as Rasputin) shows up with brother John and sister Ethel. Laurel & Hardy are there, as are The Marx Brothers. Maurice Chevalier sings (sadly, not "You Brought a New Kind of Love to Me"), as do Eddie Cantor, dressed as *The Kid from Spain* (1932); Jimmy Durante; an unlikely trio of Jean Harlow, Joan Crawford, and Bette Davis; and an even less likely quartet of Harold Lloyd, Clark Gable, Adolphe Menjou, and Edward G. Robinson. Sid Grauman tears tickets from George Arliss, Joe E. Brown, and Buster Keaton, while Charlie Chaplin crawls past without a ticket. A morbidly obese Groucho waddles up, and Sid asks him how he is. Chico, Zeppo, and Harpo pop out of Groucho's jacket, answering, "Oh we're fine," even Harpo, and they scatter. Finally, Mickey rolls up with his crew: his girlfriend Minnie, his dog Pluto, Horace, and Clarabelle.

The show begins, *Galloping Romance*. In the cartoon-within-the-cartoon, Mickey is playing on his xylophone while Minnie tickles the ivories. She is "mousenapped" by Peg Leg Pete, who escapes on horseback. Mickey gives chase on his wheeled xylophone, then by turtle, five-legged mollusk (pentapus), and finally kangaroo. He dispatches Pete with cannon shot and rescues Minnie.

Will Rogers pulls Mickey onstage with his lasso. The audience, which has found this to be the funniest film of all time, congratulates Mickey. Greta Garbo showers him with kisses. Mickey wakes up to find he is actually being licked by Pluto!

Other celebrities caricatured include Mae West, Ed Wynn, Wheeler & Woolsey, Bela Lugosi, Lon Chaney, Boris Karloff, Douglas Fairbanks, John Gilbert, Fredric March, Rudy Vallee, William Powell, Will Hays, Janet Gaynor, Constance Bennett, Gloria Swanson, and Marlene Dietrich.

Joe Grant was a caricaturist at the *Los Angeles Record*, where he was discovered by Disney and brought to this project. He became supervisor of the Character Model Department.

FUN FACTS: *Mickey's Gala Premier* was the last show on the BBC Television Service before it stopped broadcasting on September 1, 1939, two days before the United Kingdom declared war on Germany. It was shown in its entirety. It was thought that the VHF signal from the broadcast would serve as a homing beacon for the enemy planes closing in on London. On June 7, 1946, the BBC resumed broadcasting with *Mickey's Gala Premier*. The story that the 1939 broadcast was interrupted and the 1946 broadcast picked up where the first left off is an urban legend. The continuity announcer, Jasmine Bligh, introduced the cartoon by saying, "Now then, as we were saying before we were so rudely interrupted."

Reedited and released for home exhibitions under the title *Movie Star Mickey* (1933). New animation is included in *Galloping Romance*. *Galloping Romance* has never been available as a stand-alone cartoon.

Some sources (including the DVD menu for *Mickey Mouse in Black and White*) would have it *Mickey's Gala Premiere*, but the actual title card lacks the final "e".

● ● ● ● ● ● ● ● ●

Pin Feathers (July 3, 1933)

Walter Lantz Productions. Directed by Walter Lantz, Bill Nolan. Produced by Walter Lantz. Animated by Walter Lantz, Bill Nolan.

Pooch the Pup is walking along when a young bird passes him, chasing a worm. The worm turns and eats the bird. Pooch unzips the worm and lets the bird out.

The bird goes home and his mother gives him a book of *Flying Lessons* and demonstrates for him. The bird attempts to fly and falls to the ground. Pooch tries to catch the bird in his hat, but the bird goes right through. Pooch borrows a few tail feathers from a passing turkey and gives them to the bird to use as wings.

That mission accomplished, the bird has to take music lessons from Prof. Coo Coo. The professor is unimpressed and literally kicks the bird out. Pooch attempts to teach the bird to sing and eventually gives him a whistle to swallow so he can sing, well, like a bird. An Ed Wynn bird and an Eddie Cantor bird stop to appreciate his song. A Harpo Marx bird plays along on his tail like a harp. The bird also attracts the attentions of a hungry cat, who lures him in by pulling the fur down on his tail and pretending it is a worm.

As the cat tries to get away with the bird, Pooch passes forks to other birds, which they shoot at the cat using the harp-tail of the Harpo bird like a bow. The birds attack the cat with a lawn mower, a rat trap, and hot tongs. The cat runs into a cage and shuts himself in. It is the Dog Pound. Pooch and the bird happily walk away.

Although the Ed Wynn and Eddie Cantor birds are good caricatures, the harp-playing bird bears no resemblance at all to Harpo, and this film's status as a Marxtoon is questionable. A reported Marxtoon of unknown vintage, *Lessons for Birds*, not seen by this author, is believed to be this cartoon edited for the home movie market.

• • • • • • • • •

Cubby's World Flight (August 25, 1933)

Van Beuren Studios. Directed by Hugh Harman, Rudolf Ising. Produced by George Stallings. Animated by Isadore (Friz) Freleng, Paul Smith.

After Harman and Ising cut all ties with Leon Schlesinger and Warner Bros. over money, they were offered a contract to produce the Cubby Bear cartoon series at Van Beuren. Cubby was Van Beuren's answer to Mickey Mouse.

Cubby Bear embarks on a world flight to much fanfare, including The Four Marx Brothers as Boy Scouts. They all sing his praises, even Harpo. Even Charles Lindbergh comes to see him off. "Why don't you come up sometime?" asks Cubby. The enthusiasm seems misplaced, since Cubby seems to be unfamiliar with his own airplane, let alone the principles of aviation. Although Cubby barely makes it off the ground, he crosses most of the conterminous United States before tunneling through the earth to China. He never said he was flying around the world. He flies over Germany, where he is toasted by President Paul von Hindenburg, Chancellor Adolf Hitler, and a third Nazi (Joachim von Ribbentrop?). Lotsa Nazis in this movie. In France, a statue of Napoleon comes to life, morphs into Maurice Chevalier, and serenades Cubby. (Sadly, not "You Brought a New Kind of Love to Me.") Over the Atlantic, his plane is repeatedly struck by lightning, but he flies literally by the seat of his pants and lands on the Statue of Liberty, where he is hailed by New Yorkers and King Kong.

FUN FACT: Although *Bosko's Picture Show* (1933) is sometimes credited with the first appearance of Hitler in a narrative film, this cartoon predated it.

● ● ● ● ● ● ● ● ●

Bosko's Picture Show (August 26, 1933)

Warner Bros. Directed by Hugh Harman, Isadore (Friz) Freleng. Produced by Hugh Harman, Rudolf Ising. Animated by Isadore Freleng, Carman "Max" Maxwell. Written by Manny Gould, Ben Harrison. Music: Frank Marsales. Cast: Rochelle Hudson (Honey), Johnny Murray (Bosko).

Bosko is running the titular picture show, and plays the Furtilizer Organ along with "The Golddiggers' Song (We're in the Money)". This is followed by a newsreel with footage of The Four Marx Brothers from *Bosko's Dog Race* (1932). Also in the newsreel are caricatures of Jack Dempsey, Jimmy Durante, and Adolf Hitler. Next up is a "Haurel and Lardy" short. The feature is a "TNT Picture" entitled *"HE DONE HER DIRT" (And How!)*. Honey is riding her bicycle, followed by The Four Marx Brothers (again) on a four-seat tandem bike (again). Uncharacteristically for him, but not for Bosko movies, Harpo sings (again!). Honey is kidnapped by Dirty Dalton, who jumps a train with her. She calls for help and Bosko runs up on stage and puts his head through the picture of Dalton on the screen, neutralizing him.

This was the last Bosko Looney Tune. Harman and Ising learned from the experiences of Disney, their former boss, who lost the rights to his beloved character, Oswald, and they copyrighted Bosko when they were at Warner Bros. and brought him with them to Metro-Goldwyn-Mayer (MGM). Friz Freleng is believed to have been an uncredited co-director on this movie.

FUN FACT: Bosko apparently calls Dalton a "dirty fuck."

• • • • • • • • •

Movie Struck (September 8, 1933)

Columbia Pictures. Directed by Dick Huemer. Produced by Charles Mintz. Animated by Art Davis. Music: Joe DeNat.

Scrappy and Oopy's reading of "Twinkle, Twinkle Little Star" gets them a Hollywood contract with The Terrific Huge Collosal [sic] Gigantic Moving Picture Corporation working in the Lunch Room. They meet Laurel & Hardy, Adolphe Menjou, Eddie Cantor, Douglas Fairbanks, and Groucho Marx, among others. In the Lunch Room are Roscoe Ates, Greta Garbo, Jimmy Durante, George Arliss, and Harold Lloyd. The Four Marx Brothers eat soup and dance. Joe E. Brown has a big mouth.

• • • • • • • • •

Soda Squirt (October 12, 1933)

Celebrity Productions, Inc. Directed by Ub Iwerks. Produced by Ub Iwerks, Pat Powers. Animated by Ub Iwerks. Music: Carl Stalling.

Ub Iwerks left Disney after a series of disputes and was replaced by Burt Gillett. Iwerks was offered the princely sum of $300 a week to open his own cartoon studio by Pat Powers of Celebrity Productions, Inc. Iwerks hired composer Carl Stallings and animators Grim Natwick, Max Fleischer, Rudy Zamora, Al Eugster, and Shamus Culhane. Chuck Jones was given a job as a cel washer. The first series, in 1930, was to feature Tony the Frog, but Iwerks changed the name to Flip. *Fiddlesticks* (1930) used two-strip Technicolor, making it the first color sound cartoon. The films were distributed by (MGM), who decided to produce them in black and white. This was to be the last cartoon for Flip, who had worn out his welcome at MGM.

It's the Grand Opening of Flip's Drug Store, complete with klieg lights, red carpet, and a live radio broadcast. On the red carpet are Laurel & Hardy, Jimmy Durante, Buster Keaton, Lionel Barrymore (as Rasputin), and The Four Marx Brothers. Harpo honks for the radio. Then Mae West walks by, and all four Marxes take off after her.

Inside, the celebrities place their orders. The Marx Brothers have an orange coke with four straws. Joe E. Brown has an ice cream cone, which he eats with his big mouth, followed by almost an entire cake.

An effeminate man interrupts Flip's flirtation with Mae West by ordering a chocolate soda. Flip spikes the drink with hair tonic, castor oil, tacks, Flit, and ink. When the effeminate man drinks it, he turns into Fredric March as Mr. Hyde. The Four Marx Brothers disappear behind the counter, leaving behind only their wigs and hats and Groucho's glasses, mustache, and cigar.

Limos leave Flip's Drug Store in reverse. Mr. Hyde trashes the drug store. Flip tries to stop him, but is grabbed by Mr. Hyde, who shakes Flip over and over again, hitting an atomizer bulb for the perfume "Eau de Pansy". This changes him back into his old self, and he dances away. Flip, in his ruined store, hits the cash register, ringing up a "No Sale" and destroying it.

• • • • • • • • •

Stratos Fear (November 11, 1933)

Celebrity Productions, Inc. Directed by Ub Iwerks. Produced by Ub Iwerks. Music: Carl Stalling. Cast: Jane Withers (Voice Actor).

Willie Whopper was the next series after Flip the Frog for Ub Iwerks' animation studio. Willie was a boy who told outrageous "whoppers" or lies. His catch phrase was, "Say, did I ever tell ya this one?" Willie's character was redesigned for this short by Iwerks, and from this point, he and the series were more widely praised. The shorts were released by MGM until MGM and Iwerks ended the series by mutual agreement. Iwerks was later replaced by Harman and Ising with their Happy Harmonies series.

Willie is not cooperating with the dentist, who gives him gas to put him under. The already balloon-like Willie inflates and floats away through outer space, where he is spotted by aliens on another planet. A meteor shoots Willie down and he starts his descent. The aliens suck him in with a giant vacuum cleaner.

The head alien shows Willie a dentist's chair, and Willie runs into another room, only to have the door nailed shut behind him. He falls down a trap door into a room where hybrids of aliens and instruments play music. A ghostly Harpo Marx plays a peacock's tail like a harp.

Willie's tap dancing awakens an Egyptian-style vamp from a coffin. She sounds a little like Mae West but looks like Theda Bara. Theda Bara's silent film *Cleopatra* (1917) is a lost film (a few frames survive), but it is quite possible the animators in 1933 had seen it in its entirety. Willie goes off with her, and she morphs into the head alien. Willie tries to run away, but he is trapped in the ribcage of a skeleton. He wakes up still in the dentist's chair. It was all a dream!

● ● ● ● ● ● ● ● ●

Hollywood Babies (November 11, 1933)

Columbia Pictures. Directed by Dick Huemer. Produced by Charles Mintz. Animated by Art Davis.

Scrappy and Oopy are making a movie and they enlist the help of the babies of Jimmy Durante, Joe E. Brown, The Four Marx Brothers, Laurel & Hardy, Greta Garbo, Will Rogers, Marie Dressler, Wallace Beery, Ed Wynn, Eddie Cantor, Ben Turpin, Charlie Chaplin, and others. All of them look remarkably like their parents.

● ● ● ● ● ● ● ● ●

The Merry Old Soul (November 27, 1933)

Walter Lantz Productions. Directed by Walter Lantz, Bill Nolan. Produced by Walter Lantz. Animated by Walter Lantz, Bill Nolan. Cast: Bernice Hansen (Voice).

Oswald the Lucky Rabbit was created by Ub Iwerks and Walt Disney at the Walt Disney Studio. As detailed above, Walt Disney lost the rights to the character when his contract ended with Charles Mintz. George Winkler took over for Disney and hired Hugh Harman and Rudolf Ising to animate. When Walter Lantz took over production of the Oswald cartoons, he brought in his own animators and Harman and Ising were out of a job.

Oswald is getting his teeth pulled by the dentist, who bops him on the head with a mallet. Then a bulletin comes over the radio: Old King

Cole has the blues! Oswald goes to his car and rides through the streets, shouting "Old King Cole has the blues!" He rouses Greta Garbo, who decides to stay home. Fire Chief Ed Wynn drives his hook and ladder truck there with Charlie Chaplin, Buster Keaton, Joe E. Brown, and Laurel & Hardy. Will Rogers rides sidesaddle on a pig.

Apparently, Old King Cole has the blues because his Jester is really unfunny. Oswald arrives and introduces Paul Whiteman and the all-Paul Whiteman Orchestra. Songs of nursery rhymes are sung by Roscoe Ates, Edna May Oliver, W. C. Fields, Al Jolson, and Mae West. The King is entertained, as the jealous Jester looks on, fearing for his job.

Laurel & Hardy throw pies at each other, which makes the King laugh, but not as much as when he gets hit with a pie. Soon, pies are flying everywhere. They hit Jimmy Durante, Harold Lloyd (whose glasses have built-in wipers), ZaSu Pitts, and The Four Marx Brothers (Groucho ducks, but is hit with another pie).

The Jester "rabbitnaps" Oswald, ties him to a chair, and begins to torture him. It turns out the real torturer is the dentist. It was all a dream!

Academy Award Nominee, Best Short Subject, Cartoon, 1934.

● ● ● ● ● ● ● ● ●

Scrappy's Auto Show (December 8, 1933)

Columbia Pictures. Directed by Sid Marcus. Produced by Charles Mintz. Animated by Art Davis. Music: Joe DeNat.

Scrappy and Oopy go to the auto show, which inspires them to build their own car out of ordinary household items: half a tub, sausages, a door, etc. They literally crash the auto show with their creation. Oopy is the call boy announcing the features of the car, including an automatic windshield and nose wiper, which is demonstrated on The Great Schnozzola himself, Jimmy Durante. They inexplicably win first prize, which is awarded by Henry Ford. The four herald trumpeters seen throughout the cartoon are revealed to be The Four Marx Brothers. Instead of driving away, Scrappy and Oopy are carried off in their car.

• • • • • • • • •

The Autograph Hunter (January 5, 1934)

Columbia Pictures. Directed by Manny Gould, Ben Harrison. Produced by Charles Mintz. Animated by Allen Rose, Preston Blair. Written by George Herriman. Music: Joe DeNat.

Krazy Kat is waiting outside The Brown Derby and asks for John Barrymore's autograph. Krazy is then run over by The Four Marx Brothers. Denied access by a bouncer, Krazy enters through the back door, where he finds Laurel & Hardy in the kitchen washing dishes. In the restaurant are Edward G. Robinson, Mae West, Jimmy Durante, Greta Garbo, Joe E. Brown, Eddie Cantor, Wallace Beery, Marie Dressler, Charlie Chaplin, and Maurice Chevalier. The bouncer chases Krazy all around the restaurant, but in the end, it turns out he just wants Krazy's autograph.

• • • • • • • • •

Sock-a-Bye Baby (January 19, 1934)

Fleischer Studios. Directed by Dave Fleischer. Produced by Max Fleischer. Animated by Seymour Kneitel, Roland Crandall. Cast: William "Red Pepper Sam" Costello (Voice).

Dave Fleischer was a cutter at Pathé Films. His brother, Max, invented the Rotoscope, which allowed live footage to be traced frame-by-frame. They teamed up to make the Koko cartoons for Paramount, which were an instant hit. With the dawn of sound films, they created a new character, Betty Boop.

Popeye, the language-mangling, spinach-eating sailor with freakishly muscular forearms, made his first appearance in the comic strip *Thimble Theatre* on January 17, 1929, in the cartoon's tenth year. He became so popular that eventually it was renamed *Popeye*. His first animated appearance was in *Popeye the Sailor* (1933), technically a Betty Boop cartoon, but he was soon headlining his own series. He was played first by William Costello, and later by Jack Mercer. The "post-synched" dialogue, (dialogue dubbed in after the animation was produced) made it seem stilted but allowed the voice actors to ad-lib under their breath, which was used to great advantage in the Popeye cartoons. His sometime girlfriend, Olive Oyl, was sometimes played by the sometime voice of Betty Boop, Mae Questel.

Popeye is baby-sitting Betty Boop's brother, Billy, and woe betide anyone who makes noise that might disturb the baby. First to incur Popeye's wrath is Harpo Marx, playing on a street corner. Popeye sends him to Heaven to play with the angels. Popeye gives his pipe to Billy, and smoking it knocks the baby out. Popeye goes on to destroy a music school, an ocean liner, a radio station, a construction site, and a traffic jam, only to himself drop a safety pin and awaken Billy.

● ● ● ● ● ● ● ● ●

The Brave Tin Soldier (April 7, 1934)

Celebrity Pictures. Directed by Shamus Culhane (uncredited), Al Eugster (uncredited), Ub Iwerks. Writing Credits (in alphabetical order): Hans Christian Andersen (fairy tale), Shamus Culhane (uncredited), Otto Englander (uncredited), Al Eugster (uncredited). Produced by Ub Iwerks, Pat Powers (uncredited). Music: Arthur Turkisher. Animators: Shamus Culhane (as Jimmie Culhane), Al Eugster. Co-layout Artist: Shamus Culhane (uncredited). Presenter: Pat Powers.

The ComiColor Cartoons were the last series produced by the Ub Iwerks studio. They were twenty-five animated shorts made from 1933 to 1936. In 1934, they lost their distributor, MGM, and this movie and others following had to be self-distributed by Celebrity Pictures. They were shot in Cinecolor, a two-strip color process. Most of them were based on fairy tales and familiar stories.

This is an entry into the popular genre Toys (or Art, or Books, or Whatnot) Come to Life. A toymaker carelessly drops a tin soldier, breaking off his leg. The toymaker throws the Soldier into the trash and goes to bed. At midnight, things begin to happen. There is a blackface doll who quotes Al Jolson, an Eddie Cantor jack-in-the-box, and Laurel & Hardy wobbly toys. The Soldier crawls out of the trash, and limps along, using his rifle as a crutch. The other toys laugh at him, but a Ballerina toy says, "Aw, poor soldier," and he is instantly smitten. A Harpo Marx jack-in-the-box pops up and honks his horn, startling the soldier, and causing him to fall into some letter blocks, which rearrange on his head to spell, "NUTS TO YOU." The Ballerina pushes the blocks off his head and helps him up.

Elsewhere, a toy King leaves his castle with a military escort, on a carriage pulled by toy mice. He comes upon the Soldier pushing the Ballerina in the stirrup of a hobbyhorse like a swing. The King tells the Soldier to scram, which he does, reluctantly. The Ballerina receives unwanted advances from the King, so the Soldier launches a rocket into the King's butt. He tries to get away, but he is arrested by the military escort.

In court, the King asks the Soldier if he is guilty or not guilty. A Groucho jack-in-the-box pops up, and says, "Objection sustained." The King points to the hole in the seat of his robe and says, "You're guilty." The soldier says, "No!" Groucho says, "Objection overruled." The King says, "You are guilty." Groucho says, "Give him a fair trial and then we'll shoot him." The Ballerina pleads for the Soldier's life.The King says, "Execute him."

In front of the firing squad, the Soldier is offered a blindfold, but he blows his nose into it. The Ballerina throws herself in front of the Soldier, but the execution proceeds anyway, and they are both knocked into the fire. There, they melt into a red heart with a green bow. Their spirits travel up the chimney and to Toy Heaven, where St. Peter greets them on a hover board and restores the Soldier's leg. The Soldier is now able to dance, and he and the Ballerina walk through Toy Heaven's gate.

The TV/video version, *The Steadfast Tin Soldier*, has an alternate soundtrack, and eliminates dialogue, including Groucho's.

• • • • • • • • •

Wax Works (June 25, 1934)

Walter Lantz Productions. Directed by Walter Lantz, Bill Nolan. Animated by Manuel Moreno, George Grandpré, Lester Kline, Verne Harding, Fred Kopietz, and Victor McLeod. Produced by Walter Lantz. Music: James Bietrich. Cast: Bernice Hansen (Little Boy).

A "baby," who can walk and talk perfectly well, is left by his "poor penniless Mother" on the steps of Oswald's Wax Works, a museum, along with a note requesting a good home for him. Oswald briefly resists, then takes him in. After the baby tells Oswald he doesn't need to use the "salon," they go to bed.

At midnight, Art Comes to Life. The baby needs to use the salon, and grabs a candle. Afterwards, he asks Venus de Milo to button him up, then The Thinker. Nero fiddles. A discus hits Cyrano de Bergerac's nose, and he plays it like a 78 rpm record.

Romeo climbs to the top of the balcony to see Juliet, but Groucho Marx pushes him to the ground. "Not tonight, Romeo." Napoleon seeks to make whoopee with Josephine, but Groucho pushes him away. "Not tonight, Josephine." Napoleon shoots him in the head. He uses a pop gun, but it still knocks Groucho cold.

The baby is caught by The Hunchback of Notre Dame, who lives in the Horror Chamber with Bluebeard, Dracula, Frankenstein, The Mummy, Mr. Hyde, and The Invisible Man. The baby makes a run for it, and accidentally turns on a blow torch, which he uses to chase the monsters until The Invisible Man grabs it and threatens to put him into hot wax. Oswald hears The Invisible Man cackle, and rushes to investigate. The Invisible Man threatens to pour wax onto Oswald. Oswald wakes up to find the baby dripping candle wax on him. It was all a dream!

The reissue print is called *The Wax Museum*, and lacks the title song.

• • • • • • • • •

Viva Buddy (December 12, 1934)

Warner Bros. Directed by Jack Carr. Cast: Billy Bletcher (Pancho), Buddy (Jack Carr).

Buddy was the second star of the Looney Tunes series, a paler, more human version of Bosko, whose creators, Hugh Harman and Rudolf Ising, had departed for the greener pastures (and money) of MGM. (Wouldn't Harman-Ising have been a better name than Looney Tunes?) Leon Schlesinger told Earl Duvall to create a new character, and after a troubled beginning (Schlesinger rejected the first two shorts and Friz Freleng reedited them), Buddy limped forth. Bob Clampett called him "Bosko in whiteface" and "a nothing."

Buddy rides into a sleepy (literally) Mexican town and wakes up everyone in the cantina with music. Pancho, himself a caricature of

Wallace Beery from *Viva Villa* (1934), arrives and starts shooting up the place. Patrons cry out "Pancho!" Pancho shoots a Murphy bed, which opens to reveal The Four Marx Brothers (despite Zeppo having left the team in 1933) and they cry out their O-names (uncharacteristically for Harpo!). He and Buddy fight over Buddy's girlfriend, Cookie, and eventually bring the house down, literally. Pancho (in a reference to Beery's role in *The Big House* [1930] as Butch) says, "I was only foolin', Buddy."

FUN FACT: Billy Bletcher appeared in *Monkey Business* (1931).

● ● ● ● ● ● ● ● ●

Who Killed Cock Robin? (Walt Disney Studios, June 26, 1935)

Directed by David Hand. Writing Credits (in alphabetical order): William Cottrell (story), Joe Grant (story), Bob Kuwahara (story). Animators: Norman Ferguson (Judge Oliver Owl, Cuckoo on stand), Clyde Geronimi, Hardie Gramatky, Joe Grant, Bob Kuwahara, Eric Larson, Dick Lundy, Hamilton Luske (Jenny Wren and Cock Robin), Bill Roberts (Paul Parrot), Bob Wickersham. Produced by Walt Disney. Music: Frank Churchill. Cast: Billy Bletcher (Judge Oliver Owl), Pinto Colvig (Paul Parrot), Clarence Nash (Legs Sparrow), Purv Pullen (Cock Robin's Whistling), Martha Wentworth (Jenny Wren).

A Silly Symphony, based on the nursery rhyme. All characters are anthropomorphic birds. Cock Robin, a caricature of Bing Crosby, serenades Jenny Wren, a caricature of Mae West. Someone shoots him with an arrow, and he plunges to the ground in front of The Old Crow Bar. The avian Keystone Kops arrive and start rounding up the usual suspects: a mentally handicapped cuckoo, caricaturing Harpo Marx; a gangster, Legs Sparrow; and a blackbird, caricaturing Stepin Fetchit. A Kop beats on the blackbird's head, dissolving to Judge Owl pounding his gavel. Court is now in session. Paul Parrot is prosecuting. Cock Robin's body is Exhibit "A." Merritt and Kaufman write that Joe Grant said William Cottrell's story was inspired by Gilbert and Sullivan, "But the court scene is closer to the rough-and-tumble world of minstrelsy, slapstick burlesque, and the Marx Brothers—particularly *Duck Soup* [1933]—than to the refined topsy-turvy of nineteenth-century operetta." The blackbird is the first witness, as the Kops beat him mercilessly. After he says he knows nothing, he is thrown back into "Sing-Sing," the Kops beating him all the way there. Next up is Legs. Two Kops beat him on the way to the witness stand, but Legs takes them out. Legs refuses to talk. Finally, the cuckoo gives his wordless testimony. He first implicates Judge Owl, then Paul Parrot, then both, then himself. "He don't know a thing," says Parrot.

Suddenly Jenny Wren enters the courtroom, seeking justice for her dead lover. "These birds look guilty," she says. The Judge, smitten, says, "Hang 'em all!"

An arrow pierces the Judge's mortarboard. It was fired by Dan Cupid, who also shot Cock Robin—not, it turns out, fatally, but just with an arrow of love. When Robin fell from the tree, he was knocked cold. He now comes to and kisses Jenny Wren. The Kops apologize for profiling based on priors, mental defect, and race. Just kidding.

FUN FACTS: The real Paul Parrott was an actor and director at Hal Roach Studios. His older brother was Charley Chase (née Charles Parrott).

Disney released this cartoon on the DVD *Silly Symphonies Volume 1*, but only as an Easter egg because of its political incorrectness.

The first of two Marxtoons where a cuckoo Harpo is a suspect in the killing of Cock Robin.

Episode 17 of the radio show, *The Mickey Mouse Theater of the Air* (April 24, 1938), is "Who Killed Cock Robin?" but Harpo does not appear. His radio career was somewhat limited.

• • • • • • • • •

Flowers for Madame (November 20, 1935)

Warner Bros. Directed by Isadore (Friz) Freleng.

A Merrie Melodies cartoon. A flower pageant is disrupted by a fire, and the plants and insects band together to snuff it out. An anthropomorphic flower puts on a Harpo hat and plucks out a few bars of "Oh! You Beautiful Doll" on a spider web.

• • • • • • • • •

Mr. and Mrs. Is the Name (January 19, 1935)

Warner Bros. Produced by Leon Schlesinger. Directed by Isadore (Friz) Freleng. Music by Bernard B. Brown, Norman Spencer. Film editing by Treg Brown. Painter: Betty Brenon. Sound Supervisor: Bernard B. Brown. Sound Effects Editor: Treg Brown. Animators: Ben Clopton, Cal Dalton, Robert Clampett, Rod Scribner. Cast: Jack Carr (Buddy), Bernice Hansen (Cookie).

This is sometimes considered the first Buddy color short, and the only Buddy in the Merrie Melodies series, although Buddy and Cookie are not named, and are half fish (the bottom half). "Buddy" finds a sunken ship and dresses up as a merman Charlie Chaplin. "Cookie"—this is the last time we will use those annoying quotation marks—plays the title song on the harpsichord and is accompanied by an anthropomorphized lobster version of Harpo. Uncharacteristically for Harpo, but not for Buddy movies, Harpo sings along. Cookie is "mernapped" by a five-legged sea creature—the dreaded pentapus. Buddy gives chase and eventually bests the pentapus and wins Cookie.

Robert Clampett was originally hired by Harman and Ising to animate their Merrie Melodies cartoons.

• • • • • • • • •

Mickey's Polo Team (January 4, 1936)

Walt Disney Studios. Directed by David Hand. Produced by Walt Disney. Animated by Art Babbitt, Johnny Cannon, Grim Natwick, Dick Huemer. Cast: Walt Disney (Mickey Mouse) (uncredited), Clarence Nash (Donald Duck) (uncredited), Ned Norton (Max Hare).

It's the Movie Stars: Stan Laurel, Oliver Hardy, Harpo Marx (riding an ostrich), and Charlie Chaplin (riding a pantomime horse) vs. the Mickey Mousers: Mickey, Goofy, The Big Bad Wolf, and Donald Duck (riding a burro). The crowd includes Shirley Temple, Clark Gable, Edna May Oliver, Charles Laughton (as Henry VIII), Eddie Cantor, Harold Lloyd, W.C. Fields, and Greta Garbo. Cartoon characters include Max Hare,

Clarabelle Cow, Pluto, Fifi the Peke, two Easter Bunnies from *Funny Little Bunnies* (1934), The Wise Little Hen, The Flying Mouse and his mother, Peter and Polly Penguin, King Midas and Goldie the Elf from *The Golden Touch* (1935), Ambrose Puss the Cat and Dirty Bill the Dog Robber from *The Robber Kitten* (1935), and Cock Robin and Jenny Wren from *Who Killed Cock Robin?* (1935).

Referee Jack Holt throws out the first ball, leading to a massive pileup. Ollie is thrown off his mount and showered with horse shoes. It looks like The Wolf is going to score a goal, but Chaplin steals the ball with his cane and everyone heads down the field. Harpo's ostrich gets freaked out and sticks his head in the ground. So does Harpo, as the players thunder around him.

Stan tries to help Ollie back on his horse. They are ultimately successful, but now the horse won't move. Stan pulls out a needle to prick the horse. The horse bolts, leaving Ollie behind, and the needle goes into Ollie's behind.

The Wolf breaks his mallet, so he blows the ball toward the goal as Shirley Temple and the Three Little Pigs razz him. The Wolf blows down their bleachers. Harpo steals the ball from Donald and they collide. Donald quacks at Harpo, who launches a boxing glove from his top hat and honks Donald's butt like a horn. Donald continues to quack, so Harpo launches yet another boxing glove from his butt and pulls a blowtorch from his trench coat and sears Donald. Then, he takes a squawker blowout and literally blasts the end down Donald's throat, sending him rolling back to his burro. Suddenly, the ball lands between Donald's feet. He makes a tee out of dirt, puts the ball on top of it, mounts his burro, and then the players come by and Goofy steals it. Donald blames his burro and starts beating and kicking him. The burro kicks back, knocking Donald into the ground. His exposed butt becomes a tee and Stan hits the ball off it. As Donald stands there quacking, Stan knocks the ball down his throat. Harpo kicks the ball, now in Donald, down the field. The Wolf knocks Donald onto Harpo's ostrich, and Harpo hits Donald with the ostrich's head.

The players continue to chase Donald and the ball down the field. Donald finally takes refuge with Jack Holt (where's he been all this time?). There is a massive collision, and when the dust clears, the mounts are riding the players.

FUN FACTS: Harpo would actually ride an ostrich in *At the Circus* (1939).

Animator Dick Huemer, who did many Marxtoons at Columbia, was Joe Grant's writing partner. Joe Grant designed the celebrity caricatures in this cartoon, although he is not credited. His original sketches of Harpo, Chaplin, and Laurel & Hardy can be seen at the Smithsonian Institution National Portrait Gallery. Walt Disney admired his drawing of Jack Holt so much that he kept it in his home and sent Grant a thank you note. A model sheet from 1935 shows mounts for Harpo, Laurel & Hardy, Holt, and Will Rogers, but not Chaplin. Rogers was an avid polo player and one of the most famous men in the world at the time: the highest-paid movie star of the day, a comedian, radio personality, and syndicated columnist. Presumably, after Rogers died in a plane crash on August 15, 1935, he was replaced by Chaplin.

• • • • • • • • •

Doctor Bluebird (February 5, 1936)

Columbia Pictures. Produced by Charles Mintz. Animated by Manny Gould. Written by Ben Harrison. Music: Joe DeNat.

"A Columbia COLOR RHAPSODY in Full TECHNICOLOR," the poster crows. Following the success of Walt Disney's Silly Symphonies, Charles Mintz launched the Color Rhapsodies series at Columbia. Prior to 1935, these were done in two strip Technicolor, but thereafter, due to Disney's rights to the process expiring, they were produced in the full three strip Technicolor process. The vivid blues here would not have been possible under the old two strip Technicolor.

Scrappy is blue (get it?) because his leg is broken and he can't go fishing. Some bluebirds get wind of this and cheer him up with a bluebird show, featuring an all-bluebird orchestra, bluebird Laurel & Hardy, a bluebird Chaplin, and bluebird Marx Brothers. They heal his foot with—wait for it—ultraviolet rays and send him on his way.

• • • • • • • • •

Duck Hunt (March 8, 1936)
Directed by Walter Lantz. Written by Walter Lantz, Victor McLeod. Animated by LaVerne Harding, Dick Bickenbach, and Jack Dunham (Artists). Produced by Walter Lantz. Cast: Bernice Hansen (Oswald).

Oswald goes duck hunting. A flock of ducks flies overhead, followed by a black Harpo duck with hat and horn. Oswald fires several shots at him, which miss but turn him white (with fright?). Oswald's sixth shot blows the feathers off him. The seventh shot for some reason festoons him with a washboard, a pair of scissors, a hairbrush, an alarm clock, and a checkered flag. I don't get it either. The score appears to musically quote the songs "The Organ Grinder" and "I'm Daffy Over You."

• • • • • • • • •

The Novelty Shop (August 15, 1936)
Columbia Pictures. Directed by Art Davis. Produced by Charles Mintz. Animated by Art Davis. Written By Ben Harrison. Music: Joe DeNat.

A Color Rhapsody cartoon. This is another entry into the popular genre Toys Come to Life. Gags feature Laurel & Hardy, The Dionne Quintuplets, The Three Stooges, and The Marx Brothers.

• • • • • • • • •

The Merry Mutineers (October 2, 1936)
Columbia Pictures. Produced by Charles Mintz. Animated by Manny Gould. Written by Ben Harrison. Music: Joe DeNat. Cast: The Radio Rogues (Voices).

Most Color Rhapsodies were one-offs, but this one stars our old pals Scrappy and Oopy. They are sailing their toy boats in a fountain. Onboard Oopy's boat are Wallace Beery as Long John Silver from *Treasure Island* (1934), Charles Laughton as Captain Bligh from *Mutiny on the Bounty* (1935), The Three Stooges, and W.C. Fields. Scrappy's crew includes

The Marx Brothers, Jimmy Durante, Laurel & Hardy, Bing Crosby, Fred Astaire, and Joe E. Brown. Toys Come to Life.

● ● ● ● ● ● ● ● ●

The CooCoo Nut Grove (November 28, 1936)

Warner Bros. Directed by Isadore (Friz) Freleng. Produced by Leon Schlesinger. Animated by Robert McKimson, Sandy Walker, T. Hee. Written by Sid Marcus. Music: Carl W. Stalling. Cast: Verna Deane (Additional Voices) (uncredited), Bernice Hansen (Dionne Quintuplets) (uncredited), Peter Lind Hayes (Ben Birdie) (uncredited), Tedd Pierce (W.C. Fields) (uncredited), The Rhythmettes (Additional Voices) (uncredited), Wini Shaw (Helen Morgan) (uncredited), and Danny Webb (Mouse) (uncredited).

A Merrie Melodies cartoon. The Coo-Coo Nut Grove (as it is spelled in the sign in the cartoon) is a parody of The Cocoanut Grove—note archaic spelling of "coconut"—a nightclub in the Ambassador Hotel in Los Angeles, California. Here, celebrities are sometimes portrayed as anthropomorphic animals. "Ben Birdie" (a parody of Ben Bernie, the Old Maestro) is the bandleader. An avian Harpo pursues a comely blonde, who, when caught, turns out to be Groucho in drag. Harpo then takes off. Later, Helen Morgan sings a torch song, which makes everyone cry, even Harpo, who presses a button in his hat to activate the windshield wiper for his eyes. The tables in the club float away, including a table with Harpo and Groucho, still in drag.

Other celebrity caricatures include Charles Laughton, Joe E. Brown, Lionel Barrymore, John Barrymore, Walter Winchell, George Raft, Katharine Hepburn, W.C. Fields, Johnny Weissmuller, Gary Cooper, The Dionne Quintuplets, Hugh Herbert, Ned Sparks, Mae West, Clark Gable, Edward G. Robinson, Wallace Beery, Edna May Oliver, George Arliss, and Laurel & Hardy.

T. Hee, the character animator, was called in to Warner Bros. by Frank Tashlin after Tashlin saw Hee's celebrity caricatures in the *Los Angeles Examiner*. However, it was Friz Freleng who hired Hee for this cartoon. Freleng was put in charge of the color Merrie Melodies in 1936 when Schlesinger hired Tex Avery to do the black and white Looney

Tunes. Freleng later recalled, "I had a man working for me who was a great caricaturist by the name of T. Hee (later prominent at the Disney studio.) He caricatured everybody around the studio so well that I started using that in cartoons. It was difficult for some animators who could not imitate the drawings that closely. A caricature, as you know, would be an exaggeration of a feature, and if that feature moved out of place, the character didn't look right. But we had a very good model sheet that showed two or three different angles that the animator was able to follow. If it was a difficult kind of caricature, you were very limited in what you could do."

• • • • • • • • •

Scrappy's News Flashes (December 8, 1937)
Columbia Pictures. Produced by Charles Mintz. Animated by Harry Love. Written by Tedd Pierce. Music: Joe DeNat.

A parody of newsreels. At a Baby Parade in Hollywood, we see Baby Katharine Hepburn, Baby Clark Gable, and Baby Marx Brothers. Groucho looks like George S. Kaufman before he applies his peanut butter and jelly mustache. Chico tickles miniature ivories and Harpo plays a tiny harp.

• • • • • • • • •

Hollywood Picnic (December 29, 1937)
Columbia Pictures. Produced by Charles Mintz. Animated by Art Davis. Written by Sid Marcus. Music: Joe DeNat.

Scrappy Presents A Color Rhapsody cartoon, but he's not in it. Charles Laughton, Mae West, Jimmy Durante, Clark Gable, and others ride a merry-go-round. Laurel & Hardy play on the seesaw. Shirley Temple swings. W. C. Fields sells hot dogs. At the ballgame, Joe E. Brown pitches, The Marx Brothers bat—all at once—and The Three Stooges catch—all at once. Others caricatured include John Barrymore, Eddie Cantor, Marlene Dietrich, Stepin Fetchit, Katharine Hepburn, Hugh Herbert, Boris Karloff, Martha Raye, and Edward G. Robinson.

• • • • • • • • •

String Bean Jack (August 26, 1938)

Terrytoons. Directed by John Foster. Writing Credits (in alphabetical order): John Foster (uncredited), Paul Terry (uncredited). Produced by Paul Terry. Music by Philip A. Scheib. Animators: John Foster (uncredited), Jerry Shields (uncredited), Carlo Vinci (uncredited). Cast: Arthur Kay (Jack's Mother) (uncredited).

Terrytoons (originally spelled Terry-Toons, sometimes spelled TerryToons), located in the "K" Building in downtown New Rochelle, produced theatrical animated cartoons from 1930 to 1971. Founder Paul Terry said, "Disney is the Tiffany's in this business, and I am the Woolworth's." This was the first color Terrytoon.

The Old Woman in the Shoe has fallen on hard times and now lives in a trailer. She sends her son, Jack, to the market to get what he can for their old cow. The proprietor of the Used Cow lot, a caricature of W. C. Fields, gives Jack some magic beans "in six delicious flavors: lemon, lime, raspberry, and pineapple." Jack's mother tosses the beans into the yard.

The next day, Jack sees a vine growing from the beans and decides to climb it. He comes to a castle in the clouds and enters through a window. The owner of the castle, a Russian-accented two-headed giant, enters, and Jack follows him to the Gold Room, where a hen lays golden eggs which the Giant cuts into coins with an egg slicer. An anthropomorphic Harpo Marx harp plays "The Blue Danube" on itself. "Get hot," orders the Giant, and Harpo switches to jazz. Jack grabs the hen, which squawks. "Fee fi fo fooey, something here's a little screwy," says the Giant. The chase is on.

Jack escapes the castle and slides down the vine, managing to chop it down before the Giant finishes descending, killing him. He presents the hen to the Old Woman, saying, "Mother, we're rich." The family moves out of their old trailer into a doublewide.

FUN FACT: The "harp" music on the soundtrack is actually Philip A. Scheib playing the piano because Paul Terry was too cheap to pay a harpist.

• • • • • • • • •

Hollywood Bowl (October 5, 1938)

Walter Lantz Productions. Directed by Elmer Perkins. Produced by Walter Lantz. Animated by Frank Tipper, Merle Gilson. Written by Victor McLeod, Alex Lovy. Music: Frank Churchill. Cast: Sara Berner (Katharine Hepburn/Martha Raye/Various), Jack Mercer (Various).

Opening night at the Hollywood Bowl. Edward G. Robinson, William Powell, and Clark Gable are there. Hugh Herbert mugs. Greta Garbo sits by a treetop, "vanting" to be alone. Turns out Groucho Marx is also in the treetop. He offers her a banana. Clark Gable and Charles Laughton play their characters from *Mutiny on the Bounty* (1935). Edna May Oliver, Joe Penner, Ned Sparks, Bing Crosby, Katharine Hepburn, Joe E. Brown, W. C. Fields with Charlie McCarthy, and others also appear. Leopold Stokowski attempts to conduct Schubert's "Unfinished Symphony," which is—you guessed it—unfinished. Ben Bernie, Fats Waller, Benny Goodman, Cab Calloway, Martha Raye, Jack Benny, Wallace Beery, Fred Astaire, and others complete it.

• • • • • • • • •

The Glass Slipper (October 7, 1938)

Terrytoons. Directed by Mannie Davis. Produced by Paul Terry. Music: Philip A. Scheib.

Cinderella's sisters go to the Prince's ball without her. Cinderella's Fairy Godmother, Mae West, appears and gives her a gown, slippers, and a carriage. "Turn in your glad rags by midnight, Toots, or I'll have to charge you for another day." The Prince, in all honesty, bears little resemblance to Harpo Marx, but he is red-haired, mute, and honks a horn. He and Cinderella jitterbug all evening until she exits just before the stroke of midnight, leaving behind one of her glass slippers. The Prince comes to Cinderella's house, and his footman asks Cinderella, "Does this slipper belong to you?" Mae West appears and says, "That slipper belongs to me." The Fairy Godmother and Prince Harpo live happily ever after.

• • • • • • • • •

Mother Goose Goes Hollywood (December 23, 1938)
Walt Disney Studios. Directed by Wilfred Jackson (uncredited). Writing Credits (in alphabetical order): T. Hee, Dick Rickard. Character Designer: T. Hee. Animators: Jack Campbell (uncredited), Ferdinand Horvath (uncredited), Ward Kimball (The Marx Brothers, Fats Waller with the Marx Brothers) (uncredited), Isadore Klein (uncredited), Grim Natwick (uncredited), Don Patterson (uncredited), Robert Stokes (uncredited). Layout Artist: Terrell Stapp. Produced by Walt Disney. Music: Edward H. Plumb. Cast: Al Bernie (Voice), Thelma Boardman (voice), Dave Weber (Voice), Dave Barry (Groucho Marx/Eddie Cantor/Spencer Tracy/Hugh Herbert/Ned Sparks/Joe Penner/Charles Laughton/W.C. Fields/Charlie McCarthy/Edward G. Robinson/Joe E. Brown/Oliver Hardy) (uncredited), Sara Berner (Katharine Hepburn/Martha Raye/Greta Garbo/Freddie Bartholomew), The Four Blackbirds (Vocal Group), Clarence Nash (Donald Duck) (uncredited), Danny Webb (Fats Waller/Stepin Fetchit) (uncredited).

The third to last Silly Symphony, and the last to use a Silly Symphony title card. Joe Grant and William Cottrell were developing a story called *The Hollywoods*, where the forest was full of birds and animals who were celebrity caricatures. After Warner Bros. did the similar *The CooCoo Nut Grove* (1936), Disney hired T. Hee, who designed the caricatures for that film and combined *The Hollywoods* with another story in development, *Mother Goose Land*, where nursery rhymes are set to jazz music.

Mother Goose appears in a dig at the MGM logo. A title card reads, "Any resemblance of characters herein portrayed to persons living or dead, is purely coincidental." Little Bo-Peep (Katharine Hepburn) has lost her sheep. Rally she has. Old King Cole (Hugh Herbert, with Ned Sparks as the Jester) calls for his fiddlers three: The Marx Brothers, who break their fiddles over their knees. He calls for his bowl, which turns out to be duck soup brought in by Joe Penner, who says, of course, "You wanna buy a duck?" The unlucky duck is Donald.

The three men in a tub are Charles Laughton as Captain Bligh and Spencer Tracy and Freddie Bartholomew as their characters in *Captains Courageous* (1937). Little Bo-Peep putters by in a makeshift motorboat, still looking for her sheep. Humpty Dumpty (W. C. Fields) is annoyed by Charlie McCarthy and eventually takes a swing at him, falling off the wall onto a toadstool, which morphs into an egg cup.

Simple Simon (Stan Laurel) is catching worms using a fish as bait. The Pieman (Oliver Hardy) whistles just enough of their theme song, "Dance of the Cuckoos," to avoid plagiarism. The pie Simon wants is in the middle of the stack, so he successfully plays Pie Jenga to get it. When the Pieman tries it, the pies go south, literally. He throws his one remaining cherry pie at Simon. It hits Bo-Peep and for some reason makes her face brown. She asks in Southern Black dialect, "Is any of you old folks seen my sheep anywheres?"

Margery Daw (Greta Garbo) is on the seesaw with Edward G. Robinson, but she "vants" to be alone, so Robinson gets off the seesaw, and she falls to the ground.

Little Jack Horner (Eddie Cantor) sings a song of sixpence. Four and twenty blackbirds (the actual Four Blackbirds, plus caricatures of Cab Calloway, Stepin Fetchit, and Fats Waller) are baked in a pie. Wallace Beery is Little Boy Blue and blows his horn. Edna May Oliver, Mae West, and ZaSu Pitts play along, as do Clark Gable on flute and George Arliss on bass sax. Groucho and Chico join Fats on the piano until he pushes them away. The piano keys seem to move by themselves. Fats lifts up the piano cover and finds Harpo plucking the strings like a harp. Fred Astaire dances. Martha Raye sings. Joe E. Brown has a big mouth. In his mouth is Little Bo-Peep, who has yet to find her sheep.

Nominated for an Academy Award for Best Short Subject, Cartoon; but lost to *Ferdinand the Bull* (1938).

● ● ● ● ● ● ● ● ●

Art Gallery (May 13, 1939)

MGM. Director: Hugh Harman (uncredited). Cast: Mel Blanc (Laughing Cavalier/Henry VII/Town Crier (uncredited), Kent Rogers (Ned Sparks) (uncredited).

Harman and Ising were fired by MGM when their Happy Harmonies series ran over budget and they were replaced with Fred Quimby. Quimby later hired them back.

Art Comes to Life. Nero persuades three monkeys to set fire to Rome, which they do. This leads to varying reactions from the other works of art. Dr. Jekyll turns into Mr. Hyde. The Three Musketeers turn into The Marx Brothers in *The Spirit of '76*. Stan Laurel cries. The Town Crier (Alexander Woollcott) tries to rouse the community. Other celebrity caricatures include Herbert Hoover, Mae West, and Ned Sparks.

FUN FACTS: Alexander Woollcott "The Town Crier" was quite well-known at the time as a writer, actor, and radio personality. Today, he is best-known, if at all, for being the first New York critic to champion The Marx Brothers on Broadway in *I'll Say She Is* (1924), leading to a lifelong friendship with Harpo.

The Marx Brothers emulate *The Spirit of '76* in *The Cocoanuts* (1929).

● ● ● ● ● ● ● ● ●

Hollywood Sweepstakes (July 28, 1939)

Columbia Pictures. Directed by Ben Harrison. Produced by Charles Mintz. Animated by Manny Gould. Written by Melvin Millar. Music: Joe DeNat.

A Color Rhapsody cartoon. At Santa Anteater Park, despite a huge downpour, all the stars have come out: Laurel & Hardy, Clark Gable, Ned Sparks, Edward G. Robinson, Bing Crosby, and more. Hugh Herbert is the starter. The Marx Brothers are the judges. A pony ridden by a turtle jockey wins the race, if you must know. I guess he's a mudder.

FUN FACTS: The real Santa Anita Park was where *A Day at the Races* (1937) was shot. Chico frequently went there to lose his paycheck. Footage from this cartoon was later reused in *A Hollywood Detour* (1942).

● ● ● ● ● ● ● ● ●

The Autograph Hound (September 1, 1939)

Walt Disney Studios. Directed by Jack King. Written by Harry Reeves. Assistant Directors: Bob Newman, Harry Teitel (uncredited). Layout Artist: Bill Herwig. Animators: Edwin Aardal, Paul Allen, Preston Blair, Johnny Cannon, Larry Clemmons, Rex Cox, Shamus Culhane (as Seamus Culhane), Nick DeTolly, Ed Dunn, John W. Dunn (as John Dunn), John

Elliotte, Andy Engman, Osmond Evans, Emery Hawkins, Ward Kimball, Ed Love, Lee Morehouse, Kenneth Muse, Ray Patin, Ken Peterson, Dunbar Roman, Don Schloat, Claude Smith, Robert Stokes, Judge Whitaker. Music: Oliver Wallace (uncredited). Produced by Walt Disney. Executive In Charge of Production: David Hand (uncredited). Cast: Clarence Nash (Donald Duck), Sara Berner (Greta Garbo/Shirley Temple/Bette Davis/ Katharine Hepburn/Martha Raye/Joan Crawford) (uncredited), Billy Bletcher (Security Guard) (uncredited).

Mickey Mouse became a role model for children in the 1930s, and Walt Disney was looking to create an edgier protagonist. Donald Duck is a funny animal character, who made his first appearance in *The Wise Little Hen* (1934), but found his niche as a foil for Mickey and a third wheel with Mickey and Goofy. He got his own series in 1937. Clarence Nash provided the semi-intelligible voice.

At Hollywood Studios, which looks a lot like Paramount, the policy is "No Autograph Hounds," and the Security Guard throws Donald out. Donald hitches a ride on the rear wheel arch of Greta Garbo's car and passes by the Guard, who thinks he's in the cab with Garbo. Donald is snagged on the old-fashioned turn signal of a truck and gets deposited right at the Guard's feet. The chase is on.

Donald ducks into Mickey Rooney's dressing room. Mickey does some sleight-of-hand for Donald. Donald makes an egg "disappear" into his hat. Mickey smashes the egg onto Donald's head, who becomes so hot with rage, he fries the egg. Donald hops up and down, and Mickey places a fiddle and bow in his hands and Donald plays a jig. He throws the fiddle at Mickey, misses, and hits the Guard.

Donald runs into the revolving doors of the commissary as a waiter (a caricature of Henry Armetta) and comes out with a covered serving platter.

"Have you seen a duck?" asks the Guard.

"No, Flatfoot," answers Donald from the platter.

"Have ye got a duck in there?" the Guard asks Armetta.

"No duck, boss, roast beef," says Armetta, and lifts the cover to reveal nothing but gravy and a few scraps. Donald is in the cover with the roast, which he throws onto the platter, covering the Guard and Armetta with sauce.

Donald finds himself on the set of a Sonja Henie movie. She autographs the ice with the blades of her skates. Donald takes the block of ice, but it melts when he walks through a desert set. In a tent on that set are silhouetted three exotic dancers, who turn out to actually be The Ritz Brothers. They autograph Donald's butt. Donald throws a can of paint at them, misses, and hits the Guard.

Donald literally bumps into Shirley Temple on the set of her movie, who asks for his autograph. The Guard grabs him, and Shirley says, "You leave him alone! He's Donald Duck!"

Word travels quickly through the studio that Donald Duck is there. In addition to Groucho and Harpo Marx, stars shown include Clark Gable, The Andrews Sisters, Charlie McCarthy, Stepin Fetchit, The Lone Ranger on his horse Silver, Joe E. Brown, Martha Raye, Hugh Herbert, Irvin S. Cobb, Edward Arnold, Katharine Hepburn, Eddie Cantor, Slim Summerville, Lionel Barrymore, Bette Davis, Mischa Auer, Joan Crawford, and Charles Boyer. They bury Donald and the Guard in autograph books.

"Your autograph, sir," says the Guard, handing Donald a fountain pen. "Let me have it." "Okay, flatfoot," says Donald, spraying the Guard with ink and leaving an autograph on his shirt.

FUN FACT: Henry Armetta would later appear with The Marx Brothers in *The Big Store* (1941).

● ● ● ● ● ● ● ● ●

Mother Goose in Swingtime (December 18, 1939)

Columbia Pictures. Directed by Manny Gould. Produced by Charles Mintz. Animated by Ben Harrison. Written by Allen Rose. Music: Joe DeNat. Cast: Elvia Allman (Baby Snooks), Sara Berner (Mother Goose/Martha Raye/Greta Garbo), Mel Blanc (Various), Dave Weber (Various).

A Color Rhapsody cartoon. Baby Snooks (originally played by Fanny Brice on the radio) asks her father for a bedtime story. Soon she is transported to the land of Mother Goose (Edna May Oliver), where she teaches everyone how to swing, including Little Boy Blue (Cary Grant), Tweedle Dum and Tweedle Dee (Laurel & Hardy), and Old King Cole's fiddlers three (Guess Who, reprising their roles from *Mother Goose Goes Hollywood* [1938]).

Some of the other celebrity caricatures: Martha Raye, George Raft, Edward G. Robinson, Claudette Colbert, James Cagney, Katharine Hepburn, Ned Sparks, Joan Crawford, Herman Bing, Shirley Temple, Hugh Herbert, Greta Garbo, Mickey Rooney, Cary Grant, Benny Goodman, W.C. Fields, Joe E. Brown, Bing Crosby, William Powell, John Barrymore, Jack Benny, Clark Gable, Leopold Stokowski, Fred Astaire, Ginger Rogers, Wallace Beery, May Robson, Edward Everett Horton, Akim Tamiroff, Kay Francis, Tyrone Power, Robert Taylor, Jeanette MacDonald, and Nelson Eddy.

FUN FACT: Kay Francis is largely forgotten today, but she starred with The Marx Brothers in *The Cocoanuts* (1929).

• • • • • • • • •

Nellie of the Circus (1939)

Walter Lantz Productions. Directed by Alex Lovy. Written by Victor McLeod, James Miele. Cast: Mel Blanc (Dauntless Dan, Rudolf Ratbone).

The Nellie series, burlesques of nineteenth century melodrama, was Walter Lantz's attempt to replace his Oswald the Lucky Rabbit franchise. Nellie wasn't so lucky, she'd soon be replaced by Woody Woodpecker. In this episode, she has been kidnapped into the circus by Rudolf Ratbone. Her childhood sweetheart, Dauntless Dan, searches the world for her. At one point, he tries to flag down a passing four-seat tandem bicycle (shockingly, not ridden by The Marx Brothers) and then a passing Harpo Marx, who only has a bicycle horn. In case you wondered, Dan finds Nellie and defeats Ratbone.

• • • • • • • • •

Busy Bakers (February 10, 1940)

Warner Bros. Directed by Ben Hardaway, Cal Dalton. Produced by Leon Schlesinger. Written by Jack Miller. Animator: Richard Bickenbach. Cast: Mel Blanc (Swenson/Blind Man Elf/Crossed-Eyed Elf/Colonna Elf) (uncredited), The Sportsmen Quartet (Vocalists) (uncredited).

From the Merrie Melodies series. Swenson the baker is not so busy. He has no money, no supplies, and no stock but for one doughnut, which he gives to a blind beggar. The beggar goes back to an old windmill and reveals himself to be an elf. He wakes up his fellow elves, including caricatures of Harpo Marx and Jerry Colonna, and gets them to go back to Swenson's Bakery with supplies. "We must work fast, before he wakes, and fill his store with pies and cakes!"

Cue singing elves. Harpo drops a cake on its top and labels it "Upside-down cake." Eventually, Swenson wakes up and the elves scatter. The bakery opens and it is a huge success.

The elf returns in blind beggar drag and asks for a crust of bread. Swenson gives him a pie and tells him there's a 5¢ deposit on the pan. The elf throws the pie in Swenson's face. "That's gratitude for ya," says Swenson.

● ● ● ● ● ● ● ● ●

Springtime in the Rockage (August 30, 1940)

Fleischer Studios. Directed by Dave Fleischer. Written by Dan Gordon. Produced by Max Fleischer, Adolph Zukor. Animated by Myron Waldman, Dick Williams.

One of a series of twelve Stone Age Cartoons by Fleischer Studios. As in *The Flintstones* (1960), much of the humor comes from prehistoric iterations of modern technology. A caveman is feeding his flowers when a locust the size of a Komodo dragon starts eating his other plants. When the caveman shows the locust his "Keep Off" sign, the locust eats it. Then, the locust steals the caveman's net, breaks it in half, and chases him off with the handle. "I just get things planted and then insects come along and eat it," says the caveman. He then morphs into Groucho Marx to deliver the line, "Why last year, I didn't get as much as one tomato." Someone throws a tomato in his face.

The caveman is cooking a delicious dinner and bees try to get in by pretending to be Fuller Brush men. The caveman is not fooled. The bees booby-trap the door and bean the caveman on the head the next time he answers. They hold a mock funeral procession with a bee Harpo playing a "harp" and lock him in the closet while they eat his food. The caveman escapes, and the bees knock him out. The last few bars of the score seem to musically quote the title theme from *Horse Feathers* (1933).

• • • • • • • • •

Puttin on the Act (August 30, 1940)

Fleischer Studios. Directed by Dave Fleischer. Story: Bill Turner (as William Turner). Animators: Tom Golden, Dave Tendlar. Produced by Max Fleischer. Music by Sammy Timberg (uncredited). Cast: Margie Hines (Olive Oyl) (uncredited), Jack Mercer (Popeye) (uncredited).

Olive Oyl bursts into the apartment of Popeye and Swee'pea with a newspaper. The headline is "Vaudeville Coming Back!" Popeye goes up to the attic to get his props and costumes from his theatrical trunk. Then, they rehearse their act, "Half Song, Half Wit." Swee'pea is the call boy, handling the title cards. After their theme song, Popeye and Olive model swimsuits and do a balancing act in "The Body Beautiful."

Next up is "Impoiskonations." Popeye molds his face into Jimmy Durante and Stan Laurel. Then he puts on a mustache and glasses and trades his pipe in for a cigar and plays Groucho Marx, entering to the tune of "I'm Daffy Over You." "The first morning I was there, I shot an elephant in my pajamas. How he got in my pajamas, I'll never know. Suddenly, we came upon a beautiful pool. I raised my weapon. I shot. It was the eight ball in the side pocket." A pool stick is thrown onstage. "Well, I guess this is my cue to leave."

In "The Adagio," Popeye twirls Olive like a baton and throws her like a javelin right out the window. More concerned about the act than Olive's welfare, Popeye runs down several flights of stairs and catches her. Meanwhile, Swee'pea, who apparently has better reading comprehension than anybody else in this cartoon, notes the date on the headline, "Vaudeville Coming Back!": August 1, 1898. Womp womp.

FUN FACTS: When the elderly rabbit climbs out of Popeye's old magic hat, the music is "Silver Threads Among the Gold," a song frequently played by Chico.

Popeye and Olive's theme song was written by Sammy Timberg, who was reportedly the Marxes' musical director in Vaudeville.

● ● ● ● ● ● ● ● ●

Popeye Meets William Tell (September 20, 1940)

Fleischer Studios. Directed by Dave Fleischer. Animation Director: Shamus Culhane (uncredited). Story: Dan Gordon. Produced by Max Fleischer. Music by Winston Sharples (uncredited), Sammy Timberg (uncredited). Cast: Pinto Colvig (High Governor) (uncredited), Jack Mercer (Popeye/Announcer) (uncredited), Carl Meyer (William Tell) (uncredited).

Popeye is walking along when someone starts shooting arrows at him. He is impressed to learn it is THE William Tell. "Where's your son?" asks Popeye. Tell confesses that he shot his son from under an apple. He produces a locket with a picture of his son. It is an animated photo of Groucho Marx.

The High Governor commands all "lowbrows" must bow down to his "high hat" (a hat on a pole). William Tell refuses, and he is brought before the High Governor, who commands him to shoot an apple off his son's head or lose his own. William Tell sputters that he hasn't any son, but Popeye pretends to be his son. William Tell takes the pipe out of Popeye's mouth and smacks him. "Smokin' again!" The High Governor hits William Tell, and Popeye hits the High Governor and some cops.

Dissolve to Popeye standing in front of a tree with an apple on his head, knees shaking. William Tell attempts to shoot the apple standing next to Popeye. The High Governor demands he step back ten paces. He takes eight baby steps. The High Governor picks him up and moves him ten giant steps. William Tell fires the arrow through Popeye's shirt. William Tell is taken away by the cops to the executioner.

The arrow has been stopped by a can of spinach in Popeye's shirt. He beats up the cops, the High Governor, and the executioner. William Tell thanks him by stealing his pipe and spanking his "son" for smoking.

This is one of the most reviled Popeye shorts. Animation director Shamus Culhane agrees. "If you look at the picture, you'll see that I was trying to use an editing approach and some acting, but it really didn't go with Popeye."

• • • • • • • • •

Mississippi Swing (February 7, 1941)

Terrytoons. Director: Connie Rasinski. Story: John Foster.

The lives of African-American sharecroppers in a sleepy riverside cotton town are brightened by the arrival of a showboat, which produces a minstrel show. A caricature of Bill "Bojangles" Robinson tap dances up and down a staircase. A pianist plays and a Black Harpo Marx pops out of the upright piano, plays the harp, and honks the pianist's nose.

"Scarlett O'Hara from Tara," a heavyset African-American woman, sings a song to her butler. The butler carries her up the steps and drops her. She goes crashing through the floor. The butler plays the slot machine and it pays off in watermelons.

FUN FACTS: Harpo, Groucho, and Chico played in blackface (using axle grease) in *A Day at the Races* (1937). The Four Marx Brothers parodied minstrel shows in *Duck Soup* (1933).

• • • • • • • • •

Abdul the Bulbul-Ameer (February 22, 1941)

MGM. Directed by Hugh Harman. Produced by Fred Quimby. Music: Scott Bradley. Cast: Cliff Nazarro, Harry Stanton, Leon Belasco, Hans Conried.

"Abdul the Bulbul-Ameer"—there are variant spellings—was a song written during the Russo-Turkish War. Abdul is either a Turk or a Persian or an Arab whose toe is stepped on by the Russian soldier, Ivan Skavinsky Skavar. Tensions escalate, and Ivan challenges Abdul to a fight. A news crew arrives to document this event. The crew is supposed to be Groucho Marx, Al Ritz, and Lou Costello, but "Groucho" wears no glasses, and the vocal imitations are terrible. A ferocious battle ensues, and Ivan's friend puts a bomb down Abdul's pants. This blows both men sky high, and when they land, they crash through the ice of the lake and emerge frozen solid.

Truly bizarre. Russia and the United Kingdom would invade Iran later that year. Maybe that's what this is all about. Maybe not.

FUN FACTS: Leon Belasco would later play the violinist in *Love*

Happy (1949). Harry Stanton is no relation to Harry Dean Stanton, although they would appear together in *Petticoat Junction* (1963).

● ● ● ● ● ● ● ● ●

Hollywood Steps Out (May 24, 1941)

Warner Bros. Directed by Tex Avery. Produced by Leon Schlesinger. Animated by Rod Scribner. Written by Melvin Millar. Music: Carl W. Stalling. Cast: Dave Barry (Cary Grant/Clark Gable/James Cagney/Bing Crosby/Lewis Stone/Ned Sparks/Groucho Marx), Sara Berner (Greta Garbo/Coat Check Girl/Henry Fonda's Mother/Dorothy Lamour), Mel Blanc (Jerry Colonna/Peter Lorre), Kent Rogers (Jimmy Stewart/Mickey Rooney/Henry Fonda)

Tex Avery, whom Joe Adamson called "King of Cartoons," started out painting backgrounds for Oswald cartoons at Walter Lantz Studios. As a director for Schlesinger, he created or helped develop the characters of Bugs Bunny, Daffy Duck, and Porky Pig.

A Merrie Melodies cartoon. At Ciro's in Los Angeles, where the De Luxe Dinner is "$50.00 and up, with Easy Terms, 6 months to pay, small down payments," Cary Grant buys cigarettes from cigarette girl Greta Garbo, who lights one by scratching a match on her really big shoe. Later, Harpo gives her a hotfoot (and we know how big those feet are), to which she barely reacts. A comely blonde catches Clark Gable's eye. "Sally Strand," a parody of Burlesque dancer Sally Rand, does her bubble dance. She was Sally Rand earlier in the cartoon, when she handed over all her clothes to the Coat Check Girl, but is renamed here to avoid a lawsuit. With a slingshot, Harpo bursts her bubble, exposing her wearing only a barrel. Gable finally asks the blonde for a kiss. It is—again—Groucho, who says, "Fancy meeting you here." In the original release, Gable kisses him anyhow. This was cut from the reissue print when Gable complained it would hurt his career.

Other celebrity caricatures include Mischa Auer, Wallace Beery, Humphrey Bogart, James Cagney, Jerry Colonna, Bing Crosby, Henry Fonda, Errol Flynn, Judy Garland, Laurel & Hardy, Sonja Henie, J. Edgar Hoover, Boris Karloff, Buster Keaton, Kay Kyser, Dorothy Lamour, Peter Lorre, Myrna Loy, William Powell, Tyrone Power, George Raft, Cesar

Romero, Mickey Rooney, Ann Sheridan, C. Aubrey Smith, Ned Sparks, Jimmy Stewart, Leopold Stokowski, Lewis Stone, The Three Stooges, Spencer Tracy, Arthur Treacher, and Johnny Weissmuller. Also, Leon Schlesinger and his assistant Henry Binder appear.

FUN FACT: The building that once housed Ciro's is now the home of the Comedy Store.

● ● ● ● ● ● ● ● ●

Popeye Meets Rip Van Winkle (May 9, 1941)

Fleischer Studios. Directed by Dave Fleischer. Story: Dan Gordon. Animators: Sidney Pillet, Myron Waldman. Produced by Max Fleischer. Music by Winston Sharples, Sammy Timberg (uncredited). Cast: Jack Mercer (Popeye/Rip Van Winkle/Dwarves) (uncredited).

Popeye is walking past a house when a piano lands on the front lawn, followed by a stool. The stool is ridden by Chico Marx, who shoots the piano keys. Chico and a fellow moving man load the piano onto a wagon. Next, they load the bed, and Rip Van Winkle falls out, still asleep. The Sheriff posts a Dispossess Notice on the door for nonpayment of rent for twenty years. Popeye decides to take Rip, blunderbuss and all, home with him so Rip can sleep in Popeye's bed.

While Popeye is making him a hot drink, Rip sleepwalks away. Popeye finds him asleep in a dwarves' bowling alley. A dwarf yells at Popeye to get out. Popeye tries to shush him, afraid he'll wake Rip. The dwarves gang up on Popeye, but he refuses to fight back, even when they pound him down to their size. Popeye eats some spinach, which restores him to normal. He grabs Rip, and gets out.

Back at his house, Popeye puts Rip back into bed and removes his pants, which he folds over a chair, causing a coin to fall out, which awakens Rip. "Oh, a pickpocket, eh?" he says, and shoots at Popeye with his blunderbuss.

FUN FACT: A rare solo cartoon appearance for Chico. Coincidentally, starting in 1941, Chico would make many appearances without his brothers for the war effort and he would front a big band.

• • • • • • • • •

The Wizard Of Arts (August 8, 1941)

Fleischer Studios. Directed by Dave Fleischer. Produced by Max Fleischer, Adolph Zukor. Animated by Tom Johnson, Jack Ozark. Written by Jack Ward.

Animated Antics, which evolved from Max Fleischer's *Gulliver's Travels* (1939), was one of the last series created by Dave Fleischer. It consisted of eleven black and white cartoons, each one less than seven minutes long, and distributed through Paramount from 1939 through 1941.

The title character, a caricature of Jerry Colonna, takes us on a tour of his studio, which mostly produces spot gags. "Paradise" is a pair of dice. "Vice" is a vise. "Salome" is salami. "Defeat"—you get the idea. "Hope" is a bust of Bob "Frequent Jerry Colonna Collaborator" Hope. "Silly, isn't it?" asks Colonna. The background music is Hope's theme, "Thanks for the Memories."

On the mezzanine are the higher arts, but not necessarily better jokes. "The Four Seasons" are pepper, salt, mustard, and vinegar. "The Five Senses" are a quintet of pennies. "Lost Souls"—I can't. "The next painting is a beautiful statue," says Colonna.

The familiar strains of "I'm Daffy Over You" are played as The Sphinx is revealed. It's Harpo Marx. Only a few more gags before Colonna settles into his grave and plants a flower on top. (I'm not making this up.)

• • • • • • • • •

Who's Zoo in Hollywood (October 17, 1941)

Columbia Pictures. Directed by Art Davis. Produced by Charles Mintz. Written by Melvin Millar. Music: Eddie Kilfeather.

A Color Rhapsody, and the last of that series produced by Charles Mintz. A trip to the Hollywood Zoo, where all the animals are anthropomorphic celebrity caricatures. The poster portrays The Marx Brothers as monkeys: See No Evil (Chico), Hear No Evil (Groucho), and Speak No Evil (Guess). This cartoon is presumed lost and was not previewed for this book.

• • • • • • • • •

Red Riding Hood Rides Again (December 5, 1941)
Columbia Pictures. Directed by Sid Marcus. Animated by Bob Wickersham, Bill Hamner. Written by Michael Maltese. Music: Eddie Kilfeather.

The Big, Bad Wolf tries to catch Red by disguising himself as Clark Gable, Mickey Rooney, and Groucho Marx, among others. He beats her to Grandma's House, but Grandma leaves to go to a Jimmy Dorsey concert with her boyfriend. Just as he is about to eat Red, he is drafted into the army.

Academy Award Nominee, Best Short Subject, Cartoon, 1941.

• • • • • • • • •

A Hollywood Detour (January 23, 1942)
Columbia Pictures. Written and Directed by Frank Tashlin. Animator: Emery Hawkins. Layout Artist: Clark Watson. Produced by Ben Schaib. Music by Paul Worth. Cast: Paul Frees (Narrator).

A Color Rhapsody cartoon. The title card features caricatures of The Marx Brothers, W. C. Fields, Joan Crawford, Katharine Hepburn, Charles Laughton, Edward G. Robinson, Ned Sparks, George Raft, and many others.

A mock travelogue that takes viewers behind the scenes at "The Brown Darby" (a parody of Groucho's real-life hangout The Brown Derby), Columbia Studios, Grauman's Chinese Theatre (obligatory Greta Garbo big feet joke), Santa Anteater Park, Malibu, and a baseball game with The Three Marx Brothers at bat. Stock footage is used heavily in this cartoon, and the latter sequence is from *A Hollywood Picnic* (1937).

A running gag is autograph hounds mobbing "The Great Profile" John Barrymore until he finally produces a Tommy gun and sends them all to Heaven. Heaven? Really?

Other caricatured stars include Bing Crosby, Fred Astaire, Rita Hayworth, Clark Gable, Edna May Oliver, Joe E. Brown, and The Three Stooges.

FUN FACTS: The writer/director of this cartoon, Frank Tashlin, would later go on to be a writer on *Love Happy* (1949), which starred The Marx Brothers, and to direct *Will Success Spoil Rock Hunter?* (1957), which featured a cameo by Groucho.

Paul Frees would later do the voices of Chico and Zeppo in the Napoleon sketch on *The Mad, Mad, Mad Comedians* (1970).

● ● ● ● ● ● ● ● ●

Slick Hare (November 1, 1947)

Warner Bros. Directed by Isadore (Friz) Freleng. Produced by Edward Selzer. Animated by Virgil Ross, Gerry Chiniquy, Manuel Perez, Ken Champin. Written by Tedd Pierce, Michael Maltese. Music: Carl Stalling. Cast: Mel Blanc (Bugs Bunny/Waiter/Bartender/Ray Milland), Dave Barry (Humphrey Bogart) (uncredited), Arthur Q. Bryan (Elmer Fudd).

In 1944, Leon Schlesinger sold his animation studio to Warner Bros. and it was renamed Warner Bros. Cartoons, Inc., with Edward Selzer the new head. Frank Tashlin left in September 1944, and Robert Clampett in October 1946. Robert McKimson took over first Tashlin's unit, then Clampett's.

Bugs Bunny's first appearance is generally considered to be Tex Avery's *A Wild Hare* (1940). He is an anthropomorphic rabbit voiced by Mel Blanc. Bugs Bunny is often said to have been inspired by Groucho, and indeed, sometimes utters, "This means war!" as does Groucho in *Duck Soup* (1933) and *A Night at the Opera* (1935). However, Friz Freleng sometimes maintained Bugs was inspired by Clark Gable's carrot-chomping character in *It Happened One Night* (1934). In the radio sketch "The Spiwit of Spwing" (1945), "Groucho adopts a pseudo-adolescent tone that sounds disconcertingly like Bugs."

A Merrie Melodies cartoon. At the Mocrumbo, where dinner is only $600, with a small down payment and no co-signers necessary (that joke never gets old), Humphrey Bogart wants fried rabbit and gives waiter Elmer Fudd twenty minutes to bring it. Elmer finds Bugs in the kitchen, eating carrots, and tells him Bogie would like to have him for dinner. Bugs puts on his tie and tailcoat, but when he realizes he's the main course, he takes off through the restaurant. He puts on a Groucho disguise and hides in plain sight at a table with Chico and Harpo. Elmer, in Harpo drag, chops up his cigar with a butcher knife. Bugs tries to get away, but bounces off Sydney Greenstreet's stomach. Bugs then hides in Carmen Miranda's hat and takes over her act. Back in the kitchen, Bugs pretends to be a waiter, orders pies, then throws them in Elmer's face. Elmer finally catches on, throws a pie at Bugs, and misses, hitting Bogie. Time's up, and Bogie wants his rabbit. Elmer confesses he doesn't have one. "Baby will just have to have a ham sandwich instead," says Bogie. When Bugs hears the word "Baby," he happily submits to being eaten by Lauren Bacall.

FUN FACT: The Mocrumbo is a parody of real-life Hollywood nightclub, the Mocambo.

• • • • • • • • •

The Baby Sitter (November 28, 1947)

Famous Studios. Directed by Seymour Kneitel. Writing Credits (in alphabetical order): Marjorie Henderson Buell (as Marge) (Comic Strip); Larry Riley, Bill Turner (Story). Produced by Seymour Kneitel, Izzy Sparber. Animators: Al Eugster, Tom Golden, Martin Taras, Dave Tendlar. Music by Winston Sharples. Cast: Cecil Roy (Little Lulu) (uncredited).

Kathryn Allamong Jacob, curator of the Schlesinger Library, wrote, "Lulu was born in 1935, when *The Saturday Evening Post* asked Buell to create a successor to the magazine's Henry, Carl Anderson's stout, mute little boy, who was moving on to national syndication. The result was Little Lulu, the resourceful, equally silent (at first) little girl whose loopy curls were reminiscent of the artist's own as a girl. Buell explained to a reporter, 'I wanted a girl because a girl could get away with more fresh stunts that, in a small boy, would seem boorish.'" She appeared in a series of shorts in the 1940s, which replaced the Superman shorts.

Lulu is called by Mrs. Jones to babysit her son, Alvin. Lulu packs her "Baby Pacifier," a large mallet. At the Jones house, Alvin saws his way out of the crib. Lulu gets him back in and boards up the hole. Alvin intimates that he has to use the bathroom and locks Lulu out. She fishes him out through the transom and boards up the top of the crib. Alvin slips out through a trap door on the bottom. Lulu gives chase and runs into a wall, where a falling picture knocks her out.

When she wakes up, she finds herself at the Stork Club. Alvin gets out of a limo. This "Stork Club" is run by storks for babies. The babies are versions of W. C. Fields, Bob "Diaper and Top Hat Wearing" Hope, Miriam Hopkins, Jerry Colonna, Frank Sinatra, Bing Crosby, and Harpo Marx. The band is led by a baby Cab Calloway.

Lulu comes to back at the house when Alvin dumps a fishbowl on her head. It is nine o'clock, the hour Mrs. Jones is set to return. She pays Lulu, who leaves. Mrs. Jones finds Alvin in the crib inside a locked birdcage.

● ● ● ● ● ● ● ● ●

Felix the Fox (March 10, 1948)

Terrytoons. Directed by Mannie Davis. Story: John Foster. Animators: Mannie Davis, James Tyer, Carlo Vinci (uncredited). Produced by Paul Terry. Music by Philip A. Scheib. Cast: Dayton Allen (Dimwit/Felix the Fox) (uncredited).

Felix the Fox, pursued by hounds, jumps a stone fence and makes a sharp right. All the hounds go straight except for the last one over the fence, Dimwit, who manages to pick up Felix's scent, and the chase is on.

Felix hangs from a branch. Dimwit jumps up and holds onto the branch and Felix darts into the hollow tree. He tickles Dimwit with a squawker blowout, causing him to let go. Dimwit shimmies up the tree and Felix cuts the bark away with a pair of scissors, sending the hound to the ground. Dimwit falls for this twice, really living up to his name.

Felix is standing on a hollow tree balanced on a rock. Dimwit tries to hit Felix with an axe, and goes launching through the air into a tree. Doors appear in trees and Felix darts in and out of them, finally slamming a door on Dimwit's head.

Dimwit pursues Felix into a bush and thinks he has grabbed Felix's tail, but it's just fur on a roller. Dimwit finally pulls the roller out of the bushes. Felix pops out of the roller and hits Dimwit on the head with a mallet.

Felix leads Dimwit up a hollow tree. Felix exits the tree through a door. Dimwit climbs to the top and Felix launches a skyrocket up his butt.

Felix dons glasses, eyebrows, and mustache and places a cigar in his mouth and poses as a renter of fox suits using a Groucho Marx voice. "Ah, so you want to attract a fox? Well, there's nothing like being frank about it. On the other hand, Frank never attracted anybody. Maybe you better be Mary. Ah, well I remember Mary. She was always attractive. Hey, you know, with another face, you could attract anything. But who wants to be two-faced? Then again, it might be an improvement." He gives Dimwit a red dress and a vixen mask. "You know, with that disguise, you could even fool me. On second thought, I think I'll fool him."

Dimwit lures Felix to a love seat, and then folds it up on him and pushes it into a house, locks the door, and swallows the key. Then, he takes off his disguise. "I'm no fox, I'm a dog."

Felix replies, "That's all right. I'm no fox either. I'm a skunk," and removes his fox disguise. Dimwit escapes by crashing through a window.

FUN FACT: Dayton Allen rose to prominence as a Groucho imitator. In 1963, he famously impersonated Groucho's voice on *I've Got a Secret* (1952). The secret was that Groucho wasn't speaking to the blindfolded panel.

• • • • • • • • •

The Golden State (March 12, 1948)

Famous Studios. Directed by Seymour Kneitel. Story: Larz Bourne, Larry Riley. Cast: Charles Irving, Jack Mercer, Sid Raymond.

Fleischer Studios released 36 Song Car-Tunes series, among the earliest sound films. These shorts invited the audience to sing along to the bouncing ball and featured popular melodies. In 1945, Famous Studios, successors to Fleischer, revived Screen Songs as an all-animated series in color.

This is a gaggy history and travelogue about California. Harpo's footprints uproot themselves from Grauman's Chinese Theatre and chase after a pretty girl.

The song is "California, Here I Come." Follow the bouncing citrus.

• • • • • • • • •

Out Again, In Again (November 1, 1948)

Terrytoons. Directed by Connie Rasinski. Story: John Foster, Tom Morrison. Cast: Dayton Allen (Heckle/Jeckle/Dimwit/Narrator/Warden), Roy Halee (Other Voices).

Heckle and Jeckle are anthropomorphic yellow-billed magpies created by Paul Terry, who considered their cartoons the studio's best. Like The Marx Brothers themselves, Heckle and Jeckle "were basically antagonistic," and it was perhaps inevitable that Dayton Allen would play them.

Incarcerated Heckle and Jeckle escape from jail by sewer. They are pursued by dogs, and the Warden, who is also a dog, to a railroad trestle, where Heckle and Jeckle hop the train. The Warden takes off after them on a handcar. Dimwit, the conductor, another dog, throws them off the train because they don't have tickets. Heckle and Jeckle disguise themselves as American Indians, headhunters, and a mother and daughter before being thrown out again. They manage to grab the back of the caboose, but now the Warden and his dogs are hot on the trail. Dimwit pulls the brake, causing the handcar to collide with the train. The Warden and Dimwit chase Heckle and Jeckle through the train. Jeckle (disguised as Groucho) and Heckle (disguised as Harpo) are in the dining car. Jeckle insults Dimwit, who chases them to the engine, which blows up, propelling Heckle and Jeckle right back to jail. The Warden plays "There's No Place Like Home" on his fiddle, and Heckle and Jeckle sing along.

• • • • • • • • •

Toys Will Be Toys (July 15, 1949)

Famous Studios. Directed by Seymour Kneitel. Animated by Myron Waldman, Gordon Whittier. Written by Izzy Klein. Music: Winston Sharples. Cast: Jackson Beck, Jack Mercer.

A Screen Song and another Toys Come to Life cartoon. Beads thread themselves into a Carmen Miranda doll. Harpo Marx pops up from a jack-in-the-box and honks his horn at her. Tiny langlaufers schuss down the schnozz of a bust of Bob "Ol' Ski Nose" Hope. A toy Popeye makes an appearance. A toy soldier comes upon the beautiful Queen of Toyland, and invites the audience to join him in singing "Oh! You Beautiful Doll." Follow the bouncing ball!

• • • • • • • • •

Strolling Thru the Park (November 4, 1949)
Famous Studios. Directed by Seymour Kneitel. Story: I. Klein. Animation by Myron Waldman, Larry Silverman.

A Screen Songs cartoon. Although set in the 1890s, Abbott and Costello appear on penny farthing bicycles, as do The Four Marx Brothers on a—wait for it—four-seat tandem. The Marxes are riding along a lake when their reflection in the water hits a rock. They keep going and eventually the reflection catches up, then overtakes them, before they get synchronized again. The title song is played. Follow the bouncing ball!

• • • • • • • • •

Movie Madness (November 7, 1951)
Terrytoons. Directed by Connie Rasinski. Story: Tom Morrison. Animators: Connie Rasinski, James Tyer. Produced by Paul Terry. Music by Philip A. Scheib. Cast: Roy Halee (Heckle/Jeckle), Dayton Allen (Heckle/Jeckle).

Heckle and Jeckle walk into Wacky Studios and are thrown out by the guard. They return dressed as chauffeur and director in a limousine. The guard welcomes them in and then discovers the limo is fake. He chases Heckle and Jeckle through sets for *Romeo and Juliet* and *Arctic Adventures* (they play penguins). "You can't throw us out, we've got talent!" says Heckle. "Why look!" They imitate Jimmy Durante and Groucho Marx. "That boy will certainly go a long way. And the farther he goes, the better I'll like it. They say he's got talent. How does Talent feel about this?" Another chase ensues, and Heckle and Jeckle end up locking themselves in a paddy wagon which presumably will take them off to jail.

• • • • • • • • •

Blue Hawaii (January 13, 1950)

Famous Studios. Directed by Seymour Kneitel. Animated by Al Eugster. Music: Winston Sharples.

A Screen Song and another mock travelogue. Spot gags about Diamond Head and Pearl Harbor. Jimmy Durante gets a lei thrown around his nose. A floral shirt sprouts in the rain. A shark eats a surfer. Poi is untouched by the hands of humans, only monkeys'. At a luau, Groucho Marx rolls his eyes at the native girls in their grass skirts. Follow the bouncing ball along with the title song. Afterwards, Harpo Marx chases the grass-skirted natives with a lawnmower.

• • • • • • • • •

Forest Fantasy (November 14, 1952)

Famous Studios. Directed By Seymour Kneitel. Animated By Myron Waldman, Larry Silverman. Written By Izzy Klein. Music: Winston Sharples. Cast: Jack Mercer (Owl/Frogs) (uncredited).

The Kartune series followed the Screen Songs series after Paramount, the distributor, lost the rights to that name.

Night falls, and the owl wakes up to conduct a symphony by firefly light. Cue spot gags. A spider Harpo Marx plays his web. A ten-legged centipede plays five violins. Frogs sing along, voiced by Jack Mercer! A skunk plays xylophone on a hippo's teeth. A pelican plays the bluebells, and her chick plays the drums in her pouched bill. A giraffe plays turtles with his ossicones. Insects form a violin and bow. An elephant's tusks turn into keyboards. A scarecrow dances with a haystack. A bird charms a worm, Indian-style out of a hole by playing his bill like a pungi. Before the bird can grab him, the worm knocks the bird down with a trombone. A mother kangaroo plays the flute, while its joey plays Sousaphone. Spider Harpo appears again.

Now it's time to follow the bouncing ball, although Paramount couldn't use the term "Bouncing Ball" anymore. The song is "By the Light of the Silvery Moon." Over and over.

When day breaks, a hen ejects her rooster husband from bed to crow. However, he has a Victrola with a record of crowing, and goes back to sleep.

• • • • • • • • •

The Case Of The Cockeyed Canary (December 19, 1952)
Famous Studios. Directed by Seymour Kneitel. Animated by Steve Muffatti, Morey Reden. Written by Izzy Klein. Music: Winston Sharples. Cast: Mae Questel (Audrey).

When Paramount decided not to renew the license to Little Lulu, Famous Studios created Little Audrey, designed by the same animator, Bill Tytla, and, like Lulu, inspired by his daughter.

Little Audrey fancies herself a detective and reads herself to sleep with murder mysteries. She even does machine-gun sound effects, to the distress of her pet canary, Mary. Her sleep is interrupted by a news bird with an Extra edition: Cock Robin is dead.

Private Eye Audrey arrives at the scene of the crime and she suspects everyone. A Jimmy Durante parrot says, "I only moiders the English language." She asks a Bob "Tuxedo Wearing" Hope penguin what he has up his sleeve. It turns out to be stolen silverware, and a gag stolen from Harpo Marx. All the odder because the next celebrity we meet is a cuckoo Harpo, who once again is a suspect in the murder. Audrey follows his tracks right into a tree. Harpo is in the tree. Audrey shoots him down with popcorn and then arrests him at gunpoint for murder. Then Audrey's canary confesses to the "crime." The arrow is actually a valentine. Cock Robin wakes up and sweeps Mary off her feet. Little Audrey wakes up laughing from her "dream" to find Mary's cage is empty. She looks out the window and sees Mary sharing a nest with Cock Robin, and they have already hatched an egg.

• • • • • • • • •

Wideo Wabbit (October 27, 1956)
Warner Bros. Directed By Robert McKimson. Written By Tedd Pierce. Animated By George Grandpré, Ted Bonnicksen, Keith Darling, Russ Dyson. Produced By Edward Selzer. Musical Director: Carl Stalling. Cast:

Mel Blanc (Bugs Bunny/QTTV Producer/Elmer Fudd Yelping), Arthur Q. Bryan (Elmer Fudd), Daws Butler (Bugs as Groucho/Bugs as Norton).

Robert McKimson started in 1932 as an animator for Leon Schlesinger, who promoted him to director in 1946. The McKimson unit at Warner Bros. Cartoons, Inc. had smaller budgets than the Chuck Jones cartoons, and relied more on jokes and dialogue than slapstick.

A Merrie Melodies cartoon. Bugs answers a "Help Wanted" ad at station QTTV, where the producer is a caricature of Frank Nelson. It turns out to be for *The Sportsman's Hour*, starring Elmer Fudd, and Bugs is to be the prey. Bugs takes off and runs through the studio sets, Elmer in pursuit. On the set of *You Beat Your Wife*, Bugs impersonates Groucho. Finally, Bugs tricks Elmer into putting on a bunny suit while Bugs dons Elmer's hunting clothes and turns the tables on him on *The Sportsman's Hour*. Elmer sputters with rage, but Bugs, channeling Art Carney, says, "Hey! Take it easy! Have a cigar!" Bugs puts the cigar, nose, eyebrows, and glasses disguise he was previously wearing on Elmer and notes, "Gee. What a Groucho!"

● ● ● ● ● ● ● ● ●

Injun Trouble (September 20, 1969)

Warner Bros./Seven Arts. Directed by Robert McKimson (as Bob McKimson). Story: Cal Howard. Animators: Ted Bonnicksen, James Davis (as Jim Davis), Laverne Harding (as La Verne Harding), Ed Solomon. Produced by William L. Hendricks (as Bill L. Hendricks). Music by William Lava. Cast: Larry Storch (Cool Cat).

The last executive in charge of Warner Bros. Cartoons, Inc. was David H. DePatie, appointed in 1961, and ordered to shut down the studio in 1962. In 1963, he and Friz Freleng opened Depatie-Freleng Enterprises in the old Warner Bros. Cartoons studio. They outsourced cartoons for three years before bringing production back in-house. They were unable to lure Robert Clampett out of retirement, and Alex Lovy, former animator at Walter Lantz Studio and Hanna-Barbera, was appointed director. Shortly thereafter, Seven Arts Associates bought Warner Bros. and the studio was renamed Warner Bros.-Seven Arts Animation. Robert McKimson, who took a two year break when Warner Bros. shut down its cartoon division, was hired back.

This was the last of the Merrie Melodies until 1979, the last Warner Bros. theatrical cartoon until 1987, and the 1,000th cartoon short released by Warner Bros.

Cool Cat is driving through the desert in his dune buggy when an Indian on horseback starts pursuing him. Cool Cat makes it over a canyon on a log, but the horse and Indian fall in. The horse grabs the edge of the cliff, and the Indian grabs the horse, who knocks him off. Cool Cat rescues the horse, who in turn helps him save his dune buggy when it starts to roll away.

Spot gags. A brave gifts Cool Cat with a young, fat squaw. Cool Cat calls him an Indian giver. A brave puts a bucket on his head and calls himself "Pailface." A young, slim squaw invites Cool Cat to Indian wrestle. He agrees, only to be beaten up by a large Indian brave.

Another Indian stops him and asks, "Why?"

"I thought Indians always said how," says Cool Cat.

"Me know how," replies the Indian, producing a cigar. "Now I wanna know why." He wiggles his eyebrows and Groucho-walks away.

Cool Cat arrives in Hotfoot, where men are men and horse doctors really are horses. He walks into a topless bar and orders a root beer from the shirtless male bartender. A rough cowpuncher named Gower Gulch comes in and Cool Cat cuts out literally, with a pair of scissors. He sticks his head back through his outline, saying, "So cool it, now, ya hear?"

Because of its political incorrectness, this cartoon has never been released on video or shown on broadcast television.

● ● ● ● ● ● ● ● ●

Great (Isambard Kingdom Brunel) (1975)

British Lion Film Corporation, Bob Godfrey Films. Directed by Bob Godfrey, Jeff Goldner, Ann Jolliffe. Written by Bob Godfrey, Joseph McGrath, Robyn Smyth, Richard Taylor, Paul Weisser. Animated by John Challis, Mark Shepherd, Bob Godfrey, Graeme Jackson, Ian Moo-Young, Denis Rich, Kevin Attew, Hester Coblentz, Chris Jelley. Produced by Bob Godfrey. Cast (in credits order): Richard Briers (Isambard Kingdom Brunel), Harry Fowler (Narrator), Barbara Moore (Queen Victoria),

Angus Lennie (Voice), Peter Hawkins (Voice), Dick Graham (Voice), Imogen Claire (Voice), Cyril Shaps (Voice).

Isambard Kingdom Brunel, an English engineer, helped develop the SS *Great Britain*, the largest ship built up to that time, among many other engineering marvels.

This blend of traditional and cutout animation with live action tells Brunel's story with comedy, song, and dance. It is more than a little bit like *Monty Python's Flying Circus* (1969). Toward the end of the movie, a singer, supposedly quoting Queen Victoria, croons, "A bigger thing than this, my dear, has surely never cruised/And just as soon as I'm aboard, I could be quite amused." Queen Victoria dons a Groucho Marx disguise and wiggles her eyebrows.

Winner of the Academy Award for Best Animated Short Film, 1976; and Best Animated Film, BAFTA Awards, 1976.

● ● ● ● ● ● ● ● ●

About Face (1978)

Written and drawn by Chris James. Music: Claude Jouvin. Camera: Julian Holdaway. Produced with financing by The Arts Council of Great Britain.

Description: "*About Face* (1978)... features caricatures of Henry... VIII, Mick Jagger, Oscar Wilde, Lord Alfred Douglas, Queen Elizabeth [II], Prince Philip, Prince Charles, Adolf Hitler, Idi Amin, Pablo Picasso, Salvador Dali, The Marx Brothers, David Bowie and a worm. The film was runner-up in the Grierson Award for Best Short Film of 1978 and was screened on the inaugural day of Channel Four television in November 1982. Other showings include The Arts Council Film Tour and the film festivals of Annecy, Zagreb, Los Angeles, Tampere, Varna, Lucca, Wellington and more."

● ● ● ● ● ● ● ● ●

Grease (June 16, 1978)

Paramount Pictures. Directed by Randal Kleiser. Writing Credits: Jim Jacobs and Warren Casey (original musical), Bronte Woodard (screenplay) (as Bronté Woodard), Allan Carr (adaptation). Cast (in credits order): John Travolta (Danny), Olivia Newton-John (Sandy), Stockard Channing (Rizzo), Jeff Conaway (Kenickie), Barry Pearl (Doody), Michael Tucci (Sonny), Kelly Ward (Putzie), Didi Conn (Frenchy), Jamie Donnelly (Jan), Dinah Manoff (Marty), Eve Arden (Principal McGee), Frankie Avalon (Teen Angel), Joan Blondell (Vi), Edd Byrnes (Vince Fontaine), Sid Caesar (Coach Calhoun), Alice Ghostley (Mrs. Murdock), Dody Goodman (Blanche), Sha Na Na (Johnny Casino & The Gamblers), Susan Buckner (Patty Simcox), Lorenzo Lamas (Tom Chisum), Fannie Flagg (Nurse Wilkins), Dick Patterson (Mr. Rudie), Eddie Deezen (Eugene)

The song "Grease," written by Andy Gibb and sung by Frankie Valli, plays under the main titles, designed and animated by John Wilson. They are a mixture of animation, stills, caricature, and photos. We see the stars: Travolta, Newton-John, Channing, and Conaway. There are pictures of Elvis, hula hooping, a Davy Crockett hat, an "I Like Ike" button, Groucho Marx and the duck with the secret word (guess), comic books, Marilyn Monroe, Lucille Ball, Jackie Gleason, Joseph Stalin, *MAD* magazine, General Douglas MacArthur, *Playboy* Magazine, and the Thunderbird logo. Cops chase cars around. The animated backdrop turns into the real high school and the movie begins. SPOILER ALERT: The girl gets the guy.

• • • • • • • • •

The Looney, Looney, Looney Bugs Bunny Movie (November 20, 1981)

Warner Bros. Directed by Friz Freleng. Writing Credits: John W. Dunn, David Detiege, and Friz Freleng (story), John W. Dunn (as John Dunn) and Friz Freleng, Warren Foster, and Tedd Pierce (stories). Produced by Friz Freleng. Cast: Mel Blanc (Bugs Bunny/King Arthur/Sir Osis of Liver/Sir Loin of Beef/Yosemite Sam/Gerry the Idgit Dragon/Daffy Duck/Sylvester/Tweety Pie/Porky Pig/Speedy Gonzales/Treasury Director/Rocky/Mugsy/Judge/Clancy/O'Hara/Cops/Pepe Le Pew/Clarence), June Foray (Granny), Stan Freberg (Big Bad Wolf/Three Little Bops/Singing Narrator). Ralph James (Narrator), Frank Nelson (Satan), Frank Welker (Lawyer/Interviewing Dog).

Partners David DePatie and Friz Freleng split up in 1980. Freleng returned to Warner Bros. to head up their first cartoon department since 1962. This was the second feature-length mashup of classic Warner Bros. cartoons linked with new animation. The program begins with Academy Award-winning short *Knighty-Knight Bugs* (1958) before going into the movie proper, which is in three acts. In "Satan's Waitin'," Yosemite Sam bargains with the devil, promising him Bugs Bunny's soul in place of his own. "The Unmentionables" is a parody of the television show, *The Untouchables* (1959). "The Oswald Awards" is a parody of The Oscars. Master of ceremonies Bugs, sans mustache and glasses, but with tailcoat, painted-on eyebrows, and carrot cigar, lopes across the stage Groucho-style and says, "Say the secret woid and win an Oswald."

FUN FACT: Frank Nelson worked with Groucho and Chico on the radio show, *Flywheel, Shyster, and Flywheel* (1932). He is parodied in *Wideo Wabbit* (1956).

● ● ● ● ● ● ● ● ●

A Sundae in New York (1983)

Motionpicker Productions. Directed by Jimmy Picker. Cast: Scott Record (Voice). Produced by Jimmy Picker.

Made in Claymation. Then-New York City Mayor Ed Koch talk-sings the theme to the movie *New York, New York* (1977). "I love to wake up in the city that, uh, never sleeps/And find I'm A-number 1, top of the list, king of the hill," Koch says, then morphing into Groucho Marx, adds, "And incidentally, a heckuva nice guy."

Celebrity cameos include Alfred E. Neuman, David Letterman, Rodney Dangerfield, Santa Claus; Toody and Muldoon from *Car 54, Where Are You* (1961); Frankenstein's Monster, and Frank Sinatra.

Winner of the Academy Award for Best Animated Short Film, 1983.

● ● ● ● ● ● ● ● ●

Dot Goes to Hollywood (1987)

Yoram Gross Films. Directed by Yoram Gross. Written by John Palmer. Produced by Yoram Gross. Music by Guy Gross. Cast: Barbara Frawley (Dot), Ross Higgins (Voice), Robyn Moore (Voice), Keith Scott (Voice).

Dot and the Kangaroo is a beloved children's book in Australia written in 1899 by Ethel Pedley. A young girl lost in the outback is befriended by a kangaroo and other mammals, who help her get home. An animated film adaptation was made in 1977 by Yoram Gross, who followed up with many sequels, including this one, a strange mixture of cel animation and live action.

Dot and her koala, Gumley, sing and dance to raise money for Gumley, who needs an operation for his eye affliction, which may kill him. She sings because she's happy, and when she's happy, she sings. It's a vicious circle. Working the streets makes her a mere pittance, though, and she decides the real money is whoring herself in Hollywood. Dot and Gumley hop into the pouch of the kangaroo, who hitches a ride on the logo of a Qantas plane.

In Hollywood, she meets an actor between jobs who works as a cabdriver, who reminisces about the olden days in Hollywood. Al Jolson, his back to the camera lest we see his blackface makeup, sings a song in front of the *You Are The Star* mural on Hollywood Boulevard at Wilcox Avenue. It depicts Robert Redford, Paul Newman, Sidney Poitier, Woody Allen, several dwarfs, Mae West, Mickey Rooney, Judy Garland, Marilyn Monroe, Shirley Temple, W.C. Fields, Lassie, James Dean, Charlie Chaplin, Fred Astaire, Ginger Rogers, and others. Chaplin becomes animated and performs with animated Keystone Kops and an animated Fields. The animated Three Stooges run past, and animated Marilyn dances. An animated Groucho Marx says, "Ridiculous." He pursues Marilyn, but an animated Harpo throws a banana peel in his path, causing him to slip. Harpo slips on the same peel, as animated Chico watches.

Dot meets Laurel & Hardy, who, for some reason, insist on using their first names, unlike in their movies. The Laurel & Hardy scenes alternate awkwardly between awkwardly dubbed stock footage from the public domain feature *Flying Deuces* (1939) and awkwardly animated linking segments. They tell her about a talent contest at a Hollywood studio, and she decides to enter.

Unfortunately, the studio does not allow koalas, so Dot and Gumley have to sneak in, with the guards in hot pursuit. While Dot is auditioning, the guards catch Gumley and have him sent off to the zoo. Hardy tells her what has happened and she leaves in mid-song.

A Walter Brennanesque veterinarian at the zoo realizes Gumley needs an operation but rules it too expensive. Gumley is thrown into a cage by himself.

Dot arrives at the zoo just as it is closing, but she breaks in, and with the help of a Jimmy Stewartesque elephant, a Jimmy Duranteesque lion named Leo, and a monkey named Kong, she is reunited with Gumley.

Meanwhile, despite her early departure, Dot has won the talent contest. She's not that scary talented, but to be fair, everyone else we've seen has been comparatively awful. However, Dot is nowhere to be found. The director figures out that she is at the zoo, and finds her. The vet decides to perform the operation on Gumley after all.

Dot's film debut, with stock footage of Jimmy Cagney and Shirley Temple, is a success. She is reunited onstage with the now-cured Gumley, Laurel & Hardy, Leo, Kong, Dr. Brennan, and the elephant. Groucho lopes in and says, "Whoops! I think I'm in the wrong production." I'll say he is.

● ● ● ● ● ● ● ● ●

Aladdin (November 25, 1992)

Walt Disney Pictures. Directors: Ron Clements, John Musker. Writing Credits: Ron Clements & John Musker and Ted Elliott & Terry Rossio (screenplay), Burny Mattinson, Roger Allers, Daan Jippes, Kevin Harkey, Sue C. Nichols (as Sue Nichols), Francis Glebas, Darrell Rooney, Larry Leker, James Fujii, Kirk Hanson, Kevin Lima, Rebecca Rees, David S. Smith, Chris Sanders, Brian Pimental, Patrick A. Ventura (story). Animated by Ken Duncan, Tom Sito. Supervising Animators: Duncan Marjoribanks (Abu), Glen Keane (Aladdin), Will Finn (Iago), Eric Goldberg (Genie), Andreas Deja (Jafar), Mark Henn (Jasmine), Dave Pruiksma (Sultan), Randy Cartwright (Carpet), Aaron Blaise. Character Animator: Barry Temple. Lead Animator: T. Daniel Hofstedt (Gazeem, Achmed). Effects Animator: Ted Kierscey. Produced by Ron Clements. Music by Alan Menken. Cast: Scott Weinger (Aladdin), Robin Williams (Genie/Peddler), Linda Larkin (Jasmine), Jonathan Freeman (Jafar), Frank Welker (Abu/Cave of Wonders/Rajah), Gilbert Gottfried (Iago), Douglas Seale (Sultan), Charles Adler (Gazeem/Melon Merchant/Nut Merchant) (as Charlie Adler), Jack Angel (Additional Voices), Corey Burton (Prince Achmed/Necklace Merchant), Philip L. Clarke (Additional Voices) (as Philip Clarke), and Jim Cummings (Razoul/Farouk).

Joe Grant left Disney in 1949 and went on to run a ceramics company and a greeting card business. In 1988, Disney's Feature Animation Division was trying to find out how the story development process worked in the 1930s so they could recreate it. They visited Jack Kinney, a former associate of Joe Grant's. Since Kinney was in poor health, his wife asked Grant to come to the meeting, also. The meeting led Thomas Schumacher, producer of *The Rescuers Down Under* (1990), to invite Grant to see the work-in-progress. Grant set foot on the Disney lot for the first time in more than thirty years. They liked his ideas, and more invitations followed. In 1991, he was offered part-time employment. His wife, Jennie, who had had a lung ailment for three years, urged him to accept. She died on June 10, 1991. After a period of mourning, Grant accepted the offer. For *Aladdin* (1992), Disney's thirty-first animated feature, and part of the "Disney Renaissance," Grant created, among other things, the character of Aladdin's monkey sidekick, Abu. Abu would be played by Frank Welker, one of the most prolific voice actors, who frequently played Groucho Marx and other roles in television Marxtoons.

Aladdin, trapped in a dark pit, rubs a lamp and the Genie appears and grants him three wishes. The Genie morphs into Groucho Marx and says, "No substitutions, exchanges, or refunds." The duck from *You Bet Your Life* (1950) flies down with the secret word: "REFUNDS." The Genie gets Aladdin and Abu out on a magic carpet.

Aladdin wishes for the Genie to make him a Prince so he can court the lovely Princess Jasmine, who must be wed in three days. Meanwhile, the Royal Vizier, Jafar, is scheming to marry Jasmine himself and has Aladdin dropped off a cliff into the water. He is rescued by the Genie and returns to the palace to confront Jafar. Jafar is arrested, but escapes. He gets his parrot, Iago, to steal the lamp for him and his first wish is to be made Sultan and he disrupts the Sultan's announcement of the wedding of Aladdin and Jasmine. His second wish is to be made a sorcerer and he sends Aladdin to "the ends of the earth." Aladdin gets back to Agrabah on his magic carpet. He tricks Jafar into wishing to become a genie and traps him in his own lamp. Aladdin uses his last wish to free the Genie. Aladdin and Jasmine get engaged.

In addition to Groucho, Williams impersonates Arnold Schwarzenegger, Ed Sullivan, William F. Buckley, Jr.,; Señor Wences, Robert De Niro, Carol Channing, Arsenio Hall, Walter Brennan, Mary Hart, Ethel Merman, Rodney Dangerfield, Jack Nicholson, and Peter Lorre. The design for most characters was based on the work of Al Hirschfeld, who caricatured The Marx Brothers numerous times.

• • • • • • • • •

Looney Tunes: Back in Action (November 14, 2003)

Warner Bros. Directed by Joe Dante. Written by Larry Doyle. Produced by Bernie Goldmann, Joel Simon, Paula Weinstein. Music by Jerry Goldsmith. Cast: Brendan Fraser (DJ Drake/Himself/Voice of Tasmanian Devil and She-Devil), Jenna Elfman (Kate), Steve Martin (Mr. Chairman), Timothy Dalton (Damien Drake), Joe Alaskey (Bugs Bunny/Daffy Duck/Beaky Buzzard/Sylvester/Mama Bear), Jeff Bennett (Yosemite Sam/Foghorn Leghorn/Nasty Canasta) (as Jeff Glenn Bennett), Billy West (Elmer Fudd/Peter Lorre), Eric Goldberg (Tweety Bird/Marvin the Martian/Speedy Gonzalez), Bruce Lanoil (Pepe Le Pew), June Foray (Granny), Bob Bergen (Porky Pig), Casey Kasem (Shaggy), Frank Welker (Scooby-Doo), Danny Chambers (Cottontail Smith), Stan Freberg (Baby Bear), Will Ryan (Papa Bear), Danny Mann (Robo Dog & Spy Car), Mel Blanc (Gremlin Car) (archive footage).

Technically the last traditionally animated Warner Bros. film, although it also contains computer animation and live action.

Daffy says, "I'm afraid the brothers Warner must choose between a handsome matinee idol, or this miscreant perpetrator of low burlesque," and points to Bugs wearing Groucho glasses. Studio executive Kate Houghton fires Daffy, and she and Bugs spend the rest of the movie trying to get him back.

There are two other Marx references in the movie. Daffy is liquefied by a ray gun and then sucked up in a turkey baster. Kate says, "You're going to put him back, right? Because I can't go back to LA with duck soup." When Bugs is "incapacitated" by Marvin the Martian's Bubble Gun, he says, "Of course, you realize this means war."

The movie's failure caused Warner Bros. to hold back the release of new completed Looney Tunes shorts and to cancel those in production.

• • • • • • • • •

Sausage Party (August 12, 2016)

Annapurna Pictures, Columbia Pictures, Point Grey Pictures. Directed by Greg Tiernan, Conrad Vernon. Writing Credits: Kyle Hunter, Ariel Shaffir, Seth Rogen, Evan Goldberg (screenplay); Seth Rogen, Evan Goldberg,

Jonah Hill (story). Produced by Megan Ellison, Evan Goldberg, Seth Rogen, Conrad Vernon. Music by Christopher Lennertz, Alan Menken. Cast: Alistair Abell (Mariachi Salsa/Gefilte Fish), Iris Apatow (Berry Good Candies/Grape #3/Coconut Milk), Sugar Lyn Beard (Baby Carrot/Cookies), Michael Cera (Barry), Ian James Corlett (Apple/Tickilish Licorice/Relish/ Bag of Dog Food), Michael Daingerfield (Chunk Munchers Cereal/Light Bulb/Indian Chutney), Brian Dobson (Italian Tomato/Lettuce), Michael Dobson (Queso), James Franco (Druggie), Bill Hader (Firewater / Tequila / El Guaco), Salma Hayek (Popped Cherry Mixer/Plum #1/ Loretta Bun/ Frozen Fruitz), Jonah Hill (Carl), Anders Holm (Troy), Nick Kroll (Douche), David Krumholtz (Lavash), Danny McBride (Honey Mustard), Edward Norton (Sammy), Nicole Oliver (Sally Bun/Ice Cream/Watermelon/Female Shopper #1), Craig Robinson (Grits), Seth Rogen (Frank/Sergeant Pepper), Paul Rudd (Darren), Kristen Wiig (Brenda), Harland Williams (Ketchup/ Drug Dealer/Baba Ganoush).

Groceries begin every day that Shopwell's begin each day by singing a hymn to their gods—the shoppers who pick them up and take them to the paradise of The Great Beyond. Frank, a hot dog, learns from Firewater, one of the Immortals (unperishable goods) that foodstuffs are actually taken home and eaten. Firewater even wrote the original lyrics to the hymn, although he bemoans the fact that others have changed the words to suit their own agenda. In particular, the Nazi sauerkraut, for example, sing ethnic slurs against the Juice, whom Firewater has always liked. Apple and Orange Juice are anthropomorphic versions of Harpo and Groucho Marx. Frank leads a revolt and kills all the shoppers, but then Firewater tells him that this is all just a cartoon. At the end, the groceries go through a star gate to get their revenge on the filmmakers in *Sausage Party II.*

The transition from trained voice actors to stars is almost complete here. All the major roles and many tiny ones are filled by actors who could open a movie on their own. What's a voice actor like Frank Welker to do? Go to television.

TELEVISION MARXTOONS

● ● ● ● ● ● ● ● ●

The Quick Draw McGraw Show Season 2, Episode 10 "Scooter Rabbit" (November 12, 1960)

Hanna-Barbera Studios. Directed by Joseph Barbera, William Hanna. Written by Michael Maltese. Animators: Dick Lundy,Lewis Marshall. Produced by Joseph Barbera, William Hanna. Cast: Daws Butler (Quick Draw McGraw/Baba Looey/Scooter).

William Hanna and Joseph Barbera were hired by Harman and Ising at the MGM cartoon studio in 1939 within weeks of each other. There, they worked on several shorts in the Tom and Jerry series and the Droopy series. In 1957, MGM decided to close the cartoon studio. Hanna and Barbera failed to persuade MGM to do their proposed animated TV series, so they started their own studio with the backing of live-action film director George Sidney, who got Screen Gems, Columbia Pictures' TV subsidiary, to make a distribution deal with them. Many former MGM animators joined the production staff, as did voice actors, such as Daws Butler. The first two shows were *The Ruff and Reddy Show* (1957) and *The Huckleberry Hound Show* (1958).

The Quick Draw McGraw Show (1959) was Hanna-Barbera's next cartoon production. Quick Draw was an anthropomorphic horse that generally played a sheriff. Daws Butler, veteran voice actor and Groucho Marx impersonator, played the leading role.

The Mayor is facing reelection and he needs Quick Draw to help him by capturing Scooter Rabbit. Scooter, who doesn't look like Groucho Marx but is played by Daws Butler with a Grouchoesque voice, says, "Welcome to *You Bet Your Life You Won't Catch Me.*" Quickdraw gets Snuffles the hound dog to help in the search by appealing to Snuffles' addiction to dog biscuits. Scooter pretends he is a doctor and puts Snuffles to bed. Quickdraw and Baba Looey get Scooter under control with dog biscuits. The Groucho-like repartee is written by Michael Maltese, who was a writer on *Slick Hare* (1947). He left Warner Bros. circa 1958, and was replaced by John W. Dunn.

• • • • • • • • •

The Yogi Bear Show (Snagglepuss) Season 1, Episode 16 "Remember the Daze" (May 15, 1961)

Hanna-Barbera Studios. Directed by William Hanna, Joseph Barbera. Written by Michael Maltese. Animated by William Keil. Music: Hoyt Curtin. Produced by William Hanna, Joseph Barbera.

Snagglepuss was a pink anthropomorphic mountain lion character that began his career on *The Quick Draw McGraw Show* (1959) as Snaggletooth before becoming the star of a regular segment on *The Yogi Bear Show* (1961) in thirty-two episodes. His voice, performed by Daws Butler, was an imitation of Bert Lahr's. Snagglepuss frequently tangles with Major Minor, a tiny big game hunter.

In "Remember the Daze," Major Minor's testimonial dinner is interrupted by TV host Turner Backward, who is doing an episode of his show, *This Is Your Strife*. Turner points out that the Major has never bagged Snagglepuss, so Major Minor tries to kill the lion. Snagglepuss leads the Major on a chase through the TV studio, where various ill fates befall him. On *What's the Secret Word*, Snagglepuss, with cigar, mustache, and bad toupee, tells the Major he will win a new hat if he says the secret word. "Huh" turns out to be the secret word, and the Major's old hat is blown off. Snagglepuss says, "Exit stage right," before exiting stage left. Finally, on the *Man Into Space Show*, the Major is launched away in a rocket.

Sometime later, Snagglepuss checks his mail and finds Turner Backwards in the box, telling him *This Is Your Strife*. Snagglepuss says, "Exit stage left," before exiting stage right.

The Grouchoesque banter is once again by Michael Maltese, and Butler does Snagglepuss doing Lahr doing Groucho.

● ● ● ● ● ● ● ● ●

Beany and Cecil Season 1, Episode 18 "So What And The Seven Whatnots" (1962)

Bob Clampett Studios, Snowball Studios. Directed by Robert Clampett. Written by Dale Hale, Robert Clampett, Jack Kinney. Animated by Bud Hester, Bill Nunes. Produced by Robert Clampett, A.C.R. Stone. Music: Jack Roberts, Hoyt Curtin, Bob Clampett, Sody Clampett. Voice Actors: Jim MacGeorge, Irv Shoemaker.

Bob Clampett created the puppet show, *Time for Beany* (1949), after leaving Warner Bros. The cartoon premiered Sunday, October 11, 1959. By 1962, it was on Saturdays during prime time, speaking to its popularity amongst adults. For the next five years, reruns were shown on Saturday mornings.

Beany and Cecil go to the entertainment capital of the world, Lost Wages, Nevada. Uncle Captain gives Cecil his year's pay, a shiny nickel. Cecil passes up Dishonest John's shady Kastle Klub to see So What and the Seven Whatnots, much to the displeasure of John, who morphs into the Witch from *Snow White* (1937) and brews up some of his poison apple juice: ant poison, uncle poison, and arsenic and old shoe lace.

So What is a toothsome blonde, and the Seven Whatnots are $tas¢h-do, a caricature of Louis Armstrong; Elfis, an elven Presley; Harpsy McChord (Guess Who); Dizzy R. Nez, a caricature of Desi Arnaz; Fred McFurry, whose name parodies Fred MacMurray; Screw-Loose Latrec, a caricature of Toulouse Latrec; and Loverachi, a caricature of Liberace.

Dishonest John places his poison apple juice on Cecil's table with a sign that reads, "For So What." Cecil accidentally inhales it. "My headache's gone," he says, parodying a contemporaneous Excedrin commercial before keeling over.

Dishonest John eliminates the middle serpent and gives his potion to So What directly. She drinks it and keels over. Cecil says to the Seven Whatnots, "Let him have it, fellers!" Fred hits Dishonest John, who bounces off Harpsy's harp into a table held in Cecil's mouth. John falls into the upright piano, exposing his underwear-clad buttocks to Loverachi, who singes them with a blowtorch. Finally, Cecil hits him with a bass saxophone and he goes through Harpsy's harp, cutting him into five pieces. They all run away.

The only thing that can awaken So What is a kiss. Cecil gives her one of his super slurp-kisses. So What and the Seven Whatnots give Cecil a parade.

FUN FACTS: Harpo Marx was a big fan of *Beany and Cecil* (1959).

Groucho Marx once wrote a letter to Clampett saying *Beany and Cecil* (1959) "was the only children's show adult enough for his young daughter, Melinda, to watch."

Jim MacGeorge went on to play the Grouchoesque character Crazy Claws.

● ● ● ● ● ● ● ● ●

The Mad, Mad, Mad Comedians (April 7, 1970)

Rankin-Bass Productions, Mushi Studios. Directed by Arthur Rankin, Jr.; Jules Bass.

Written by Romeo Muller (Special Material). Animated by Steve Nakagawa (Animation Supervisor). Caricatures: Bruce Stark. Produced by Arthur Rankin, Jr.; Jules Bass. Music: Maury Laws. Vocal Talent: Jack Benny (Himself), George Burns (Himself), Groucho Marx (Himself), The Smothers Brothers (Themselves), Flip Wilson (Himself, Christopher Columbus), George Jessel (Himself), Phyllis Diller (Herself), Jack E. Leonard (Himself), Henny Youngman (Himself), Paul Frees (Introductions, W.C. Fields, Chico Marx, Harpo Marx, Zeppo Marx, Cop, Fields' Future Mother-In-law), Joan Gardner (Secondary Characters).

Originally broadcast before the 42nd Academy Awards ceremony. Most of the comedians supplied their actual voices, except for the late W. C. Fields, the late Chico Marx, and the tardy Zeppo Marx, who were played by Paul Frees.

Jessel, Leonard, Youngman, and Diller perform interstitial material. Flip Wilson does a standup bit about Christopher Columbus. Burns and Benny perform a skit where cheapskate Benny drives his Maxwell across the river to save a fifty-cent toll. The Maxwell is not performed by Mel

Blanc, who played the auto on radio and posthumously played the AMC Gremlin in *Looney Tunes: Back in Action* (2003). W. C. Fields cons a St. Bernard out of his brandy keg. The Smothers Brothers perform a musical routine. There are musical wraparounds before each sketch.

The centerpiece of the show is "Napoleon's First Waterloo," a scene from The Marx Brothers' first Broadway hit, *I'll Say She Is* (1924), and later performed in Vaudeville. The Marx Brothers' follow-up Broadway hits, *The Cocoanuts* (1925) and *Animal Crackers* (1928), were both turned into motion pictures, but this is the only scene originally from the show that was committed to film with any of the original cast. "The Theatrical Agency" sketch that appears in *The House that Shadows Built* (1931) dates back to their pre-Broadway Vaudeville days. Groucho is seventy-nine here, and sounds it, and the script is heavily edited, but this is what we have, and its historical importance cannot be overstated.

At the court of Napoleon, a footman announces Napoleon's gentlemen-in-waiting: Alphonse (Chico), Francois (Zeppo), and Gaston (Harpo), who bypass Napoleon and go straight to Josephine.

"I must be off," says Napoleon. "And, Josephine, if I leave you here with these three snakes, I really must be off."

Josephine says, "When you go, all France is with you."

Napoleon says, "Yes, and the last time I came back, all France was with you. And a slice of Italy, too." Leaving, he drops his sword on the floor.

Alphonse begins making love to Josephine, but hides when Napoleon returns.

"I thought you were at the front," says Josephine.

"I was," says Napoleon, "but nobody answered the bell, so I came around here." Napoleon finds his sword, but drops it again upon leaving.

Gaston appears with harp. He hides under Josephine's skirt when Napoleon comes back. Napoleon knows people have been there and decides to smoke them out with Flit (snuff in the original Broadway version). Alphonse, Francois, and Gaston are caught and sent to the firing squad. Shots are heard, and Alphonse and Gaston appear in their underwear, chasing the guards with a rifle. Curtain.

Celebrity caricatures in the audience include President Richard Nixon, First Lady Pat Nixon, ex-President Lyndon Johnson, ex-First Ladies Lady Bird Johnson and Jackie Onassis, Dean Martin and Jerry

Lewis (seated together), Ray Charles, Popeye, and Joe Namath. The Beatles, minus Ringo, have a cameo.

● ● ● ● ● ● ● ● ●

Magic Shadows (1974-1987)

TVO. Series Music by Harry Forbes. Cast: Robert Godwin (Himself), Elwy Yost (Host)

Magic Shadows (1974) was a half-hour show on Canadian television that presented old movies in serialization. In the opening credits, cutout animation is used to show a series of images. Three Grouchos appear. A hand changes one of them to Harpo and another one to Chico.

● ● ● ● ● ● ● ● ●

The Electric Company Season Six, Episode 130B "Frootsie" (1977)

Children's Television Workshop. Directed by Bob Schwarz. Writing Credits: Tom Whedon (Head Writer), John Boni, Sara Compton, Tom Dunsmuir, Thad Mumford, Jeremy Stevens, and Jim Thurman. Producer: Andrew B. Ferguson, Jr.

The Electric Company (1971) was created by Paul Dooley (yup, that Paul Dooley) and employed sketch comedy and other devices (including animation) to help elementary school kids develop their language skills.

This was apparently an animated parody of the "Tootsie-Frootsie Ice Cream" scene in *A Day at the Races* (1937). There are three cels that sometimes turn up for sale online, two depicting Chico and Groucho, the other depicting Groucho in four poses. Sometimes erroneously credited to *Sesame Street* (1969). Released on VHS in 1986, never released on DVD. Not found online, not reviewed for this book, and no further information is available.

• • • • • • • • •

The Robonic Stooges Episode 27 "Dr. Jekyll and Hide Curly" (March 4, 1978)

Hanna-Barbera Studios. Written by Kathy Colburn, Tom Dagenais, Dianne Dixon, Kari Oaurs, Andy Heyward, Chris Jenkyns, Mark Jones, Joan Maurer, Michael Maurer, Norman Maurer, Jack Mendelsohn, Howie Post, Cliff Roberts, Sandy Sandifer. Story Directors: Alvaro Arce, Carl Fallberg, Cullen Blaine (as Cullen Houghtaling), Mike O'Connor, Don Sheppard, George Singer. Story Editors: Norman Maurer, Sid Morse. Animated by Sue Speak, Cecil Collins, Rodney D'Silva, Dick Dunn, Peter Eastment, John Ellis, Warwick Gilbert, Gerald Grabner, Sebastian Hurpia, Greg Ingram, Richard Jones, Cynthia Leech. Produced by Terry Morse, Jr. Executive Producers: William Hanna, Joseph Barbera. Creative Producer: Iwao Takamoto. Associate Producer: Neil Balnaves. Cast: Joe Baker (Larry), Paul Winchell (Moe), Frank Welker (Curly), David Jolliffe (Larry), John Stephenson (Sheriff Bagley), Paul Winchell (Woofer), Bob Hastings (D.D.), Patricia Stitch (Pepper), Tara Talboy (Dotty), Jim MacGeorge (Wimper).

The Three Stooges were a comedy team contemporaneous with The Marx Brothers. They started out in Vaudeville literally as stooges for Ted Healy before moving into motion pictures with the coming of sound. The trio broke away from Healy and went on to do a large number of shorts for Columbia on "Poverty Row." These shorts were made quickly and cheaply, with generous use of stock footage and stand-ins, and relied on violence for most of the comedy. The team in the movies originally consisted of Larry Fine, Moe Howard, and his brother, Shemp. Shemp left the team and was replaced by brother Curly. When Curly had a stroke, Shemp came back to do some shorts before leaving again. When Shemp left for the final time, he was replaced by Joe Besser, a fat, balding man, who played a sissy character and would later play a little boy opposite Abbott & Costello. Curly Joe DeRita later replaced Besser in a series of feature films. It was this permutation of the team that starred in the cartoon series, *The New Three Stooges* (1965), providing the voices and doing live wraparounds. The team's early shorts with Shemp and Curly had been widely syndicated to television in the meantime, making The Three Stooges huge stars all over again.

In 1977, bionic was all the rage, and unfortunately, The Three Stooges were not exempt from this fad. *The Robonic Stooges* originally aired from September 10, 1977, to December 24, 1977, as a segment on the CBS show, *The Skatebirds* (1977). Fan favorite Curly Howard came back for this show, but all the voices were impersonated since he, Moe, and Larry were dead. The characters were superheroes, who got their orders from the much put-upon Agent 000. In 1978, *The Skatebirds* (1977) was cancelled and the show got its own half-hour timeslot, along with *Woofer and Wimper, Dog Detectives*; and it ran for 16 episodes.

Dr. Jekyll, in a 1906 San Francisco prison, uses Red Hot Atomic Pepper to turn the back of his head into Mr. Hyde and breaks out, resolving to get revenge on The Robonic Stooges, especially Curly. Agent 000 orders them to capture Dr. Jekyll and hide Curly. Curly's first disguise makes him look like Joe Besser on *The Abbott and Costello Show* (1952). He finally settles on a Frankenstein's monster mask. Dr. Jekyll kidnaps them anyway.

The back of Curly's head is transformed into Mr. Hyde, and Curly sprinkles Dr. Jekyll's Red Hot Atomic Pepper on the other stooges, turning the backs of their heads into monsters. Curly uses his chemical set to try to change them back to normal. The first effort backfires, turning Curly, Larry, and Moe into Groucho, Harpo, and Chico Marx. "Say the secret woid and you win a hundred dollars," says Groucho-Curly. The second try works and they capture Hyde, but start the San Francisco earthquake.

Frank Welker plays Curly and Groucho here.

● ● ● ● ● ● ● ● ●

The Kwicky Koala Show (Crazy Claws) (1981)

Hanna-Barbera Productions, Hanna-Barbera Australia. Directed by George Gordon, Carl Urbano, Rudy Zamora, Ray Patterson, Bob Goe, Terry Harrison. Animated by Frank Andrina, Ed Barge, Tom Barnes, Susan Beak, Bob Bemiller, Lefty Callahan, Rudy Cataldi, Jesse Cosio, Zeon Davush, Ed De Mattia, Joan Drake, Dick Dunn. Produced by Art Scott. Musical Director: Hoyt Curtin. Cast: Jim MacGeorge (Crazy Claws), Don Messick (Rawhide Clyde), Peter Cullen (Bristletooth), Michael Bell (Ranger Rangerfield).

After leaving Warner Bros., Tex Avery directed at Paramount, MGM, and Lantz. Starting in 1955, he produced commercials for about twenty-three years. In 1979, he went to Hanna-Barbera to do *The Kwicky Koala Show* (1981) but he died in 1980 before it aired. It is one of his final works. The characters, who usually appeared in different segments, included Kwicky Koala, The Bungle Brothers, Dirty Dawg, and Crazy Claws. Kwicky Koala is reminiscent of Avery's Droopy, The Bungle Brothers are similar to Avery's characters George and Junior, and Dirty Dawg was played by Frank Welker. Crazy was a wildcat whose claws could be a switch blade, buzz saw, drill, or any other sharp instrument. He walks with Groucho Marx's lope, and he is played by Jim MacGeorge imitating Groucho. Rawhide Clyde, a trapper, and his dog, Bristletooth, try unsuccessfully to capture Crazy in a U.S. national park run by Ranger Rangerfield. Rawhide Clyde wears a skunk skin cap and Bristletooth is fond of beef jerky, reminiscent of Snuffles the hound dog's love for dog biscuits in *Quick Draw McGraw* (1959), another Hanna-Barbera production. Ranger Rangerfield likes to quote the rule book and spout nature facts.

• • • • • • • • •

QUOTES (from various episodes):

Crazy Claws (singing to the tune of "Oh! Susanna"): "Oh don't you cry for me/Cause the tears get on my leg and give me water on the knee."

*

Crazy Claws: I gave you guys a good plan and you messed it up. I'm insulted. In fact, I'm outsulted.

*

Crazy Claws: With all those fleas, Rawhide is really gonna have a raw hide. On second thought, scratch that last joke.

*

Crazy Claws: This ice should go on a diet. It isn't thin enough!

*

Rawhide Clyde: Are you joshing, stranger?

Crazy Claws: No, I'm Crazy Claws!

*

Clyde: It's that there cat critter!
Crazy Claws: Don't be formal, call me Crazy, or you might call me later, but if you do call me later I'll be gone!

*

Crazy Claws: Just use your head, although I must say it looks pretty well used already!

*

Crazy Claws: I just love the snow, except for those flakes!

*

Clyde: Well, godarn it, read the sign, you varmint!
Crazy Claws: Thin ice. Okay, I'll go find some fat ice! (Crazy Claws skates right over the thin ice)

*

Clyde: Now how come he didn't fall through? I just naturally don't understand it!
Crazy Claws: It's okay, folks, he just naturally doesn't understand anything!

*

Crazy Claws: Isn't that nice, it's a coming out party. I think I'll join them before they fall apart! (Clyde and The Ranger crash through a tree.)
Crazy Claws: How's that for unpacking a trunk?

● ● ● ● ● ● ● ● ●

Episode list:

Episode 1: "Crazy, It's Cold Outside" (September 12, 1981) Crazy moves into Clyde's cabin during the winter.
Episode 2: "The Claws Conspiracy" (September 19, 1981) Spot gags as Clyde tries to capture Crazy. This seems like it may have originally been the pilot.

Episode 3: "Crazy Challenges" (September 26, 1981) Clyde tries to capture Crazy during a series of challenges with Bristletooth.

Episode 4: "Clyde's Birthday Surprise" (October 3, 1981) Clyde holds a surprise party for Ranger Rangerfield to capture Crazy.

Episode 5: "The Ice Rage" (October 10, 1981) Clyde tries to capture Crazy as Crazy and Ranger Rangerfield cross the snowy park to post a sign.

Episode 6: "Claws Encounters of the Worst Kind" (October 17, 1981) Crazy and Clyde have fun with a telescope and aliens. Crazy Claws also has a guest appearance in the Bungle Brothers' wraparound in this show.

Episode 7: "Lookout Crazy" (October 24, 1981) As Ranger Rangerfield attempts to finish a lookout tower, Clyde tries to capture Crazy.

Episode 8: "Crazy Camping" (October 31, 1981) Crazy and Clyde go camping and tangle with an alligator.

Episode 9: "Gold Crazy" (November 7, 1981) Clyde thinks Crazy has a stash of gold and must keep him safe until he leads them there.

Episode 10: "See Saw Claws" (November 14, 1981) Ranger Rangerfield tries to open a new playground while Clyde tries to capture Crazy.

Episode 11: "Choo Crazy" (November 21, 1981) Ranger Rangerfield and Crazy are on a runaway train as Clyde tries to capture Crazy.

Episode 12: "Bearly Asleep" (November 28, 1981) Crazy and Clyde deal with a hibernating grizzly.

Episode 13: "Old Blowhard" (December 5, 1981) As Crazy tries to shower in a geyser, Clyde tries to capture him.

Episode 14: "Snow Biz" (December 12, 1981) Clyde tries to capture Crazy after a cold snap leaves the park covered in ice and snow.

Episode 15: "Claws Ahoy" (December 19, 1981) Clyde tries to capture Crazy on a sightseeing boat piloted by Ranger Rangerfield.

Episode 16: "Rattletrap Rawhide" (December 26, 1981) Clyde tries to capture Crazy after a rainstorm leaves the park a muddy mess.

• • • • • • • • •

Alice Through the Looking Glass (1987)

Burbank Films Australia, Jambre Productions. Directed by Andrea Bresciani, Richard Slapczynski. Writer: Jameson Brewer, based on the novel by Lewis Carroll. Produced by Jameson Brewer. Music by Todd Hayen. Cast (in credits order): Janet Waldo (Alice/The Red Queen), Townsend Coleman (Tom Fool), Phyllis Diller (The White Queen), Hal Smith (Bandersnatch/ Conductor/Horse), Jonathan Winters (Tweedledum/Tweedledee), George Gobel (Humpty Dumpty), Alan Young (The White Knight), Mr. T (Jabberwock), Clive Revill (The Snark/The Goat), Will Ryan (The Paper Man), Hal Rayle (Ed Sullivan/The Marx Brothers), Booker Bradshaw (The Centaur), Alan Dinehart (Father/The White King/The Wizard).

A British tale adapted for Australian television using American actors. There's a blizzard outside, and after her father leaves to deliver a baby, Alice is left alone with her cat, Cinder. She wonders what it would be like to go through the mirror. There is a thunderclap—during a blizzard, mind you—and she goes through the glass.

She finds herself in Chessland and meets Tom Fool, a Jester/Magician with a magic staff. He takes her to see The White Queen, who demands Tom Fool amuse her. He morphs into Ed Sullivan, and then Groucho, Harpo, and Chico Marx. The White Queen tells Alice if she can advance eight squares, The Red Queen will have to crown her queen. Alice and Tom take a flying horse to Square Two, where Tom leaves her. She then takes a submersible train to Square Three, and a land boat to Square Four. At Square 5, she meets Humpty Dumpty. At Square 6, she meets The White Knight, who promises to protect her but doesn't. Fortunately, Tom Fool rejoins her. With his magic staff, they fly over a trap set in Square 7 set by The Jabberwock and The Bandersnatch and over The Red Queen's moat into Square 8. He dissolves the guards' armor with his magic staff.

The Red Queen reluctantly crowns Alice queen. Then The Red Queen calls more guards. Suddenly, Tom's staff is powerless to beat the guards or jump the moat, until it isn't. In the jump, the staff gets broken and Alice loses her crown. The Guards, Jabberwock, Bandersnatch, and Snark chase Alice and Tom. She gets back to the mirror and goes through as Tom kisses her.

She wakes up, and Cinder is licking her. It was all a dream—or was it?

● ● ● ● ● ● ● ● ●

Jim Henson's Muppet Babies Season 4, Episode 17 "Masquerading Muppets" (January 9, 1988)

Jim Henson Productions, Marvel Productions. Directed by Ray Lee (supervising director). Writing Credits: Rich Fogel and Mark Seidenberg (writers), Jim Henson (creator), Jeffrey Scott (developer). Produced by John Ahern, Robert Shellhorn (as Bob Shellhorn). Music by Robert J. Walsh. Cast (in credits order): Greg Berg (Fozzie/Scooter), Dave Coulier (Animal), Katie Leigh (Rowlf), Laurie O'Brien (Piggy), Russi Taylor (Gonzo), Frank Welker (Kermit/Skeeter), Barbara Billingsley (Nanny).

Muppet Babies (1984) imagines what life would have been like for the Muppets if they had been brought up together. They live in a nursery and Nanny watches over them. Unlike *The Muppet Show* (1976), the series is animated, with generous use of live-action stock footage.

The babies are invited to a masquerade party and Nanny gives them a box of old clothes to look through to devise their own costumes. Baby Gonzo literally dives into the box and comes out wearing Groucho glasses. "How he got into my pajamas, I'll never know," he says, flicking an imaginary cigar. He also tries on a number of other costumes. Told to pick one, he wears the Groucho glasses on his chest, regular glasses on his face, and various other accoutrements.

● ● ● ● ● ● ● ● ●

Jim Henson's Muppet Babies Season 5, Episode 1 "Muppets Not Included" (September 10, 1988)

Jim Henson Productions, Marvel Productions. Directed by Ray Lee. Writing credits: Sindy McKay and Larry Swerdlove (written by), Jim Henson (creator), and Jeffrey Scott (developer). Produced by John Ahern. Music by Robert J. Walsh (as Rob Walsh). Cast: Greg Berg (Fozzie/Scooter),

Dave Coulier (Animal), Katie Leigh (Rowlf), Laurie O'Brien (Piggy), Russi Taylor (Gonzo), and Frank Welker (Kermit/Skeeter), Barbara Billingsley (Nanny). Appearing via archival footage: Edgar Bergen (Himself/Charlie McCarthy), Oliver Hardy (Himself), Jim Henson (Dr. Teeth), Bob Hope (Himself), Stan Laurel (Himself), Groucho Marx (Himself), Harpo Marx (Himself), Ronald Reagan (Himself), Edward G. Robinson (Himself), James Stewart (Himself), Shirley Temple (Herself), Ed Wynn (Himself).

Baby Kermit and Baby Fozzie go down to the basement to get a box for Nanny containing a mystery object. Each baby has a different idea what the object is and has a fantasy sequence. Baby Fozzie thinks it's a Mupp-O-Matic, a K-Tel-type appliance. Baby Gonzo thinks it's an Intergalactic Cheeseburger Maker. Baby Rowlf thinks it's a banjo. Baby Scooter thinks it's a dinosaur skull. Baby Piggy thinks it's a TV microphone and hosts a game show, *Celebrity Circle*, "the only game show that features one hundred Hollywood stars." The stars appear via archival footage, and in addition to those listed above include Tom Selleck, Cary Grant, Mickey Rooney, John Wayne, Gary Cooper, Mae West, and Joan Blondell. Harpo Marx honks his horn and *You Bet Your Life* (1950)-era Groucho says, in a dubbed voice, "That's the most ridiculous thing I ever hoid." Nanny reveals that the object is actually a tea strainer. The actor voicing Groucho is uncredited, but I suspect frequent Groucho impersonator Frank Welker.

• • • • • • • • •

The Real Ghostbusters Season 4, Episode 1 "The Joke's on Ray" (September 10, 1988)

Directed by Will Meugniot. Writing Credits: Dan Aykroyd, Harold Ramis (characters); Len Janson, Chuck Menville (written by). Produced by Will Meugniot. Music by Shuki Levy, Haim Saban. Cast (in credits order): Frank Welker (Slimer/Dr. Raymond Stantz), Dave Coulier (Dr. Peter Venkman), Buster Jones (Winston Zeddemore), Maurice LaMarche (Dr. Egon Spengler), Kath Soucie (Janine Melnitz).

The conceit of *The Real Ghostbusters* (1986) is that the hit live-action movie *Ghostbusters* (1984) was based on their exploits. The words "The Real" were also added as a dig against Filmation, which had a rival series,

Ghostbusters (1986), and claimed the title. The Real Ghostbusters travel all over the world, well, busting ghosts.

Ray inherits a joke shop in Queens from his Uncle Gaylord. He and Slimer go to check it out. Slimer finds a pair of Groucho glasses and says, "Say the secret woid and you get an extra dollar." Then, he sees himself in the mirror and gets spooked.

Later, the Ghostbusters answer a call at a bakery being terrorized by a giant frog. The "frog" is revealed to be a water balloon from Gaylord's Joke Shop. The Ghostbusters, disgusted, leave Ray behind.

Ray realizes that he has unwittingly released two imps from the joke shop. The Ghostbusters lure the imps back to the shop and recapture them. "No more jokes," Ray promises. "Jokes really are silly kids' stuff, and we're all a little too mature for that." He gets into the car, and Egon, Peter, and Winston are all wearing Groucho glasses.

• • • • • • • • •

Al Hirschfeld Animation—TNT Commercial (1990)

Turner Network Television used to show classic motion pictures, and an art director there got the idea to animate Hirschfeld drawings for a commercial. Groucho Marx says, in a line from *A Day at the Races* (1937), "... but for you, I'd make love to a crocodile." The caricature of "Groucho" is actually Frank Ferrante in the stage play *Groucho: A Life in Revue* (1986). Also seen and in some cases heard are Clark Gable, Katharine Hepburn, Humphrey Bogart, Cary Grant, Fred Astaire, Judy Garland, Gene Kelly, and others. This commercial ran for several years.

• • • • • • • • •

Chip 'n Dale Rescue Rangers Season 2, Episode 37 "Out of Scale" (February 8, 1990)

Directed by John Kimball, Bob Zamboni, and Alan Zaslove (supervising director). Written by David Wise. Produced by Tad Stones, Alan Zaslove. Music by Glen Daum. Cast: Corey Burton (Dale/Zipper), Peter Cullen (Ratso Ratskiwatski/Ross), Jim Cummings (Monterey Jack/Prof. Nimnul/Sgt. Spinelli/Rocco), Danny Gans (Groucho Marx Pigeon/Moose), Patti

Howeth (Bag Mouse), Tress MacNeille (Chip/Gadget), Deborah Walley (Buffy Ratskiwatski).

Chip 'n Dale are cartoon chipmunks created by Walt Disney Studios in 1943. They usually played antagonists of Goofy or Donald Duck, although they had three of their own shorts. The original idea for the then-titled *Rescue Rangers* featured two mice, but they were replaced with the established Disney characters at the suggestion of Disney CEO Michael Eisner.

A "Groucho Marx pigeon" shows up at the headquarters of the Rescue Rangers. His normal roosting spot, a thirty-foot-high statue weighing 400 tons, has been stolen, apparently in a pickup truck. The Rangers can't figure out how this was done until they discover that gangsters led by Ratso Ratskiwatski have stolen Professor Nimnul's Gigantico Ray Gun and are using it to shrink objects. The gangster's next target for shrinking down is the art museum, which Ratso gives his daughter as a present. The Rangers reverse the process on the art museum. Ratso's house is destroyed, and he, his gang, his daughter, and Professor Nimnul are rounded up by the cops.

• • • • • • • • •

Tiny Toon Adventures Season 1, Episode 116 "Fields of Honey" (November 2, 1990)

Warner Bros. Animation, Amblin Television. Directed by Ken Boyer. Produced by Richard Arons, Sherri Stoner, Tom Ruegger, Alfred Gilmeno, Steven Spielberg. Music: Bill Ross. Cast: Charlie Adler [Charles Adler] (Buster Bunny), Tress MacNeille (Babs Bunny), Cree Summer (Elmyra Duff), Joe Alaskey (Plucky Duck, Ed Sullivan), Don Messick (Hamton J. Pig, Bosko), Frank Welker (Gogo Dodo, Book Worm), Danny Cooksey (Montana Max), Greg Burson (Elmer Fudd), Noel Blanc (Porky Pig), Jeff Bergman (Bugs Bunny), B. J. Ward (Honey).

Tiny Toon Adventures (1990) was Warner Bros.' first original animated television series. Babs Bunny, Buster Bunny, Plucky Duck, Gogo Dodo, and others are attending Acme Looniversity to become the next generation of cartoon stars. Tom Ruegger joined Warner Bros. Animation to oversee production.

It's Looniversity Day. Buster Bunny and Plucky Duck have mentors in Bugs Bunny and Daffy Duck. Babs Bunny has no one to look up to. In the Film Vault, she meets the mysterious hooded Vaultkeeper and a strange voice tells her, "If you watch them, you will find her." She watches movies as months pass. Finally, she stumbles across a film reel entitled *Bosko In Person 1933*. She discovers Bosko's girlfriend, Honey, who imitates Greta Garbo, Betty Boop, Harpo Marx, and Mae West. Babs vows to find Honey and tell her how great she is. The Vaultkeeper says no one has seen Honey in over fifty years.

She checks out old newsreels about Honey. Her popularity waned after Porky Pig became Warner Bros.' first superstar. She and Bosko tried the supper club circuit with disastrous effects. In the 1960s, Ed Sullivan planned a reunion for them on his show, but Honey had disappeared. Finally, Bosko, too faded into obscurity.

The voice tells her, "If you build it, they will watch." He wants her to build a theater to show Honey cartoons, because the people's laughter will save Honey. The theater opens, but no one comes. Months pass. The voice tells her, "If you advertise, they will come." She runs commercials on every channel. Huge crowds show up. Babs says, "I only wish Honey could have been her to see this." A little old lady asks if this is where the Honey cartoons are showing and Babs ushers her in.

In the cartoon within the cartoon, a villain tries to tie Honey to the railroad tracks. Honey imitates Mae West and Groucho Marx. As the audience laughs, the years fall away from the little old lady, who is revealed to be Honey. The Vaultkeeper throws off his hood and reveals himself as Bosko. The two go off together.

● ● ● ● ● ● ● ● ●

Tiny Toon Adventures Season 3, Episode 181 "A Night in Kokomo" (September 15, 1992)

Warner Bros. Animation, Amblin Television. Directed by Byron Vaughns. Produced by Richard Arons, Sherri Stoner. Music: William Ross. Cast: Charlie Adler (Buster), Tress MacNeille (Babs), Frank Welker (Gogo).

It's Classic Comedy Team Workshop at Acme Looniversity. Toons walk by dressed as Charlie Chaplin and The Three Stooges. Babs is dressed up as Groucho Marx, Buster as Chico, and Gogo Dodo as Harpo.

Susan Writtenhouse III, an aging dowager, owns a failing hotel, Cocoanut Cabanas, and has hired the most respected hotel manager in the world, Dr. Leslie Hakinsak (Babs). Chik-O-Lina (Buster) is the chef. Pinky (Gogo) is Chick's silent sidekick.

Hakinsak comes up with a plan to save the hotel from foreclosure: invite the bank manager over for dinner and he will see a full hotel. The plan works, because Hackensack advertised a free dinner.

This is a pastiche of *The Cocoanuts* (1929), *Animal Crackers* (1930), *A Day at the Races* (1937), and *A Night in Casablanca* (1946). At one point Chik-O-Lina says the secret word, "Duck," and Plucky Duck flies down and pays him $100 in a *You Bet Your Life* (1950) reference.

Writer Sherri Stoner said, "I was never into girly-girl characters when I was young. I remember liking Groucho Marx and Harpo Marx."

• • • • • • • • •

Bonkers Season 1, Episode 19 "Poltertoon" (September 28, 1993)

Walt Disney Television Animation. Directed by Larry Latham. Written by Laraine Arkow. Produced by Robert Taylor. Music by Mark Watters. Cast: Jim Cummings (Bonkers, Lucky Piquel), Frank Welker (Elmo, Fall-Apart Rabbit, Toots), Earl Boen (Police Chief Kanifky), Sherry Lynn (Marilyn Piquel), April Winchell (Dil).

Bonkers (1993) previewed on the Disney Channel before going into first-run syndication September 4, 1993 to February 23, 1994. Reruns continued until 1995. The show was later on Toon Disney, but was taken off the schedule in 2004. There were 65 episodes.

Bonkers D. Bobcat is a washed-up former cartoon star who becomes a cop and is paired with Lucky Piquel, a human who hates toons, under the watchful eye of Chief Kanifky. In this episode, "Elmo (Frank Welker), a Groucho-like Toon ghost, moves into the Piquel house on the night Chief and Mrs. Kanifky come to dinner. Rock bottom… Welker's Groucho imitation go[es] for naught."

This episode was not reviewed for publication. It has never been released on home video and is only available on the Internet dubbed into Russian, where Welker's Groucho is lost in translation.

● ● ● ● ● ● ● ● ●

Animaniacs Season 1, Episode 25 "Hercule Yakko" (October 19, 1993)

Warner Bros. Animation, Amblin Entertainment. Director: Dave Marshall. Writer: Peter Hastings. Produced by Rich Arons, Sherri Stoner. Music by Steven Bernstein, Carl Johnson, Richard Stone. Cast (in credits order): Rob Paulsen (Yakko Warner/Pinky), Jess Harnell (Wakko Warner), Tress MacNeille (Dot Warner/Marita Hippo/Cleopatra/Pixie), Sherri Stoner (Slappy Squirrel), Frank Welker (Flavio Hippo/Runt/Chicken Boo/Furrball/Additional Voices), Maurice LaMarche (The Brain/Mark Antony/Additional Voices), Julie Brown (Minerva Mink), Bernadette Peters (Rita).

Animaniacs (1993), created by Tom Ruegger, replaced *Tiny Toon Adventures* (1990) at Warner Bros. Television. The premise was that Yakko, Wakko, and Dot Warner were three toon stars and siblings who were locked in the Warner Bros. water tower in the 1930s and escaped in the present day. Executive Producer and Head Writer Steven Spielberg said in an interview that the humor of social commentary and irreverence were inspired by The Marx Brothers. The show first aired on Fox Kids and ran from 1993–1998.

In this parody of Agatha Christie mysteries, Marita Hippo, on a Nile cruise with her husband Flavio, is missing a diamond. The porter tells her she is in luck, for the world's greatest detective, Hercule Yakko, is onboard, along with his assistants, Dr. Wakko and Number One Sister, Dot.

Dot finds prints—or rather, Prince, the singer. When Marita Hippo walks away, Yakko suddenly realizes the location of the diamond, and tells the porter to assemble all the passengers in the stateroom.

Following is a shot that quotes the one where Margaret Dumont walks to Groucho's stateroom in *A Night at the Opera* (1935). When Wakko opens the door, all the passengers fall out, including Groucho Marx. Dot laughs and says, "I hate that *Night at the Opera* [1935] bit. Funny bit."

Yakko reveals Marita has been sitting on the diamond the whole time. "I told you I'd get to the bottom of this."

● ● ● ● ● ● ● ● ●

Animaniacs Season 1, Episode 27 "You Risk Your Life" (October 25, 1993)

Warner Bros. Animation, Amblin Entertainment. Directed by Alfred Gimeno. Written by Paul Rugg. Produced by Rich Arons, Sherri Stoner. Music by Carl Johnson, Richard Stone. Cast: Jess Harnell (Wakko), Rob Paulsen (Yakko, Dr. Otto Scratchansniff), Frank Welker (Ralph the Guard).

Dr. Otto Scratchansniff is the announcer, and Yakko dresses as Groucho Marx in *You Bet Your Life* (1950), with the gray suit and red bow tie, but makes no effort to imitate him vocally. He uses a pencil in place of a cigar. The show, including cutaways to an old-timey audience, is in color. Say the secret word and Wakko will hit you over the head with a mallet. The guests are a homemaker from Madison, Wisconsin, ("What kind of homes do you make?") and the Greek philosopher, Aristotle. The secret word is "Yes," and Aristotle takes several lumps.

● ● ● ● ● ● ● ● ●

Animaniacs Season 1, Episode 65-2 "The Warners' 65th Anniversary Special" (May 23, 1994)

Warner Bros. Animation, Amblin Entertainment. Directed by Alfred Gimeno. Produced by Rich Arons, Rusty Miller, Peter Hastings, Sherri Stoner, Steven Spielberg, Tom Ruegger. Written by Paul Rugg, Tom Ruegger, Sherri Stoner. Music: Richard Stone. Cast: Jess Harnell (Wakko), Rob Paulsen (Yakko), Tress MacNeille (Dot), Frank Welker (Thaddeus Plotz), Maurice LaMarche (Spartacus), Jim Cummings (Buddy), Jeff Bennett (Weed Memlo), Paul Rugg (Lon Borax), Sherri Stoner (Slappy Squirrel), Nathan Ruegger (Skippy Squirrel), Cree Summer (Elmyra), John Mariano (Guenther), Greg Burson (Bugs Bunny). GAG CREDITS: City Desk Editor: Lou Grant. Storyboards: Bucky Beaver, Jerry Mathers as the Beaver. Sheet Timing: Jeff Hall, Monty Hall, Kids in the Hall, Norm McCabe, McCabe & Mrs. Miller, Tom Ray, Man Ray, Sting Ray, Bob & Ray, Ray Stevens, Darrin Stevens, Larry Tate. Slugger: Bill Knoll, Grassy Knoll. Louisville Slugger: Baseball Bat. Slug: Slimey Gooey Thing. B.G. Key Design: Dan McHugh,

Marty Strudler, Apple Strudler, Peach Cobbler. B.G.s.: Barry, Robin and Maurice Gibb. Spectrum Colors: Roy G. Biv. Color Key: Bunny Munns, Richard Daskas, Carolyn Guske, Robin Kane, Charles Foster Kane, Chris Naylor, Eric Nordberg, Linda Redondo, Redondo Beach, Florida. Bathroom Key: Cannot Be Duplicated. Francis Scott Key: National Anthem Writer. Key Largo: Starring Humphrey Bogart and Lauren Bacall. Mark Up: Jea DuBois, Lisa Leonardi, Valerie Walker, and Clint Walker as "Cheyenne." Mark Down: "Goof Troop" Tapes at K-Mart. Animation Checking: Jan Browning, Elizabeth Barrett Browning, Brenda Brummet, Brenda Brummet Browning, Elizabeth Brummet Browning, Jennifer Damiani, Jennifer Damiani Browning, Bunty Dranko, Elizabeth Barrett Bunty, H.M.S. Bunty, Karl Jacobs, Karl Jacobs Jingleheimer Schmidt, Howard Schwartz, John Jacob Jingleheimer Schwartz. Interest Free Checking: With a $2000 Deposit. Production Administrator: Alyson Brown, Charlie Brown, He's a Clown, That Charlie Brown. Copying and Shipping: Carlton Batten, Carlton Batten Browning, Carlton Batten Down the Hatches, Ana Durand, Duran Duran, Ana Duran Duran, Que Sera Sera, Whatever Will Be, Will Be, The Future's Not Ours to See, Ana Duran Duran, What Will Be, Will Be. Digital Production: Alan G. Brown, Sweet Georgia Brown, Sweet Elizabeth Barrett Georgia Browning. Guy Who Cuts Out All the Boring Stuff: Joe "Snippy, the Animator's Best Friend" Gall. Additional Film Editing: Al Breitenbach, Kelly Ann Foley, Theresa Gilroy-Nielson, Leslie Nielsen. Sound Reading: Bradley Carow, Denise Whitfield, Steve Siracusa, N.Y. The Sound Mix is By Thomas J. Maydeck, Russell Brower, Pat Rodman, 2nd Engineer. The Trail Mix is By: Nabisco. Monkey Screech SFX by: Russell Brower, Robert Hargreaves, Matt Thorne, "Thorny" Thornberry, Ozzy's Zany Next Door Neighbor. Dialogue Editors: Mark Keatts, Mick Brooling, Bob Lacivita, Andrew I. King, Aaron L. King, Alan King, Martin Luther King, Chicken a la King, Old King Cole, Larry King Live, Don King, Don Corleone, Don Juan, Don Quixote, Don Wilson, Dondi, Dondi Duran Duran, Whatever Will Be, Will Be. Voice Recording Engineer: Harry Andronis of the Chicago Androniseseseses: Danny Shaw, 2nd Engineer; Casey Jones, Train Engineer. Amblin Story Consultant: Douglas Wood, Mary Woods, Natalie Wood, James Woods, Ed Wood, Jr. Laboratory Services: C.F.I. Laboratory Services: CFI. Lavoratory Services: Mr. Potty Man. Kathryn Page: Kathryn Page. Episode Adopted by: Bette Midler. Production Assistants: Geno DuBois, Dustin Foster, Bobbie Page, John Morris, Paul "Godzilla is My Friend"

Trandahl. Donors $10 or More: Jon McClenahan, Dave Marshall, The Gimeno Family, Nick Hollander, Kirk Tingblad, Elizabeth Barrett Tingblad. Organ Donors: Thomas, Baldwin, Vox, Wurlitzer. Favorite Lawrence Welk Quote: "When you have a minute, I want to see you right now." If You're Counting: This Has Been Episode #65. Chicken Boo Appears Courtesy of: Zacky Farms. Promotional Fee Paid By: "Ouchies"—The Sharp, Prickly Toy You Bathe With. Special Thanks to: Ojai Constorium, Memlo Memorial Archive–Mary Margret Memlo, Curator; The Smellog Foundation, Craig T. Nelson & All His "Coach" Co-Stars, The Pew Charitable Truss. Bean Counter: Chuck Ansel. Beans Counted: 235, Definitely 235. Announcer: "Hey, Warners, you've just finished the 65th episode of Animaniacs. What are you gonna do now?" Warners: "We're going to Euro-Disney!" Executive in Charge of Production: Jean MacCurdy. Executive in Charge of Prodding: Liza-Ann Warren. Executive in Charge of Bazooka: Tim Sarnoff. Executive in Charge of Overseas Production: Ken Duer. Executive in Charge of the Writers: Barbara Simon Dierks.

This was actually the 65th episode, not an anniversary, and it was a regular episode, not a special. The Warner brothers, Yakko and Wakko, and their sister Dot are being fêted for their careers. After Viza Vizelli sings the opening song with an all-male chorus, host Bob "Maybe You Should Retire" Hope comes out to emcee. The Warner siblings started out in Buddy cartoons, hitting him over the head with a mallet, and eventually replacing him altogether. Buddy is now a nut farmer in Ohio. Other Warner Bros. cartoon stars appearing include Bugs Bunny, Daffy Duck, Foghorn Leghorn, Yosemite Sam, Porky Pig, Tweety Bird (misspelled as "Tweetie"), Elmyra Duff, and Slappy and Skippy Squirrel. Celebrities are generally referred to by their character names: Kirk Douglas (Spartacus), Bette Davis (Baby Jane), Jimmy Stewart (George Bailey), and Ronald Reagan (The Gipper). Professor Kingsfield (John Houseman) talks about how Wakko holed up with Joseph Mankiewicz to write the script for Wakko's directorial debut. This is a parody of John Houseman's memoirs, where he talks about Orson Welles writing *Citizen Kane* (1941) with Joseph Mankiewicz' brother, Herman, who also produced *Monkey Business* (1931), *Horse Feathers* (1932), and *Duck Soup* (1933). Other caricatures include John Wayne, Gary Cooper, Jimmy Cagney, Jack Nicholson, Franklin Roosevelt, Winston Churchill, Joseph Stalin, and John Travolta, who is referred to as "Lou Amalongada." The Warners appear in a "clip" from *A Really Big Shew*, a parody of *The Ed Sullivan Show* (1948), singing "Make a Gookie," a parody of Simon & Garfunkel's "The 59th Street Bridge Song (Feelin' Groovy)." Harpo Marx is not mentioned by name, but Wakko and some of the others are clearly imitating his well-known facial expression. Buddy, still bitter at being replaced, plants a time bomb in the podium, set to go off when the Warners take the stage. However, when they do, they say they wish they could share the award with Buddy. Buddy rushes onto the podium, which blows up and causes one of the two giant mallets decorating the stage to fall and crush him. The chorus boys take the stage and Yakko cuts the ropes suspending the second mallet, causing it to fall on top of the chorus boys.

● ● ● ● ● ● ● ● ●

Snow White and the Magic Mirror (1994)

Fred Wolf Films, Schwartz & Company. Directed by Tony Love. Written by Ken Koonce and Michael Merton. Produced by Bill Schwartz. Music by Dennis C. Brown, Maxine Sellers. Cast: Dan Castellaneta (Magic Mirror/Norman/Dewe/Dobbie) (uncredited), Susan Silo (Wicked Queen) (uncredited).

In this made-for-video take on the Snow White story, the Queen is one of the least beautiful people in the land. The Magic Mirror morphs into Jerry Lewis; Sammy Davis, Jr.; Jack Nicholson, Johnny Carson, Mr. Rogers, and Groucho Marx and informs her that she is #256. The Queen is furious at this state of affairs and asks the royal butcher, a kindly sort who refuses even to harm animals, to get rid of everyone more beautiful. He allows them all to escape, and, with the help of the Magic Mirror, fakes Snow's death.

Snow has to find a new place to live. She decides against Ye Bates Inn, and Dorothy's house is condemned when she leaves for Oz, presumably because of tornado damage. Snow finds an empty cottage, and after eating pie, falls asleep on one of the beds.

Soon seven dwarfs arrive. They are vocal caricatures of Jack Benny, George Burns, Ed Wynn, Rodney Dangerfield, Jimmy Durante, Buddy Hackett, and Bob "Sneezy" Hope. When Snow tells them of her plight, they agree to let her stay, in exchange for housework.

Snow is incompetent at housework, and even spooks Prince Charming and his horse with the smell of her bread baking. The Queen asks the Magic Mirror again who is the fairest. The Mirror, channeling Jacques Cousteau and Elvis Presley, tells her Snow is still alive. The Queen goes off to find her.

The Queen gains entrance to the dwarfs' cottage as a cosmetics salesperson, and gives Snow a poisoned comb, which knocks her unconscious. The dwarfs come home and revive her and warn her not to open the door for anyone.

The Queen again asks the Magic Mirror who's the fairest. The Mirror channels Billy Crystal's Fernando, Rod Serling, and John Wayne, and tells her Snow is still alive.

The Queen shows up again dressed as a hag delivering a Candy Applegram and persuades Snow to open the window for her. Snow eats the poisoned apple and falls unconscious.

The Queen asks the Mirror, channeling James Mason, again who's the fairest in the land. The mirror shows her Snow White in a glass coffin and says the Queen is the fairest, but the mirror dons a wig to make himself prettier. The Queen throws the mirror out the window into a creek. He paddles himself downriver, cackling like Walter Brennan.

Prince Charming finds Snow in the glass coffin and picks up her body to take it to his castle. She coughs up the piece of apple and comes to. Charming marries Snow, and everyone lives happily ever after. Except the Queen.

• • • • • • • • •

Garfield and Friends Season 7, Episode 3 "The Perfect Match" (September 24, 1994)

Paws, Inc. Directed by Dave Brain, Ron Myrick, Vincent Davis, James West. Produced by Vincent Davis. Written by Mark Evanier. Cast: Lorenzo Music (Garfield), Thom Huge (Jon), Gregg Berger (Odie), Frank Buxton, Gary Owens, Greg Berg, Greg Burson, Harvey Korman, Rick Ducommun, Imogene Coca, Sheryl Bernstein, and Frank Welker.

Garfield is an American comic strip cat created by Jim Davis in an effort to "come up with a good, marketable character." Garfield is a lazy, fat feline, whose owner, Jon, is socially inept. It is the most widely syndicated strip in the world and Garfield merchandise generates up to a billion dollars a year. The strip has spawned numerous movies and TV shows. This series originally ran September 17, 1988 to December 10, 1994.

In "The Perfect Match," another date leads to Jon spilling his dinner all over her. This leads him to join a computer dating service, where Garfield answers the detailed questionnaire for him. "Favorite Marx Brother?" asks Jon, using the pencil as a cigar. "Zeppo," says Garfield. (Wouldn't Gummo have been funnier?) The date, Jane Arbinkle, turns out to be an almost too perfect match. Her favorite Marx Brother is Zeppo, also, and each of them spills foodstuffs all over the other. Garfield sabotages the date by throwing a whole box of soap into the dishwasher and flooding the house. A follow-up visit to the computer dating service reveals Jon is doomed to spend the rest of his life with Garfield.

● ● ● ● ● ● ● ● ●

Bump in the Night Season 1, Episode 5 "Loss of Face" (October 8, 1994)

Danger Productions. Directed by David Bleiman, Ken Pontac. Produced by David Bleiman, Ken Pontac, Patricia Rose Duignan (Executive Producers). Written by Mark Zaslove and James Iver Mattson (story), and James Iver Mattson (teleplay). Music by Jim Latham. Cast: Jim Cummings (Mr. Bumpy), Rob Paulsen (Squishington), Gail Matthius (Molly Coddle), Scott McAfee (The Boy), Anndi McAfee (Little Sister), E.G. Daily (Germ Girl), Jeff Bennett (Gloog).

Bump in the Night (1994) was a stop-motion animated Saturday morning series on The American Broadcasting Company (ABC) network from 1994 to 1996. It focused on Mr. Bumpy, a green monster living under a bed, and his friend Squishington, a blue monster from the toilet tank.

Squishington washes his face and it comes off in the washcloth, which is stolen by silverfish. Mr. Bumpy doesn't recognize him until he writes, "I AM SQUISHINGTON" with a black magic marker. Mr. Bumpy puts Groucho glasses on him and says, "I could dance with you until the cows come home. On second thought, I'd rather dance with the cows till you come home." Then, he uses a Mr. Potato Head-type kit to turn Squishington into a Hasidic Jew, Mae West, and Elvis Presley. Finally, he just uses the magic marker to draw a face. Squishington is now able to talk and explains what happened. Mr. Bumpy and Squishington find the silverfish worshipping the washcloth like it's the Shroud of Turin. One of them is named Phil Silverfish, although he sounds more like Bert Lahr. The King Silverfish is a vocal caricature of John Wayne. He hangs Mr. Bumpy by his arms over a water pipe. Squishington accidentally wipes his face off and blindly finds the washcloth and accidentally restores his face. The King Silverfish says, "Aw, truly, he is The Foretold One," and says he will release Mr. Bumpy when Squishington leads them to The Place. Squishington leads them to the kitchen, where the silverfish feast on garbage, and everyone forgets about Mr. Bumpy.

• • • • • • • • •

The Simpsons Season 6, Episode 15 "Homie the Clown" (February 12, 1995)

20th Century Fox Television, Film Roman Productions, Gracie Films. Directed by David Silverman. Written by John Swartzwelder. Produced by David Mirkin. Cast: Dan Castellaneta (Homer Simpson, Krusty the Clown), Julie Kavner (Marge Simpson), Nancy Cartwright (Bart Simpson), Yeardley Smith (Lisa Simpson), Joe Mantegna (Fat Tony), Dick Cavett (Himself), Johnny Unitas (Himself), Hank Azaria, Harry Shearer, Pamela Hayden.

The Simpsons began life as animated segments created by Matt Groening on *The Tracy Ullman Show* (1987). In 1989, the cartoon spun off on its own, and has been running ever since. In 2016, it became the longest-running prime time series by number of episodes. Fat, dumb Homer is the head of a dysfunctional family that includes his wife, Marge, and their children: bad boy Bart; smart Lisa, and baby Maggie. The show frequently comments on pop culture and society.

TV show host Krusty the Clown starts a clown college after he gambles away all his money. Homer Simpson signs up, but is mistaken for Krusty by the mobsters that Krusty owes.

After co-hosting the Ace Awards, Dick Cavett tries to strike up a conversation with Homer/Krusty, who wants no part of it. "Heh heh," chuckles Cavett. "Your churlish attitude reminds me of a time I was having dinner with Groucho and...." Homer grabs him by the collar and says, "Look, you're going to be having dinner with Groucho tonight if you don't beat it."

● ● ● ● ● ● ● ● ●

Animaniacs Season 3, Episode 1 "Wakko's New Gookie" (September 9, 1995)

Warner Bros. Animation, Amblin Entertainment. Directed by Audu Paden. Written by Paul Rugg. Produced by Peter Hastings, Rusty Mills. Music: Richard Stone, Steven Bernstein, Julie Bernstein. Cast (in credits order): Rob Paulsen (Yakko Warner), Jess Harnell (Wakko Warner), Maurice LaMarche (Michelangelo/Bob Hope/Larry King).

Wakko is trying out a new gookie for the coming season. When Yakko tells him it isn't really a gookie, Wakko seeks other opinions. He visits Michelangelo, Bob "That's Not a Gookie" Hope, Katharine Hepburn, and *The Larry King Show* (1985), where Bob "That's Still Not a Gookie" Hope calls in, and everyone tells him basically the same thing. Yakko says everyone likes his old gookie, and he should be proud of that and not want to change it just to come up with something new.

Again, Harpo Marx is not mentioned by name, but Wakko and some of the others are clearly imitating his well-known facial expression.

● ● ● ● ● ● ● ● ●

The Twisted Tales of Felix the Cat Season 1, Episode 5 "Middle Aged Felix" (October 14, 1995)

Felix the Cat Productions, Film Roman Productions. Directed by Pamela Stalker. Produced by Timothy Berglund. Written by Martin Olson. Cast: Thom Adcox Hernandez (Felix), Cam Clarke (Poindexter), Phil Hayes (Rosco), Cree Summer (Sheba Beboporeba), Susan Silo (Sheba's Grandman), Patrick Fraley, Jennifer Hale, Jess Harnell, Janna Levinstein, Townsend Coleman, Kevin Schon.

Felix the Cat is a funny animal cartoon character created in 1919 in Pat Sullivan's animation studio. Felix was much imitated, notably by Bill

Nolan's 1935 adaptation of Krazy Kat. Pat Sullivan was slow to adopt sound, and the character was soon eclipsed by Mickey Mouse. This reboot lasted for two seasons, thirteen episodes in the first, and eight in the second, and is done in the Fleischer style.

Felix and Sheba find *Merlin's Book of Spells* while cleaning Sheba's Grandman's garage and are accidentally transported to the Middle Ages. They meet up with Merlin, who recognizes the book. When they refuse to give it back, Merlin casts a spell on two rabbits which turns them into Harpo Marx and a honking ostrich. He then turns them into two knights on horseback who attack Felix. Felix turns his tail into a snake which spooks the horses and throws the knights. Felix also defeats a dragon and The Black Plague. Sheba finds the spell to return home.

• • • • • • • • •

Duckman: Private Dick/Family Man Season 4, Episode 10 "A Trophied Duck" (March 8, 1997)

Klasky-Csupo. Directed by Jeff McGrath. Writing Credits: Everett Peck (creator); Gabor Csupo, Arlene Klasky, Ron Osborn, Jeff Reno (developers). Produced by Margot Pipkin. Music by Scott Wilk, Todd Yvega. Cast (in credits order): Jason Alexander (Eric Duckman), Nancy Travis (Bernice/Beatrice), Gregg Berger (Cornfed Pig), Dweezil Zappa (Ajax), Elizabeth Daily (Mambo) (as E.G. Dailey), Pat Musick (Fluffy/Uranus), Jeff Bennett (voice), Amy Brenneman (Lauren Simone), Jerry Houser (voice), Walt Reno, Jr. (voice).

Duckman: Private Dick/Family Man (1994), based on the comic book by Everett Peck, was animated by Klasky Csupo. It was their second animated series, after *The Simpsons* (1989). Eric T. Duckman is a family man and private dick who fails in both departments.

In this episode, Duckman heads to San Francisco with his family and his detective partner, Corny, for Dick Con 1997, where he thinks he will receive a Lifetime Achievement Award. At one of the booths, he becomes obsessed with a Groucho Marx disguise, putting it on and taking it off, showing Corny how it works. "Groucho. Not Groucho. Groucho. Not Groucho. Groucho. Not Groucho."

His award turns out to be for Lifetime Underachievement, engineered by his old rival and chairperson of Dick Con, Lauren Simone. To redeem himself, he takes a test to prove he is the best detective, but he is unable to answer a single question. He gets Corny to fill out the test while he distracts Lauren with his Groucho disguise.

• • • • • • • • •

Pinky and the Brain Season 3, Episode 3 "Pinky & the Brain… and Larry" (September 13, 1997)

Warner Bros. Animation, Amblin Entertainment. Directed by Russell Calabrese, Liz Holzman. Written by Gordon Bressack and Charles M. Howell IV. Produced by Liz Holzman, Charles M. Howell IV. Cast: Maurice LaMarche (The Brain), Rob Paulsen (Pinky), Billy West (Larry), Frank Welker (Fred Floppel).

Pinky and the Brain (1995) debuted on the second episode of *Animaniacs* (1993) and was spun off as its own show that ran on Kids' WB! Pinky and the Brain are genetically enhanced mice who live at the Acme Labs. Every night, Brain, the genius, tries to take over the world and fails, usually because of Pinky's insanity.

The executives at Kids' WB! had demanded that the producers include more characters on the show, hence the sudden and unexplained appearance of Larry, a mouse who is a caricature of Larry Fine of The Three Stooges. Larry inserts himself awkwardly into the opening theme song. Every time either Pinky or the Brain addresses the other by name, he has to add awkwardly, "And Larry." Larry's lines are mostly "Hi!" and "I'm Larry" and the like.

Brain's plan involves controlling all the remote garage door openers in the country. This will force everyone to ride bikes and destroy the oil industry. All he needs is a part available only at the White House. They decide to pose as wallpaper hangers to gain access. Three Stooges-type antics ensue, and they are thrown out.

Brain realizes the problem is Larry. Larry changes his name to Art and finds a new career singing *The Smells of Loudness* with his new partner, Paul Simon. At the end of the episode, a new mouse enters the cage at the lab. His name is Zeppo. He inserts his name awkwardly into the closing theme. The actor playing Zeppo is unbilled—Frank Welker?

• • • • • • • • •

Celebrity Deathmatch Season 2, Episode 8 "Celebrity Deathmatch: The Motion Picture" (April 22, 1999)

Cuppa Coffee Studios, MTV Animation, TakToon Enterprise. Directed by Eric Fogel. Written by A.J. Jacobs, Rick Marin. Produced by Rhonda Cox, Alison Elliott (as Alison Elliott-Yarden), John Lynn (as John Worth Lynn, Jr.) Music by Eric Perlmutter. Cast: Mills Lane (Himself), Maurice Schlafer (Johnny Gomez), Len Maxwell (Nick Diamond), Roger Jackson (Groucho Marx), André Sogliuzzo (John Wayne/Various) (as Andre), Jimmy St. Cleve (Chico Marx).

Celebrity Deathmatch (1998) used Claymation to parody professional wrestling and famous people, dead and alive. It originally ran May 14, 1998 to October 20, 2002.

A clip from "the *Celebrity Deathmatch* [1998] vaults," supposedly from the 1950s *Celebrity Deathmatch Variety Hour*, shot in black and white. John Wayne is fighting Groucho Marx because Groucho tried to pull some funny business with The Duke's lady friend at the Stork Club. Groucho is introduced as "The Vicious Vaudevillian, the Mustachioed Menace." He spies a good-looking woman in the audience and says, "A man's only as old as the woman he feels."

John Wayne enters on horseback. He punches Groucho repeatedly, so Groucho calls in the cavalry: Harpo. Harpo pulls Wayne's hat over his head and gives Mills Lane his leg. Wayne draws his guns, but Harpo has stolen them and substituted two horns. Groucho and Harpo pull the gag where Harpo gets on all fours behind Wayne, then Groucho pushes Wayne over. "I've got a good mind to join a club and beat you over the head with it," says Groucho. Harpo hands him a baseball bat out of his trench coat and Groucho hits him. They throw him out of the ring and he lands on his horse and jumps back in and lassos Harpo.

Chico stops by the broadcast booth. "You wanna violence? I gotta you violence right here," and he produces a violin.

Back in the ring, Wayne says he's going to open a canteen of whoop-ass. Groucho tells him that's the secret word. The duck flies down and spooks Wayne's horse, who throws him. Groucho kicks him and Wayne goes flying through Harpo's harp, slicing him into pieces. Groucho dances with Mills Lane.

● ● ● ● ● ● ● ● ●

Histeria Season 1, Episode 42 "Communuts" (May 8, 1999)
Warner Bros. Animation. Directed by Bob Doucette, Mike Milo, Herb Moore. Produced by Bob Doucette, Mark Seidenberg, Bobbie Page, Tom Ruegger. Written by Randy Rogel, Roger Eschbacher, Stephen Shaw, Victor Wilson. Music: Richard Stone, Julie Bernstein, Steve Bernstein, Tim Kelly, Gordon L. Goodwin. Cast: Frank Welker (Father Time, Fetch, Pule Howser), Cree Summer (Aka Pella, Kid Chorus Singer), Laraine Newman (Charity Bazaar, Miss Information, Joan of Arc, Martha Lincoln, Kid Chorus Singer), Tress MacNeille (Cho-Cho, Pepper Mills, Toast, World's Oldest Woman, Susana Susquahanna, Molly Pitcher, Kid Chorus Singer), Jeff Bennett (Lucky Bob, Napoleon Bonaparte), Nora Dunn (Lydia Karaoke, Statue of Liberty), Rob Paulsen (Mr. Smartypants, Sam Melman, Kid Chorus Singer), Nathan Ruegger (Froggo, Kid Chorus Singer), Cody Ruegger (Loud Kiddington), Luke Ruegger (Big Fat Baby, Will Rogers), James Wickline (Bill Straitman), Billy West (Horse, Chit Chatterson, Benjamin Franklin, Thomas Jefferson, Confucius, Attila the Hun), Maurice LaMarche (Christopher Columbus, George Washington, Abraham Lincoln), Paul Rugg (Nostradamus, Merlin, Sergei Eisenstein), Fred Travalena (Julius Caesar, General Ulysses Simpson Grant, Marc Antony), Jim Cummings (Attila the Hun), Don Novello (Renaissance Man).

Histeria (1998) was created by Tom Ruegger to meet FCC requirements for educational/informational content for children. It aired from 1998 to 2000 on Kids' WB.

Karl Marx as Groucho performs a song based on "Whatever It Is, I'm Against It" from *Horse Feathers* (1932). Friedrich Engels, as Chico, joins in on the Zeppo part. The actors who play Marx and Engels are not credited—Frank Welker? This was the only segment of this show viewed for publication.

"… [I]t was canceled due to low ratings, which were more or less caused by hype in the new show *Pokémon*…."

● ● ● ● ● ● ● ● ●

Pokémon Season 2, Episode 28 "The Wacky Watcher" (September 16, 2000)

Nintendo Co. Ltd., OLM-Animation Studio, Shogakukan Inc., Summit Media Group, TV Tokyo. Animation Studio: SOFTX. Directed by Kunihiko Yuyama, Masamitsu Hidaka, Yoshitaka Fujimoto. Animated by Shunya Yamada. Written by Shinzô Fujita (screenplay), based on a story by Satoshi Tajiri. Produced by Tsunekazu Ishihara, Alfred R. Kahn, Norman J. Grossfeld. Music: John Loeffler. Cast: Rikako Aikawa (Lapras), Madeleine Blaustein (Meowth), Unshô Ishizuka (Gyarados), Satomi Kôrogi (Togepi), Ted Lewis (Tracey Sketchit), Rachael Lillis (Misty/Jessie), Jerry Lobozzo (Quincy T. Quackenpoker), Rodger Parsons (Narrator) (as Ken Gates), Tara Sands (Bulbasaur) (as Tara Jayne), Eric Stuart (James), Veronica Taylor (Ash Ketchum), Ikue Ôtani (Pikachu).

At this writing, Pokémon is the second-most successful entertainment franchise in the world. By the time you read this, it will probably be number one because of the game *Pokémon GO*. The Japanese anime series is the fifth-longest running cartoon series in history.

Ashley Ketchum, Tracey Sketchit, Misty, and Pikachu are headed to the Orange League Competition when they spy a submarine piloted by Quincy T. Quackenpoker, a curly-haired, bushy-browed, bespectacled, mustachioed man. Instead of having a greasepaint mustache like Groucho Marx, Quackenpoker seems to have hair growing straight out of his nostrils. "Everybody in my family was named Quackenpoker. At least on my mother's side."

Quackenpoker and the gang head to Rind Island to study Magikarp. "When I was a boy, I woke up one morning and I saw a Magikarp in my pajamas. How a Magikarp got into my pajamas, I'll never know."

Meanwhile, Team Rocket schemes to capture the Magikarp and have them evolve into Gyarados so Team Rocket can become Pokémon masters of the world. They build a Magikarp submarine to snatch the fish right out of the water. "That's the most ridiculous Magikarp I've ever seen." The gang rescues the Magikarp and they evolve into Gyarados. Team Rocket, marooned on a small rock, are surrounded by them. "To Be Continued," but not here.

● ● ● ● ● ● ● ● ●

Clone High Season 1, Episode 6 "Homecoming: A Shot in the D'Arc" (December 1, 2002)

Directed by Ted Collyer, Harold Harris. Produced by Tom Martin, Bill Lawrence, Chris Miller, Phil Lord. Animated by Mike Moon, Dexter Smith, Carey Yost, Mark Ackland, Mark Thornton, Jan Tillcock. Written by Eric Kentoff. Music: Liam Lynch, Abandoned Pools. Cast: Will Forte (Abe Lincoln), Phil Lord (Principal Dr. Cinnamon J. Scudworth), Michael McDonald (Gandhi), Christa Miller (Cleopatra) (as Christa Miller Lawrence), Christopher Miller (JFK/Vice Principal Mr. Butlertron) (as Christopher R. Miller), Nicole Sullivan (Joan of Arc), Chris Berman (Himself), Dan Patrick (Himself), Donald Faison (Toots/Wally), Neil Flynn (Julius Caesar/Carl).

In *Clone High* (2001), historical figures such as Joan of Arc, Abe Lincoln, John F. Kennedy, and Gandhi have been cloned by the military for use in battle. Now 16, they are in high school and their evil principal, Cinnamon J. Scudworth, plans to use them to staff an amusement park, Cloney Island.

Clone High is gearing up for its annual game against Genetically Engineered Super Human High (GESH). The GESH principal bets Scudworth that Clone High won't score a single point. Joan of Arc tries to join the team, but they don't allow girls or animals. She puts on a mustache and calls herself "John Dark."

During the game, Joan takes off her mustache and reveals her true identity. Scudworth tells everyone in a fake mustache to leave. Groucho Marx exits.

● ● ● ● ● ● ● ● ●

Ghost in the Shell: Stand Alone Complex Season 1, Episode 12 "Tachikoma Runaway/The Movie Director's Dream" aka "Escape From" (March 1, 2003)

Bandai Visual Company, DENTSU Music and Entertainment, Kôdansha, Production I. G. Directed by Kenji Kamiyama. Produced by Yuichiro Matsuka, Charles McCarter, Kaoru Mfaume, Tsutomu Sugita. Executive Producers: Shigeru Watanabe, Mitsuhisa Ishikawa. Senior Producers:

Ken Iyadomi, Marvin Gleicher. Animated by Takayuki Goto. Written by Yoshiki Sakurai. Music by Yôko Kanno. Cast: Lara Jill Miller (Tachikoma), Crispin Freeman (Togusa), Rebecca Forstadt (Tachikoma), Dave Wittenberg (Saitou), Mary Elizabeth McGlynn (Motoko Kusanagi), Melissa Fahn (Tachikoma), Sandy Fox (Tachikoma), Debra Jean Rogers (Operator), Ewan Chung (Lab Tech), Lia Sargent (Tachikoma), Robert Wicks (Pazu), Michael McCarty (Ishikawa), Richard Epcar (Batou), William Knight (Daisuke Aramaki), Sherry Lynn (Tachikoma), Dean Wein (Bouma), Julie Maddalena (Tachikoma), Bill Bassett (Director), Michelle Ruff (Miki), Jonathan Fahn (Policeman), Fleet Cooper (Policeman).

An anime series based on the manga *Ghost in the Shell.* An elite law enforcement unit investigates cyber crime and terrorism aided by their Tachikoma (robots).

Batou's Tachikoma returns to its storage bay with a cyber brain containing a ghost. A lab technician links to the cyber brain and he becomes lost. Kusanagi finds the missing tech watching a movie with no beginning and no ending that makes her cry. She asks Batou if he has ever been moved to tears by a movie. He says, "You know, there was one time. I remember laughing so hard I cried from watching a Marx Brothers film."

• • • • • • • • •

Home Movies Season 3, Episode 13 "Coffins and Cradles" (May 25, 2003)

Burns & Burns Productions, Tom Snyder Productions. Directed by Loren Bouchard. Produced by Melissa Bardin Galsky, Loren Bouchard, Bonnie Burns, Linda Simensky, Brendon Small, Tom Snyder, Mary Catherine Tucker. Written by Loren Bouchard (creator), Bill Braudis, and Brendon Small. Music: Loren Bouchard, Brendon Small. Cast: Brendon Small (Brendon Small), Janine Di Tullio (Paula Small), H. Jon Benjamin (Jason Panopolis, Coach John McGuirk), Melissa Bardin Galsky (Melissa), Jonathan Katz (Erik), Ron Lynch (Mr. Lynch), and Tom Kenny (Doctor).

Home Movies (1999) is about Brendon, age eight, who makes videos with his friends Melissa and Jason in his free time. His mother is divorced, his father is remarried, and his soccer coach, John McGuirk, is a bad father figure. After a brief run on UPN, it ran for three seasons on the Cartoon Network's Adult Swim.

The Halloween party is coming up. Brendon's pregnant stepmother, Linda, is staying at Paula's house while Brendon's father is on a business trip. Coach McGuirk is visited by Stephanie, a beautiful recruiter from the Crystal Spirit Family, a new spiritual organization, who turns out to be a one-night stand from his past. Coach asks Stephanie to go to the party.

As Brendon and his friends are getting ready to leave for the party, Linda goes into labor. Coach and Stephanie are making out at his house when he has a heart attack.

The doctor in both cases at the hospital is wearing a Groucho Marx disguise, but when he takes it off, he has real glasses and mustache.

● ● ● ● ● ● ● ● ●

The Fairly OddParents Season 3, Episode 9 "Abra Catastrophe!" (July 12, 2003)

Nickelodeon Productions. Directed by Butch Hartman. Produced by Dierdre Brenner (Line Producer). Executive Producers: Butch Hartman, Fred Seibert. Written by Steve Marmel. Cast: Tara Strong (Timmy, Kid, Fairy #1, Kid #1), Daran Norris (Cosmo, Jorgen, Dad), Susanne Blakeslee (Wanda, Mom), Grey DeLisle (Vicky, Principal Waxelplax), Kevin Michael Richardson (Bad Guy, Business Man), Jason Marsden (Chester McBadbat), Gary LeRoi Gray (A.J.), Carlos Alazraqui (Mr. Crocker, Ape #2), Dee Bradley Baker (as Dee Baker) (Sanjay, Bippy, Binky, Fairy Private, Kid #2), Tom Kenny (Cupid, Another Kid, Food Cart Guy, Fairy Sergeant, Announcer), Robert Costanzo (as Bobby Costanzo) (Easter Bunny, Construction Worker Ape, Ape Truck Driver), Faith S. Abrahams (as Faith Abrahams) (Francis, Ape #1), Butch Hartman (Flashback Boy, Web Eared Guy, Third Kid, Orderly), Cara Newman Ruyle (Flashback Girl, Female Ape #1, Gorilla Business Woman), Steve Marmel (Bowling Pin, Warthog), Gary Le Mel (Fairy Cowlick, Jr.), Jim Ward (Chet Ubetcha) (uncredited).

The Fairly OddParents (2001) was created by Butch Hartman for Nickelodeon. Timmy Turner is a ten-year-old boy whose parents literally never leave him alone and videotape everything he does. One day, they pretend to leave, and Timmy calls Vicky, a babysitter. Vicky wins over the parents, and they leave for the evening. Vicky becomes the babysitter of choice, and she tortures Timmy until Cosmo and Wanda, his fairy godparents, get assigned to him to grant his wishes. Mr. Crocker, his teacher and main antagonist, had fairy godparents as a child, and has spent his adult life trying to get them back again.

At the beginning of this episode, the first TV movie of the series, it is one year since Cosmo and Wanda have been assigned to him. All the fairies are there to celebrate, and Timmy gets many magical items as gifts, including Groucho glasses, Santa's bag, and a Magic Muffin, which grants the wish of anyone who eats it.

Mr. Crocker causes Timmy to lose the muffin, and it gets mixed in with all the others at school on Muffin Monday. Eventually, Crocker ends up with the muffin and he captures Wanda and makes himself ruler of the universe.

Timmy can only fight him with the magical items he received as gifts.. He dons the Groucho glasses and uses Santa's bag as a cowl. Crocker asks him who he is. Timmy doffs the cowl, revealing himself in Groucho glasses. "I'm, uh, one of America's most beloved comedy entertainers." Crocker replies, "Fine, Shemp."

Crocker also captures Cosmo. When Crocker sees Timmy without glasses, he says, "You're not Shemp! You're not even Curly Joe!" Timmy reveals the existence of Cosmo and Wanda to his parents, causing his fairy godparents to disappear back to Fairyland. Now powerless, Crocker is defeated by Timmy's parents. Timmy gets the Magic Muffin and wishes everything was back to normal, including his fairy godparents.

● ● ● ● ● ● ● ● ●

Family Guy Season 4, Episode 24 "Peterotica" (April 23, 2006)

Fox Television Animation, Fuzzy Door Productions. Directed by Kurt Dumas. Produced by Sherry Gunther, Mike Barker, Matt Weitzman, Seth MacFarlane, David Zuckerman, Craig Hoffman, Danny Smith, Ricky Blitt, Chris Sheridan. Written by Patrick Meighan. Cast: Seth MacFarlane (Peter Griffin, Brian Griffin, Stewie Griffin, Glen Quagmire, Carter Pewterschmidt, Kool-Aid Man), Alex Borstein (Lois Griffin, Barbara Pewterschmidt), Mila Kunis (Meg Griffin), Seth Green (Chris Griffin),

Alex Breckenridge (Renee Zellweger), John G. Brennan (Mort Goldman), Mike Henry (Cleveland Brown), Tamera Mowry (Book Customer), Patrick Warburton (Joe Swanson), Ralph Garman (Ted Turner), Stacey Scowley (Renee Zellweger), Betty White (Herself), Nicole Sullivan, Fred Tatasciore, John Viener.

Family Guy (1999), which debuted on Fox after Super Bowl XXXIII, was created by Seth MacFarlane and is about Peter Griffin, a fat, ignorant Irish Catholic living in Quahog, Rhode Island with his wife, Lois (of the wealthy Pewterschmidt family); their kids, Meg, Chris, and baby Stewie; and their anthropormorphic dog, Brian. It is known for its cutaway segments, which usually have nothing to do with the plot.

Peter and his friend Quagmire go to a new adult bookshop. Carol Burnett is the cleaning lady. Quagmire sings a parody of the song *Make 'Em Laugh*:

> "Make 'em laugh, make 'em laugh,
> Don't you know all the world loves to laugh?
> I always try to find the hottest chick in the place,
> I crack her on the noggin with a lamp or a vase,
> And then when she's unconscious I do stuff to her face!
> [Pushes inflatable sex doll down out of the shot,
> when it comes back up it is wearing Groucho glasses.]
> Make 'em laugh, make 'em laugh, make 'em laugh!"
> [Puts a cigar in her mouth and lights it, the cigar explodes.]

Peter decides to start writing erotica with a $10 loan from his father-in-law, Carter Pewterschmidt. Pewterschmidt is sued and loses all his money and his wife and has to move in with the Griffins and learn the "joys" of the simple life. At the end, Pewterschmidt is rich again, his wife having married and divorced Ted Turner and taken half Turner's money.

● ● ● ● ● ● ● ● ●

Family Guy Season 7, Episode 12 "420" (April 19, 2009)

Fuzzy Door Productions, 20th Century Fox Television. Directed by Julius Wu. Produced by Sherry Gunther, Mike Barker, Matt Weitzman, Seth MacFarlane,

David Zuckerman, Craig Hoffman, Danny Smith, Ricky Blitt, Chris Sheridan. Written by Patrick Meighan. Cast: Seth MacFarlane (Peter Griffin, Brian Griffin, Stewie Griffin, Glen Quagmire, Tom Tucker), Alex Borstein (Lois Griffin, Loretta Brown, Tricia Takanawa, Barbara Pewterschmidt), Mila Kunis (Meg Griffin), Seth Green (Chris Griffin, Neil Goldman), Christa Campbell (Elizabeth Shue, Hot Chick/Blonde), Mike Henry.

Peter and his friends are sick of Quagmire talking about his cat, so as a prank, they shave the cat, which dies. The cops stop Peter, who is covered with blood on his way to bury the body, but are about to leave when Brian drops a small amount of marijuana and is busted.

Brian organizes a rally to legalize marijuana. Stewie shows him how to do it in a musical number, "Bag of Weed", complete with Groucho Marx smoking a blunt. The campaign is a success, and Mayor West legalizes marijuana in Quahog.

Carter Pewterschmidt, who is losing billions to the new hemp business, bribes Brian into making an impassioned anti-pot speech in public by printing two million copies of Brian's novel. Mayor West re-illegalizes marijuana. Brian fails to sell a single book. Peter tells Quagmire he killed the cat and collects the reward.

• • • • • • • • •

The Simpsons Season 21, Episode 8 "O Brother, Where Bart Thou?" (December 13, 2009)

Gracie Films, 20th Century Fox Television, Film Roman Productions. Directed by Steven Dean Moore. Produced by Bill Oakley, Josh Weinstein, Al Jean. Written by Matt Selman. Cast: Dan Castellaneta (Homer Simpson), Julie Kavner (Marge Simpson, Patty Bouvier, Selma Bouvier), Nancy Cartwright (Bart Simpson), Neve Campbell (Cassandra), Yeardley Smith (Lisa Simpson), Hank Azaria (Moe Szyslak, Chief Wiggum, Snake, Superintendent Chalmers), Harry Shearer (Lenny Leonard), Pamela Hayden (Milhouse), Tress MacNeille (Dolph), Jordan Nagai (Charlie), Kim Cattrall (Herself), Huell Howser (Himself), Cooper Manning (Himself), Eli Manning (Himself), Peyton Manning (Himself), Dick Smothers (Himself), Tom Smothers (Himself).

It's a snow day, but it's too cold for Bart to play outside, and then the power goes out and all the things Bart likes to do are powered by electricity. His sisters are playing Fashion Show with a flashlight and a battery-powered boom box. Bart asks if he can play with them, but Lisa tells him he will never know the close bond of a same-sex sibling because he has no brother.

Bart resists the idea, but that night, he dreams he is in Bro-Town U.S.A. The Marx Brothers ride by on a land boat. The Blues Brothers dance. The Mario Brothers chase a mushroom. The Smith Brothers cough. Sideshow Bob and his brother Cecil Terwilliger fly kites together. The Wright Brothers argue over whose turn it is to fly the plane. Peyton and Eli Manning play keep-away with their older, non-football playing brother, Cooper. The Smothers Brothers sing, but Tommy Smothers ruins Bart's dream by knocking down the Wright Brothers' plane with his yo-yo.

Bart awakens realizing he wants a brother. Homer tells him girls are easier. "I don't have to tell girls how their bodies work cause I don't know."

Bart says, "You never told me how my body works."

Homer replies, "Point and shoot."

Bart's efforts to trick his parents into making him a brother backfire. He substitutes "Tac-Tics" for Marge's birth control pills, but she catches him and points out that even if she and Homer had a child, it might be another girl. Bart realizes he can't risk this and goes to an orphanage to adopt a child. The head of the orphanage kicks him out, but Charlie, an orphan, overhears Bart and follows him home.

Bart parades Charlie around the schoolyard as his brother and teaches him hijinks and takes him to a scary movie. Chief Wiggums tries to take Charlie back to the orphanage, but Charlie assaults him with his own pepper spray. The two take refuge in a snow cave, but are found by Lisa, who tries to get Bart to return Charlie. Then a snow plow seals them in. Bart knows how to escape, though: "Point and shoot, bro!"

Back at the orphanage, Charlie is adopted by a family with six sisters. Homer and Bart spend some quality father and son time at a scary movie.

• • • • • • • • •

The Simpsons Season 22, Episode 7 "How Munched Is That Birdie in the Window?" (November 28, 2010)

Gracie Films, 20th Century Fox Television, Film Roman Productions. Directed by Michael Polcino. Produced by Bill Oakley, Josh Weinstein, Al Jean. Written by Kevin Curran. Cast: Dan Castellaneta (Homer Simpson, Grampa, Itchy), Julie Kavner (Marge Simpson), Nancy Cartwright (Bart Simpson, Todd Flanders, Nelson Muntz, Database), Yeardley Smith (Lisa Simpson), Hank Azaria (Superintendent Chalmers, Carl, Moe Szyslak), Harry Shearer (Ned Flanders, Principal Seymour Skinner, Mr. Burns, Lenny, Scratchy), Marcia Wallace (Edna Krabappel), Rachel Weisz (Dr. Thurmond), Pamela Hayden (Milhouse van Houten, Rod Flanders), Tress MacNeille (Mrs. Muntz), Russi Taylor (Martin Prince), Danica Patrick (Herself), and Gregg Berger.

The Itchy & Scratchy Show is an ancient animated cartoon in the Simpsons universe. Itchy, an anthropomorphic mouse, and Scratchy, an anthropomorphic cat, try to kill each other in hyper-violent ways. Unlike, say, the cutaways in *Family Guy* (1999), the cartoon-within-the-cartoon is always related thematically to the episode.

A homing pigeon, Raymond Bird, flies through Bart's bedroom window, breaking his wing. Lisa contacts the owner, who hangs up on him. She tells Bart he has to nurse the bird back to health because Lisa can't stand pigeons. He does so, but when the time comes to release Raymond, he refuses to go and Bart has lost his heart to him. He goes back home with Bart and is soon delivering messages all over Springfield.

Then Bart's dog, Santa's Little Helper, eats Raymond. Bart is grief-stricken and angry with his dog. He watches an episode of *The Itchy & Scratchy Show* called *Dogday Hellody of 1933*, a parody of the Mickey Mouse cartoon *Pluto's Judgement Day* (1935) and celebrity caricature cartoons of the 1930s. The title is a reference to the movie *Broadway Melody of 1936* (1935). A dog is being tried by Itchy, with an all-Scratchy jury. Edward G. Robinson riddles the dog with bullets. Will Rogers hangs him with his lasso, and the dog spews fountains of blood. W.C. Fields drinks some of the blood out of a martini glass. Harpo Marx cuts the dog's tongue off with a pair of scissors. Bing Crosby, dressed as a priest, beats the dog with a baseball bat.

The Simpsons take Bart and Santa's Little Helper to a therapist, who concludes that the Simpsons have to give the dog away. They take him to an ostrich farm upstate, and Bart says his goodbyes. "It's not my fault you're leaving, it's yours. Because you should never, ever, kill a bird! Ever!" An ostrich steals Homer's cellphone. He goes into the pen to retrieve it and the ostrich escapes and attacks Bart. Bart screams for help, but the dog is conflicted, remembering Bart's words. Bart finally strangles the ostrich, and forgives Santa's Little Helper.

The ostrich is strapped to Homer's car roof, and on the ride home, wakes up and starts strangling Homer.

FUN FACT: *Pluto's Judgement Day* (1935) was directed by David Hand, who also directed *Who Killed Cock Robin?* (1935) and *Mickey's Polo Team* (1936).

• • • • • • • • •

Family Guy Season 10, Episode 9 "Grumpy Old Man" (December 11, 2011)

Fuzzy Door Productions, 20th Century Fox Television. Directed by John Holmquist. Produced by Sherry Gunther, Mike Barker, Matt Weitzman, Seth MacFarlane, David Zuckerman, Craig Hoffman, Danny Smith, Ricky Blitt, Chris Sheridan. Written by David Ihlenfeld, David Wright. Cast: Seth MacFarlane (Peter Griffin, Brian Griffin, Stewie Griffin, Carter Pewterschmidt), Alex Borstein (Lois Griffin, Babs Pewterschmidt), Seth Green (Chris Griffin), Mila Kunis (Meg Griffin), D.C. Douglas (Superman), Danny Smith (Aquaman), and Mike Henry.

Carter Pewterschmidt falls asleep at the wheel, causing a multi-car accident, and is banned from driving. In the hospital, his family persuades him to retire.

With nothing to do, Carter is soon driving everyone crazy. Peter and Lois persuade him to look at retirement communities in Florida. Peter shows Carter how awesome retirement can be, and he agrees, so he and his wife Babs move there.

Six months later, Carter is a shell of his former self: unshaven, unclean, and muttering nonsense. Lois and Peter visit him at the home. Peter draws eyebrows and a mustache on him with magic marker, turning him into Groucho Marx. Babs finds this hilarious. Peter takes Carter back to his office and soon he is his old racist self again.

● ● ● ● ● ● ● ● ●

Little Charley Bear Season 1, Episode 44 "Patient Charley" (January 20, 2012)

Chapman Entertainment, Annix Studios, HiT Entertainment. Directed by Mark Woollard. Created by Daniel Pickering. Produced by Daniel Pickering. Script Editor and Lead Writer: Ross Hastings. Cast: James Corden (Narrator).

Daniel Pickering originally conceived of *Little Charley Bear* (2011), which teaches young children to use their imaginations, when he was an animation student in Dublin in the mid-1990s. There are 52 episodes.

Little Charley Bear is playing "Doctors and Patients" with his toys Caramel Cow, Bellarina Ballerina, Nibblit Rabbit, and Rivet Robot as patients. In a dream sequence, he finds himself sick in the hospital with Nurse Bellarina and Doctor Nibblit. Dr. Nibblit here wears Groucho Marx glasses and a greasepaint mustache. In lieu of a cigar, he carries a Harpo-style horn, which he uses in his examination. Caramel Cow brings Charley flowers, which make Nibblit sneeze. Nurse Bellarina puts him to bed, but he wants to play outside with Rivet. After his nap, he feels better.

Aired in Canada on TVO under the name *Little Wilfey Bear*.

● ● ● ● ● ● ● ● ●

Gravity Falls Season 1, Episode 3 "Headhunters" (June 30, 2012)

Directed by John Aoshima. Produced by Tobias Conan Trost, Alex Hirsch, Rob Renzetti. Written by Aury Wallington, Alex Hirsch. Music: Brad Breeck. Cast: Kristen Schaal (Mabel), Jason Ritter (Dipper), Alex Hirsch (Grunkle Stan, Soos), Coolio (Wax Coolio), Larry King (Wax Larry King), John Oliver (Wax Sherlock Holmes), Linda Cardellini (Wendy), Keith Ferguson (Deputy Durland), Kevin Michael Richardson (Sheriff Blubs), John DiMaggio (Manly Dan), Will Forte (Cute Biker), Gregg Turkington (Toby Determined).

Dipper and Mabel are twin siblings, who are sent off for the summer with their great-uncle, Grunkle Stan, who runs the Mystery Shack in Gravity Falls, Oregon. The show ran 2012–2016, first on the Disney Channel, then on Disney XD.

Years ago, Grunkle Stan stole some wax figures to display at his Mystery Shack. When their popularity waned, he locked them in a storage room where they stood for ten years, forgotten, but plotting revenge. The waxworks are accidentally rediscovered, and after Mabel creates a Wax Stan, Grunkle Stan decides to reopen the wax museum.

Wax Stan is beheaded, and at the memorial service, Mabel and Dipper discover that the wax figures did it, and Wax Sherlock Holmes tells them they must die. Mabel and Dipper realize the wax figures can be defeated with flame and heat. Dipper chops Wax Groucho Marx in half with a candle. "I've heard about a cutting remark, but this is ridiculous," says Groucho, and then, looking at his cigar-less fingers, adds, "And why is there nothing in my hand?" The actor who plays Groucho is unbilled.

● ● ● ● ● ● ● ● ●

The Garfield Show Season 3, Episodes 18-21 "Long Lost Lyman" (September 14, 2012)

Paws, Inc. Directed by Philippe Vidal. Produced by Mark Evanier, Marie-Pierre Moulinjeunc, Kim Campbell. Written by Mark Evanier. Cast: Frank Welker (Garfield), Wally Wingert (Jon Arbuckle), Gregg Berger (Odie), Laura Summer (Drusilla), Frank Ferrante (Lyman).

Garfield and Friends (1988) stopped production after the seventh season (1994-95) by mutual agreement between CBS and the production company after the network wanted to cut the budget for the show. *The Garfield Show* (2008) is a French-American CGI animated series that debuted on the Cartoon Network in the U.S.A. in 2009. It exists in a different universe than *Garfield and Friends* (1988), although it still makes references to it. Frank Welker replaced the late Lorenzo Music as "everyone's favorite fat cat," Garfield.

Lyman, in the original comic strip, was a friend and roommate of Jon's and the original owner of Odie. He first appeared on August 7, 1978, and was only active for a few months. By 1981, he was usually absent, and didn't appear at all between December 25, 1981, and June 27, 1982. By the time of his last regular appearance on April 24, 1983, he had mostly disappeared. He made only two more cameos in the following thirty years.

In the show, the character was "vocally based on Groucho," and writer/director Mark Evanier hired Frank Ferrante to play the role. In this four-parter, which lasts one hour, Lyman's disappearance is explained for the first time anywhere. Lyman left to photograph the Zabadu, a cryptid living in Franistan, and never returned. Jon watches a documentary on the Zabadu, who in a picture, is wearing a hat similar to the one Jon gave Lyman. Jon realizes Lyman may be held prisoner by the Zabadu, and goes to Franistan to find him with Garfield and Odie.

Adventurer Dirk Dinkum, who only cares about money, is also searching for the Zabadu. Jon's guide, Angie, formerly worked for Dinkum. Dinkum and his henchman, Buckley, plant a tracking device in Angie's car so they can follow her. Odie follows his nose and finds Lyman wearing a Zabadu suit.

Lyman reveals that while searching for the Zabadu, he fell and broke his leg, and a doctor in a Zabadu costume set it for him. The doctor put on the disguise to help ward off poachers. When he died, Lyman took over for him.

Dirk and Buckley take a picture of Lyman in Zabadu drag, and plan to palm it off as a picture of the real thing. They are thwarted by the real Zabadu. Although Lyman is Odie's owner, he realizes the dog is better off with Jon and Garfield, and lets him go, although he promises to visit.

• • • • • • • • •

The Simpsons Season 26, Episode 1 "Clown in the Dumps" (September 28, 2014)

Gracie Films, Film Roman, 20th Century Fox Television. Directed by Steven Dean Moore. Produced by Bill Oakley, Josh Weinstein, Al Jean. Written by Joel H. Cohen. Cast: Dan Castellaneta (Homer Simpson, Abe Simpson), Julie Kavner (Marge Simpson), Nancy Cartwright (Bart Simpson, Nelson Muntz, Ralph Wiggum), Yeardley Smith (Lisa Simpson), Hank Azaria (Chief Wiggum, Cletus Spuckler, Moe Szyslak, Comic Book Guy, Guy in Flash Mob), Harry Shearer (Principal Skinner, Kent Brockman), Pamela Hayden (Milhouse Van Houten).

Krusty the Clown is depressed after being roasted, so he goes to see his father, Rabbi Hyman Krustofski, who confesses that he finds Rabbi Rudenstein funnier than Krusty. Not only does Rabbi Krustofsky fail to give Krusty validation, he dies in mid-sentence.

Things continue to go south for Krusty at the funeral and at the office of the grief therapist. When he finally returns to his show, he quits in mid-performance.

Nothing improves in retirement, so Krusty drinks himself into a stupor. In his dream, he is in Jewish Heaven with his father, who tells him he has to help people. Krusty wakes up and says, "I gotta change my life!"

He opens "Krusty's Ark Animal Shelter" in the former Krustyburger Packaging Plant to house animals put out of work by Cirque du Soleil, but even this is unfulfilling. Bart takes him to Temple Beth Western to show him something. Rabbi Rudenstein is doing Krusty's act. Krusty realizes that his father loved his jokes. "My father respected me, but could never tell me. That's Jewish Heaven."

In Jewish Heaven, the Irving Berlin Orchestra plays. Albert Einstein dances with Golda Meir. Harpo Marx dances with Chico. Groucho dances with Karl. Rodney Dangerfield is in the Super VIP section with Jesus Christ.

● ● ● ● ● ● ● ● ●

Clarence Season 1, Episode 9 "Honk" (June 19, 2014)

Cartoon Network Studios. Directed by Nelson Boles (Post Creative Director), Raymie Muzquiz (Supervising Director). Writing Credits: Skyler Page (Creator), Mark Banker (Written by), Skyler Page, Mark Banker, and Spencer Rothbell (Story). Produced by Keith Mack. Music by Simon Panrucker, James L. Venable. Cast: Kyle Arem (Dustin), Ivy Bishop (Malessica), Tayler Buck (Courtlin), Katie Crown (Ms. Baker/Mom/Bike Shop Lady), Eric Edelstein (Chad/TV Man), Sean Giambrone (Jeff Randall), Grace Kaufman (Chelsea), Tom Kenny (Ryan 'Sumo' Sumozski/TV Artist/TV Host), Isabella Niems (Kimby/Darlie), Skyler Page (Clarence Wendle/Nathan/Mr. Reese), Gavin Pierce (Crendle), Joshua Rush (Breehn/Vu), Roger Craig Smith (Belson/Percy/TV Lawyer), Dan White (TV Guest/Principal/Teacher 1).

Cartoon Network Studios began in 1994 in name only at Hanna-Barbera studios before moving to its own space in 2000. After William Hanna's death in 2001, Hanna-Barbera was folded into Warner Bros. Animation and Cartoon Network Studios was revived as its own entity. *Clarence* was developed by Skyler Page in 2012 at Cartoon Network Studios as part of their shorts development program. It is about Clarence, a fat, none-too-bright nine-year-old, and his friends, Jeff and Sumo.

After Clarence makes a dumb joke in class, Jeff says, "Have you thought about not saying stuff like that? … You just spout words at people and hope they stick. Maybe you should look at people who are good conversationalists and try to copy what they do."

At home, Clarence channel-surfs looking for a good conversationalist. He first tries to emulate Conan O'Brien, but then he happens upon a Marx Brothers movie. Groucho and Chico also appear, but Clarence is most taken by Harpo and his horn honking. Clarence decides to honk a horn instead of talking, and buys a horn at a bike shop, which he names "Hornsby."

At first, Clarence's honking is mostly a hit, but Jeff warns him people will quickly tire of it. After Hornsby causes an accident in the chemistry lab, Jeff stages an intervention, but Clarence chooses Hornsby over rejoining society. Later, he decides to keep Hornsby in his backpack. When he gets to school, everybody has horns until they are all confiscated by a teacher. Clarence learns a valuable moral lesson: "… when you lose your horn, you buy the whistle," and he plays his new slide-whistle.

● ● ● ● ● ● ● ● ●

SpongeBob SquarePants Season 9, Episode 13b "The Executive Treatment" (September 7, 2015)

United Plankton Pictures. Creative Director: Vincent Waller. Animation Directors: Alan Smart, Tom Yasumi. Written by Jack Pendarvis. Producer: Jennie Monica. Cast: Tom Kenny (SpongeBob, Business Fish #1, French Narrator), Bill Fagerbakke (Patrick, Business Fish #2), Rodger Bumpass (Squidward, Jenkins, Business Fish #5), Clancy Brown (Mr. Krabs, Krabs Eyes, Business Fish #3, Prison Guard), Jill Talley (Business Fish #6), Frank Ferrante (Stockholder Eel).

SpongeBob SquarePants (1999) was a show created by marine biologist Stephen Hillebrand about the title character and his friends, including Patrick Star, who live in Bikini Bottom. It is the highest-rated Nickelodeon series ever, the most-distributed property of MTV, and a multi-billion dollar media franchise.

Patrick Star wants to buy a sandwich called "The Executive Treatment," but he can't without first buying a business tie and business glasses, which he happily does. Before he can eat the sandwich, he finds himself swept up into a business meeting at Business Industries, where he is told impostors are jailed as corporate spies "forever and ever and ever."

Enter Stockholder Eel, who has a mustache and bushy eyebrows. He wears a monocle instead of glasses, but his voice is a dead ringer for Groucho Marx's, and he is played by Frank Ferrante. Ferrante recalls, "I was given the role by Paul Tibbitt, producer and writer who had seen me at the Pasadena Playhouse in 1989. I think he was working at Music Plus in Pasadena at the time, and twenty-six years later, he remembered." Eel takes an instant liking to Patrick, although he says about Patrick's idea, "That's the silliest thing I've evah hoid." He gives Patrick just eighteen more chances to prove himself.

After a montage of Patrick's haplessness, Stockholder Eel says, "You know, kid, we need somebody like you around here. For me to fire." Patrick reveals he can't be fired, for he is an impostor, and he is sent to jail. SpongeBob comes to see Patrick on visiting day, and informs Patrick that since he is in charge of the laundry room on Thursdays, he is now an executive and qualifies for The Executive Treatment Sandwich. Patrick inhales the sandwich through the phone and puts on his business glasses and business tie. The guards don't recognize him, and he is able to walk out of jail a free starfish.

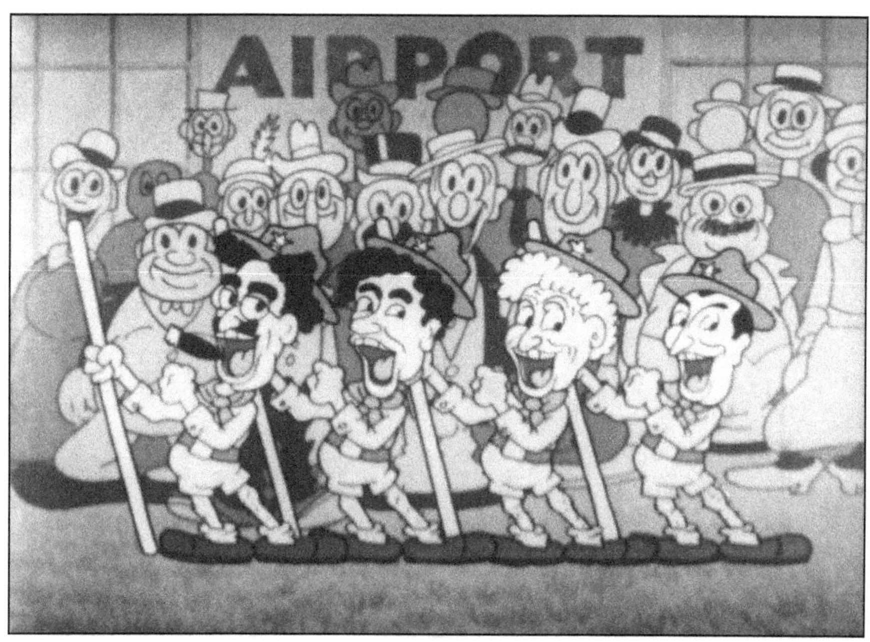

Harpo sings! A scene from *Cubby's World Flight* (1933).
Courtesy Steve Stanchfield, Thunderbean Animation.

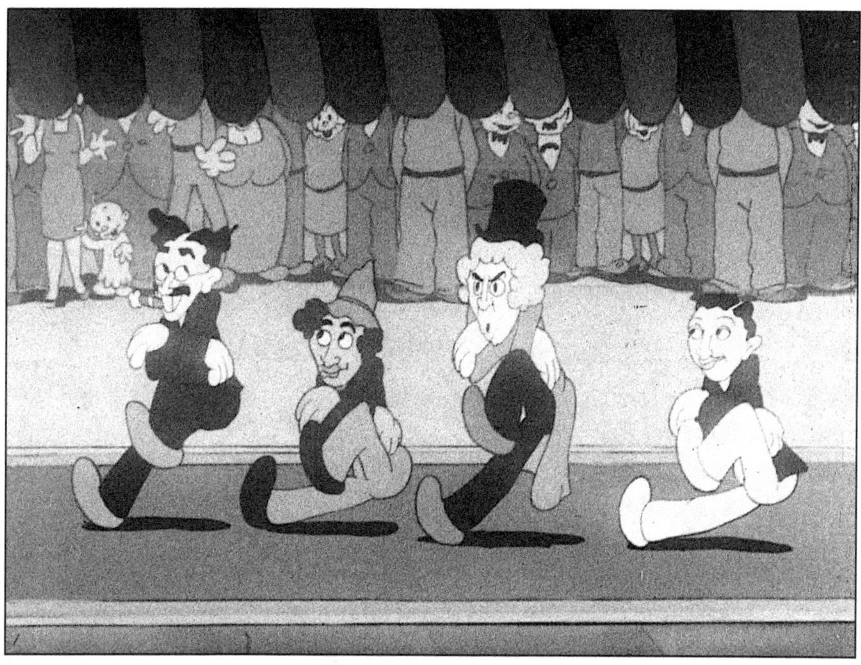

The Four Marx Brothers Cossack dance the red carpet in *Soda Squirt* (1933).
Courtesy Steve Stanchfield, Thunderbean Animation.

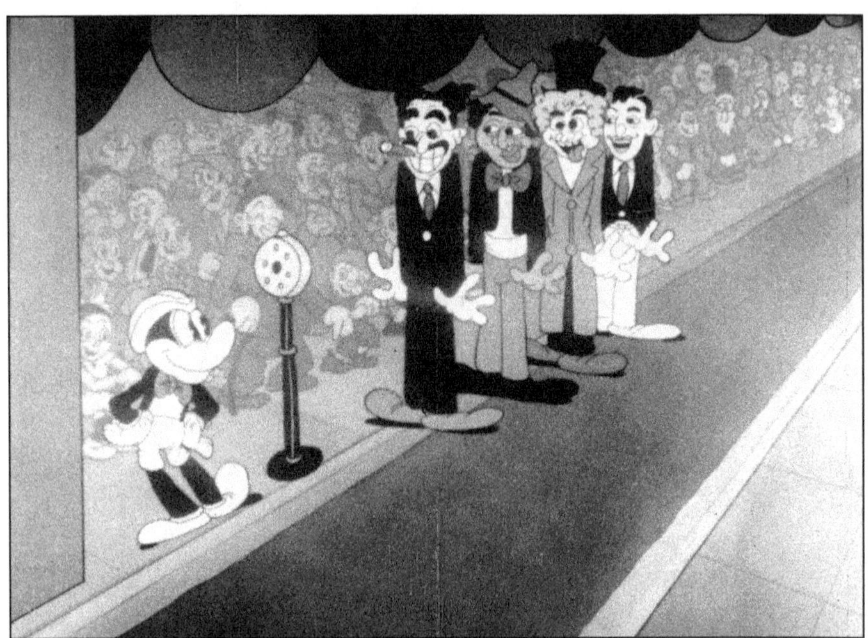

The Four Marx Brothers stop to not say a few words on the radio in *Soda Squirt* (1933). Courtesy Steve Stanchfield, Thunderbean Animation.

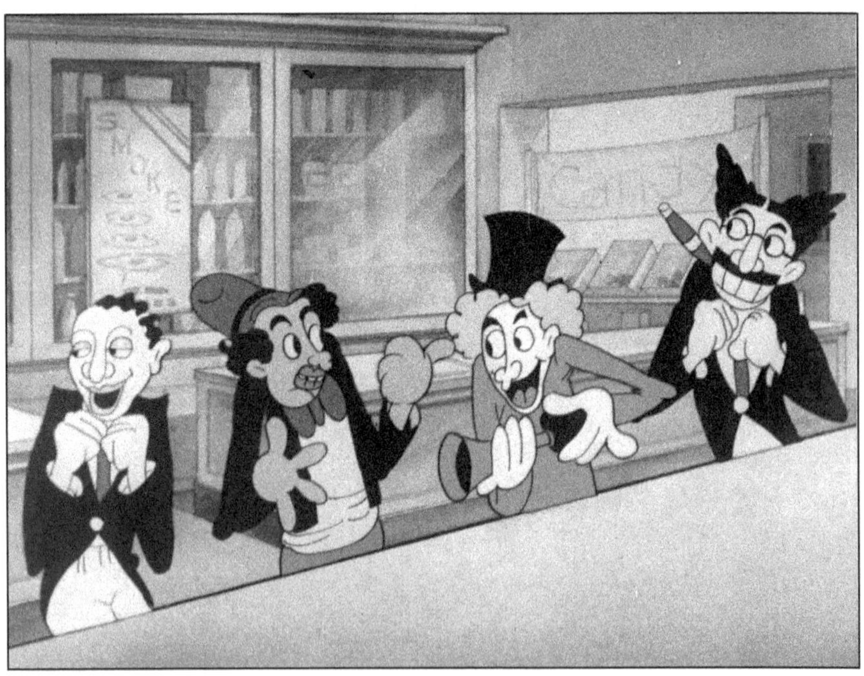

Harpo ordering three hard-boiled eggs and one duck egg in *Soda Squirt* (1933). Courtesy Steve Stanchfield, Thunderbean Animation.

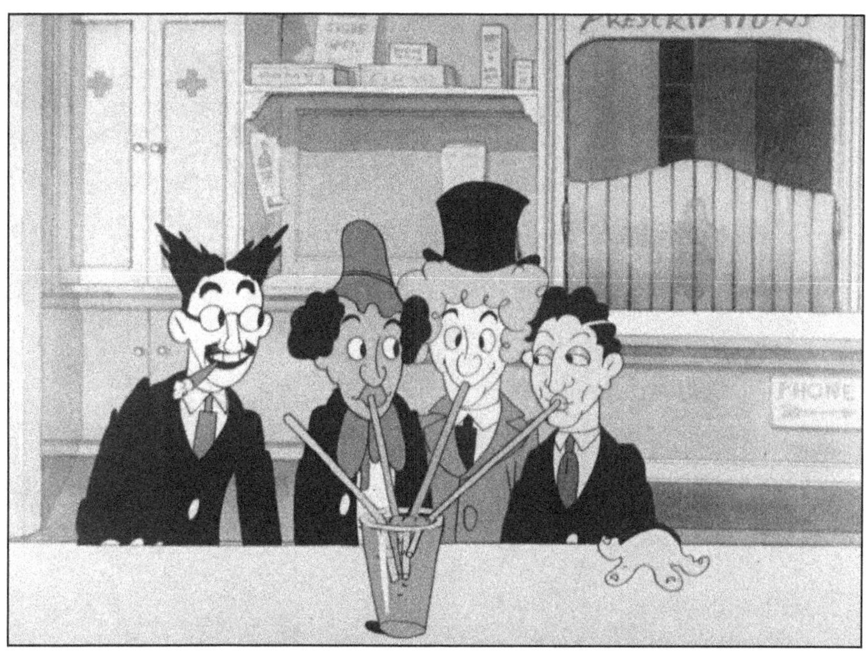

The Four Marx Brothers have an orange Coke and a smile in *Soda Squirt* (1933).
Courtesy Steve Stanchfield, Thunderbean Animation.

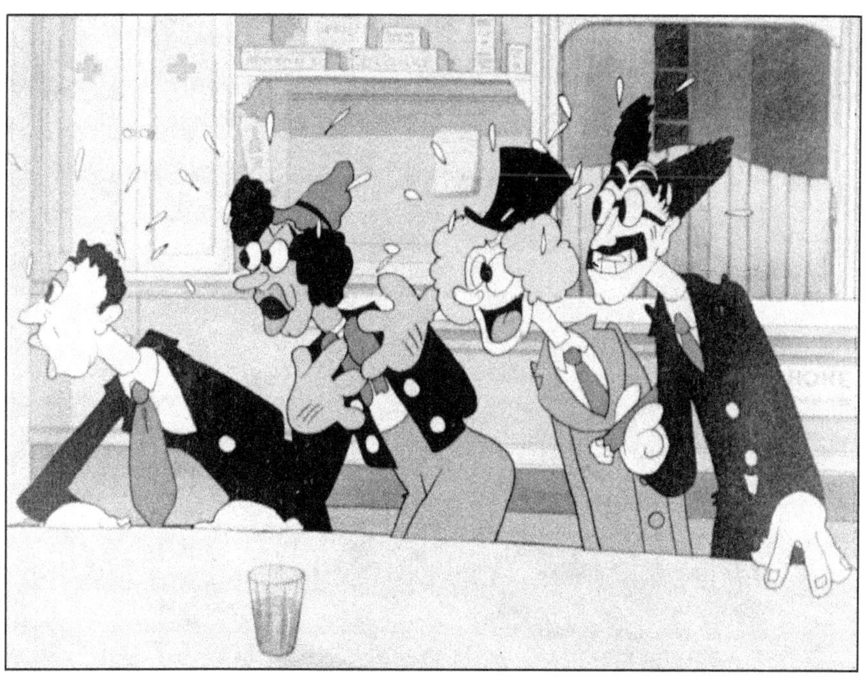

The Four Marx Brothers meet Mr. Hyde in *Soda Squirt* (1933).
Courtesy Steve Stanchfield, Thunderbean Animation.

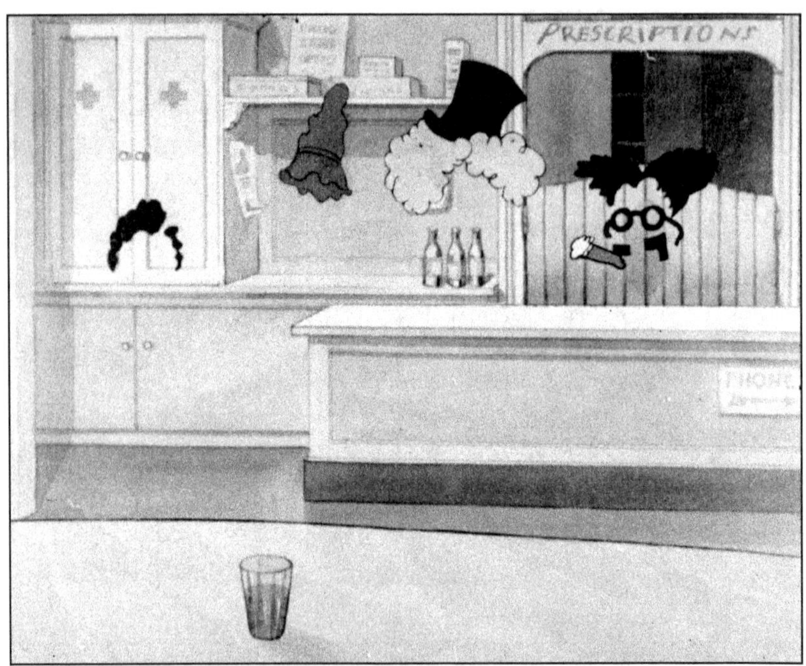

The Marx Brothers flip their wigs in *Soda Squirt* (1933).
Courtesy Steve Stanchfield, Thunderbean Animation.

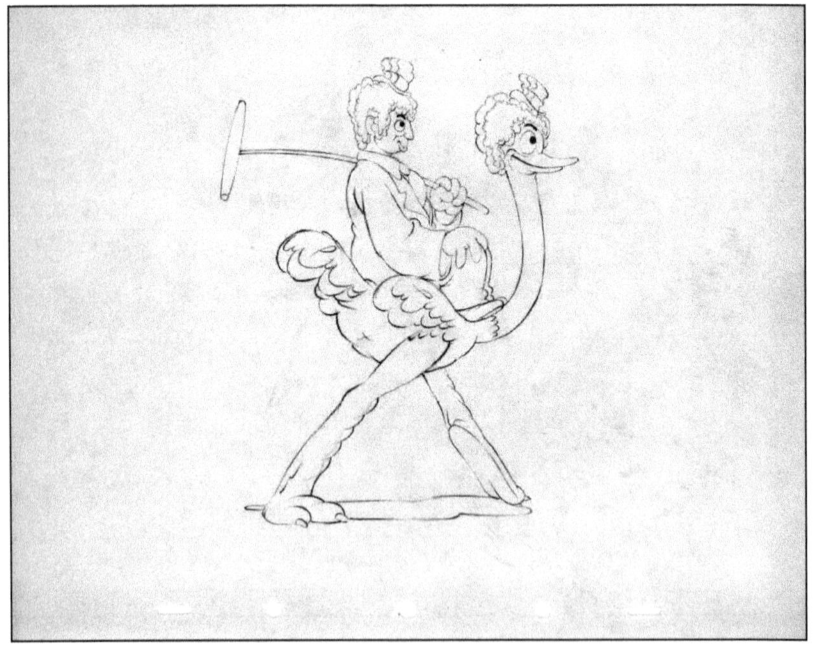

© Disney. Harpo Marx in *Mickey's Polo Team* (1936) by Joe Grant.

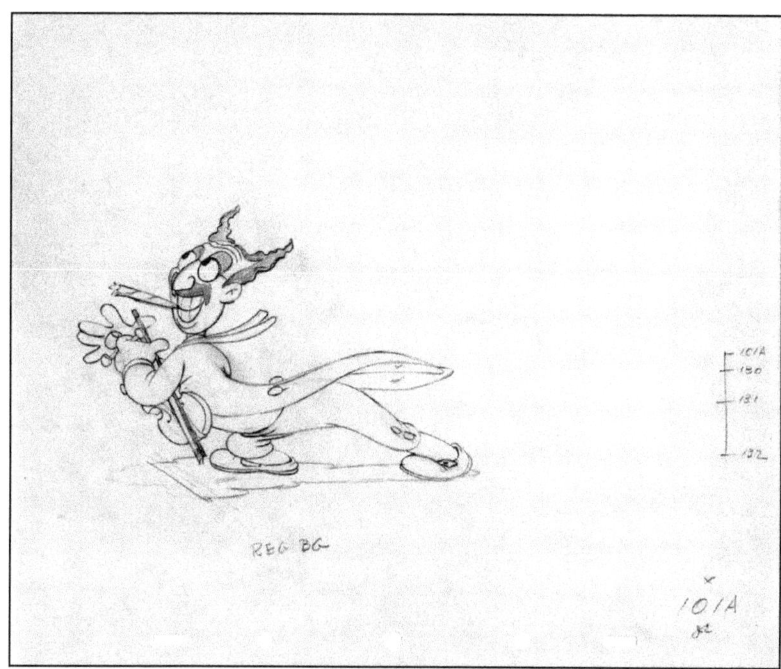

© Disney. Groucho Marx—“Fiddler” from *Mother Goose Goes Hollywood* (1939).

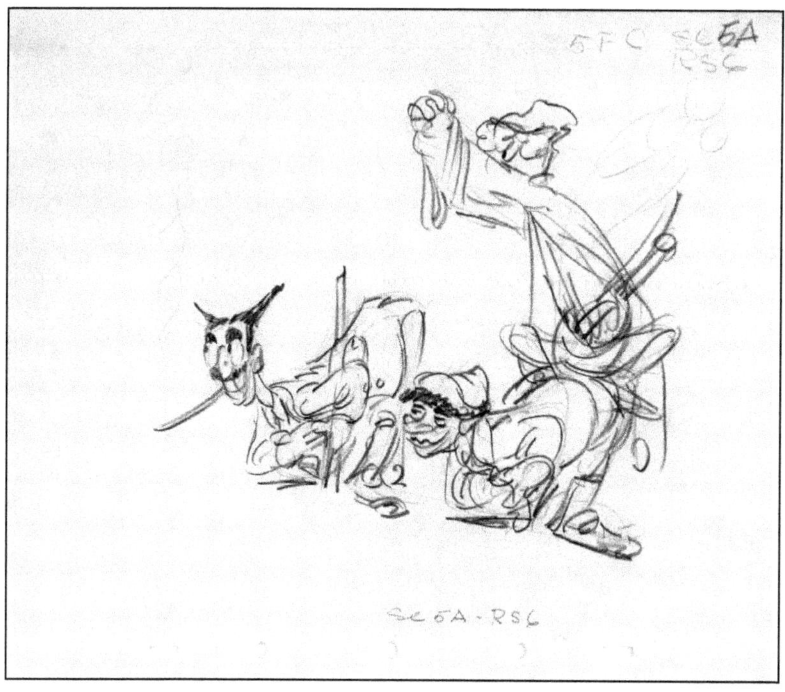

© Disney. Marx Brothers—“Fiddlers Three” from *Mother Goose Goes Hollywood* (1939).

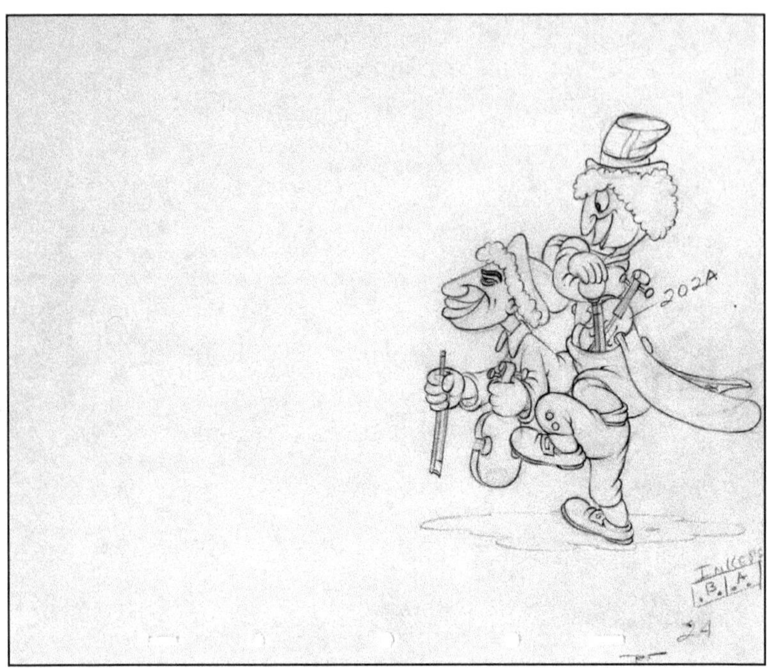

© Disney. Harpo and Chico Marx—"Two Fiddlers" from *Mother Goose Goes Hollywood* (1939).

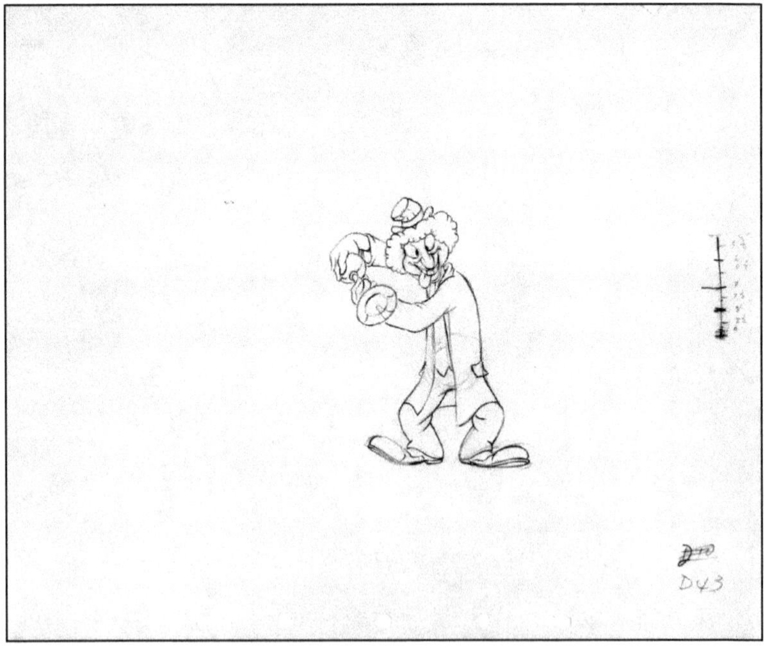

© Disney. Harpo Marx, from *The Autograph Hound* (1939). Possibly by John W. Dunn.

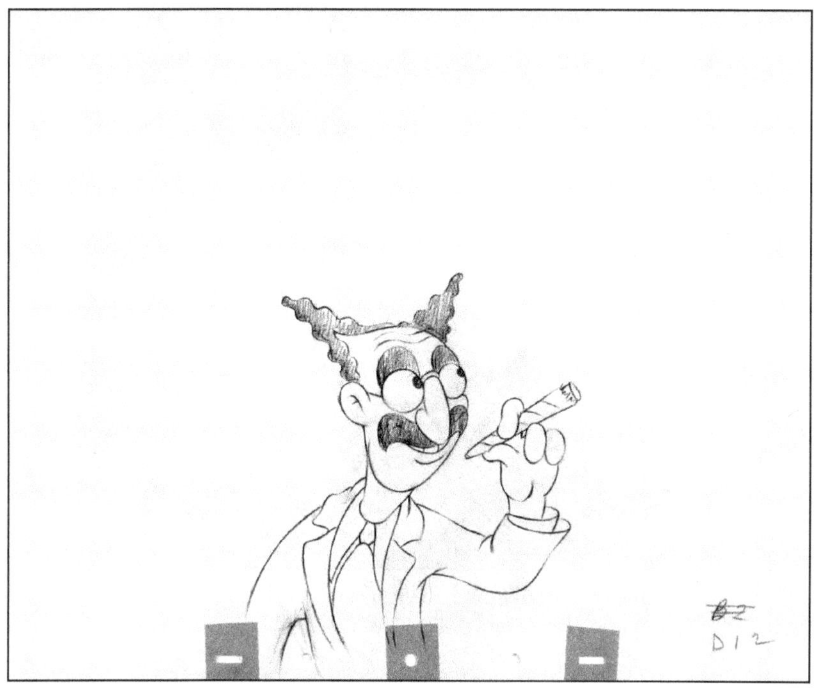

© Disney. Groucho Marx, from *The Autograph Hound* (1939). By Rexford B. Cox (Rex Cox).

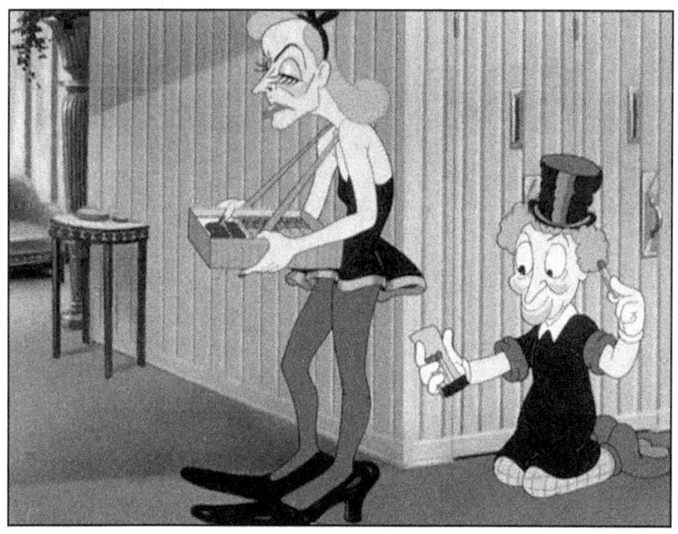

Cigars? Cigarettes? Garbo? Harpo? *Hollywood Steps Out* (1941).
From the author's collection.

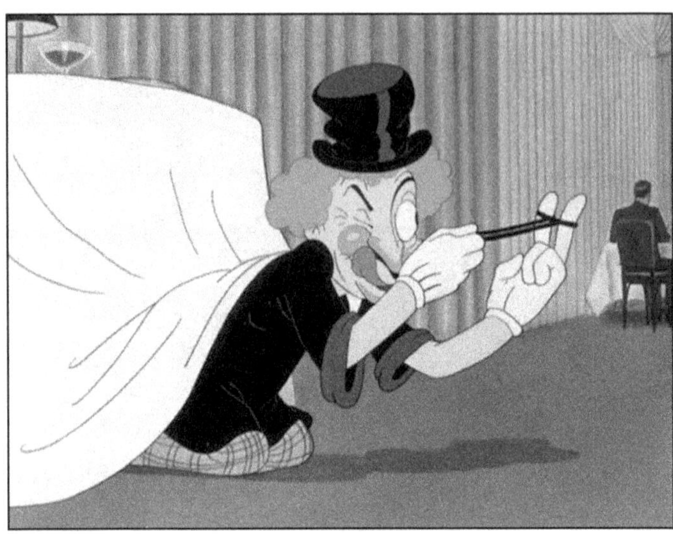

Harpo prepares to burst the bubble of Sally Rand—uh, Strand—in *Hollywood Steps Out* (1941). From the author's collection.

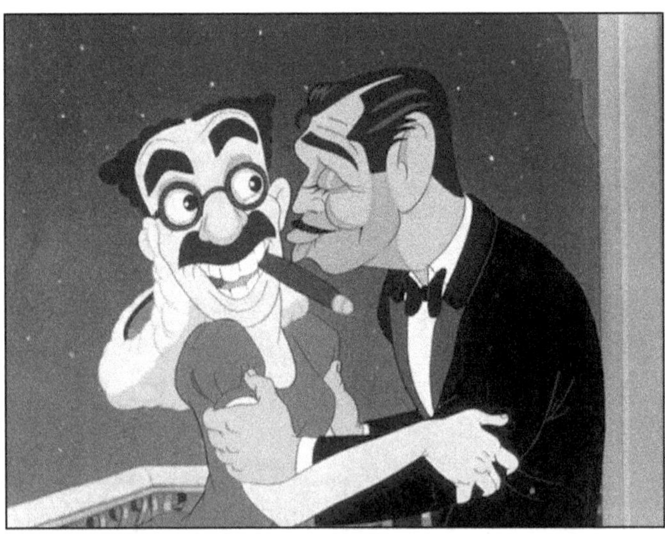

Gable's back and Groucho's got him in *Hollywood Steps Out* (1941). From the author's collection.

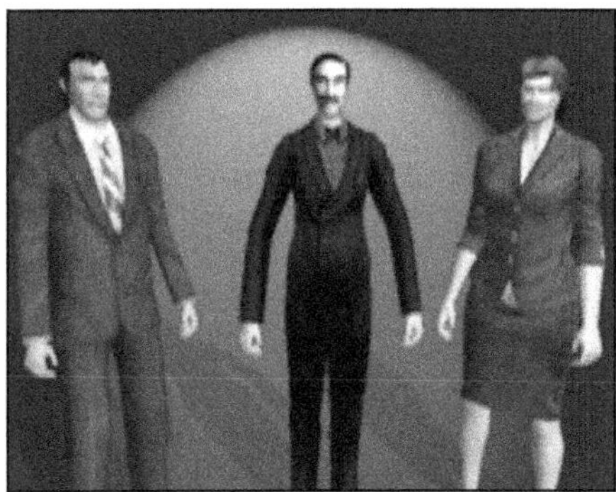

Barack, Groucho, and Hillary have a *Strange Interregnum* (2007). From the author's collection.

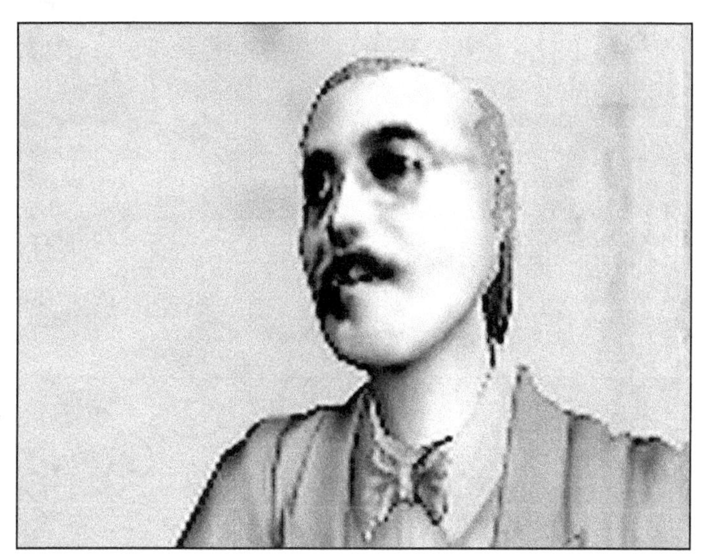

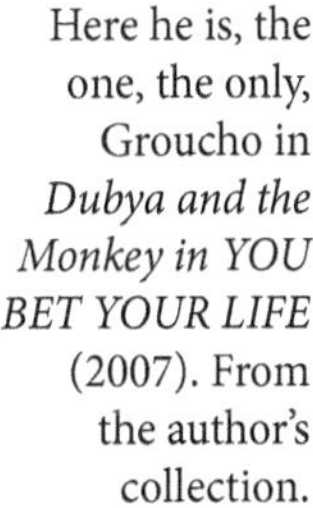

Here he is, the one, the only, Groucho in *Dubya and the Monkey in YOU BET YOUR LIFE* (2007). From the author's collection.

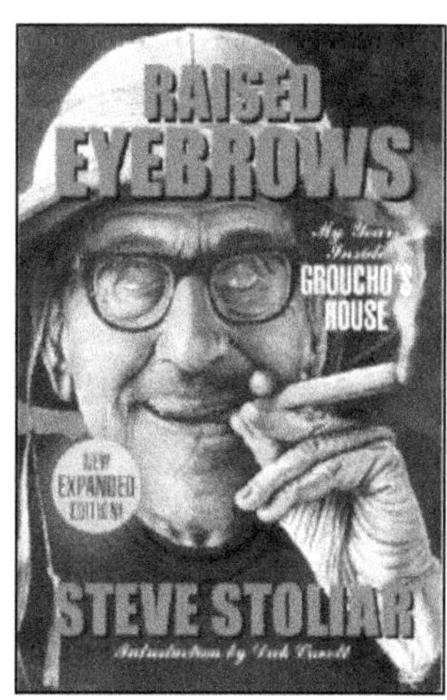

Groucho raises eyebrows in this animation by Motley PR Designs and Marketing of the original cover art by Drew Friedman from *Animated GROUCHO MARX Promo For RAISED EYEBROWS By Steve Stoliar* (2015). Courtesy of Steve Stoliar.

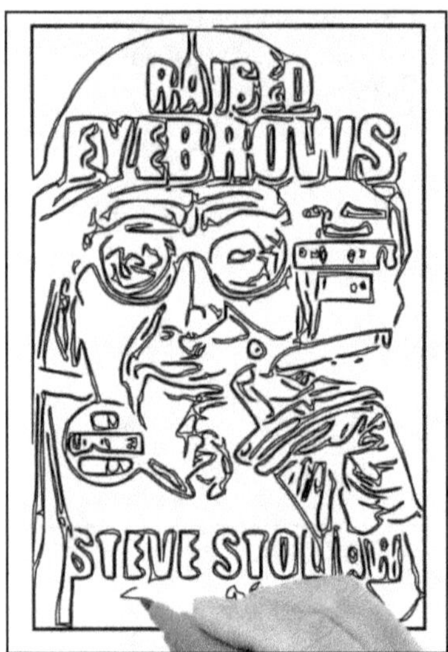

Whiteboard Animation GROUCHO Promo For RAISED EYEBROWS (2015) by Motley PR Designs and Marketing. Original cover art by Drew Friedman. Courtesy of Steve Stoliar.

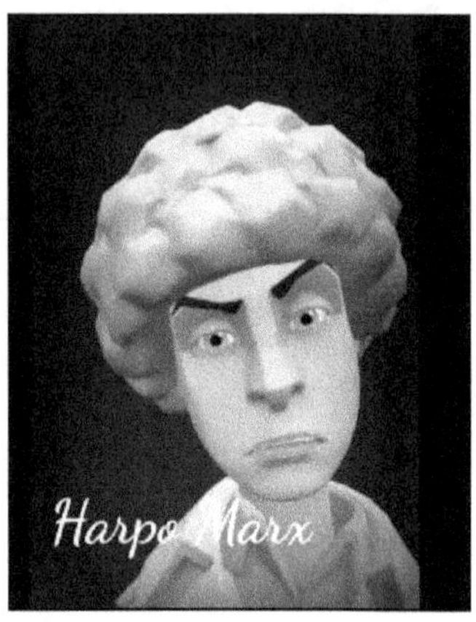

Harpo Marx has nothing to say in *Going Down, Mr. Trump?! (1936)—Marx Brothers* (2015). Courtesy Ron Jammin.

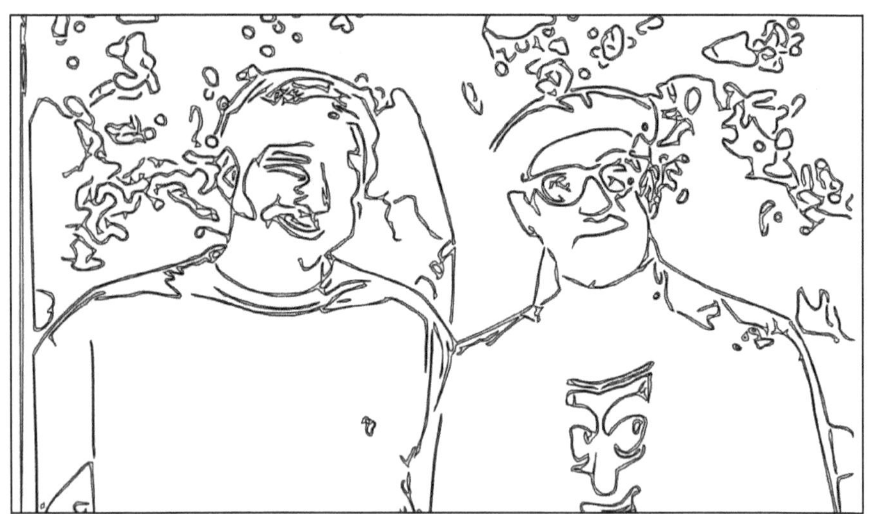

Steve Stoliar and Groucho outside Groucho's house in this whiteboard animation by Motley PR Designs and Marketing for *REMEMBERING GROUCHO Marx Promo For Steve Stoliar's Live Show* (2015). Courtesy Steve Stoliar.

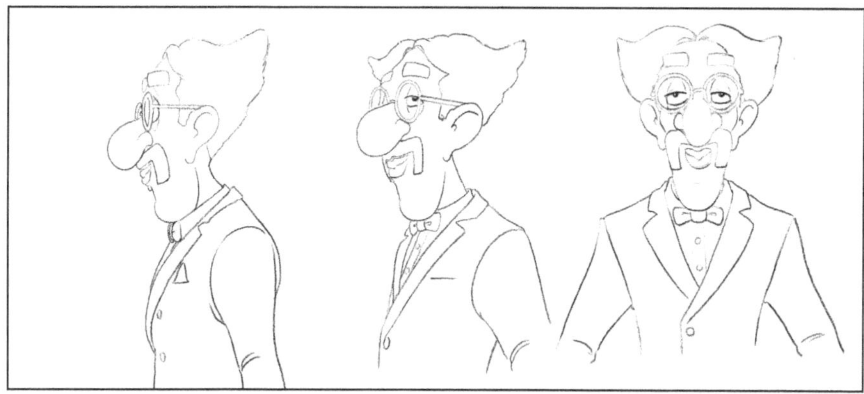

The three faces of Groucho from *Phil Hartman's Flat TV: You Bet Your Life* (2016). Character design by Brian Lemay. Courtesy of Paul Hartmann.

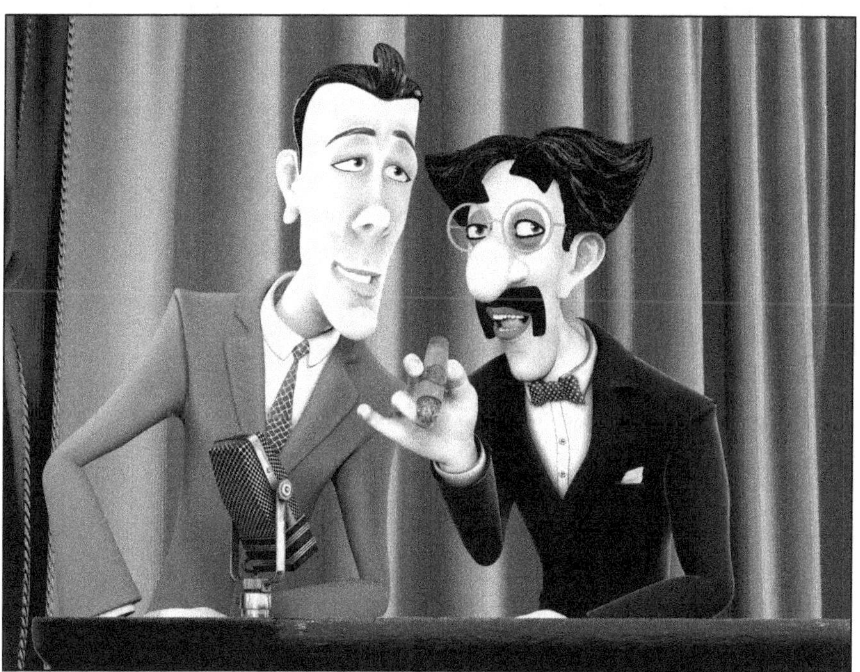

Publicity shot of George Fenneman and Groucho from *Phil Hartman's Flat TV: You Bet Your Life* (2016). Character design by Brian Lemay. Courtesy of Paul Hartmann.

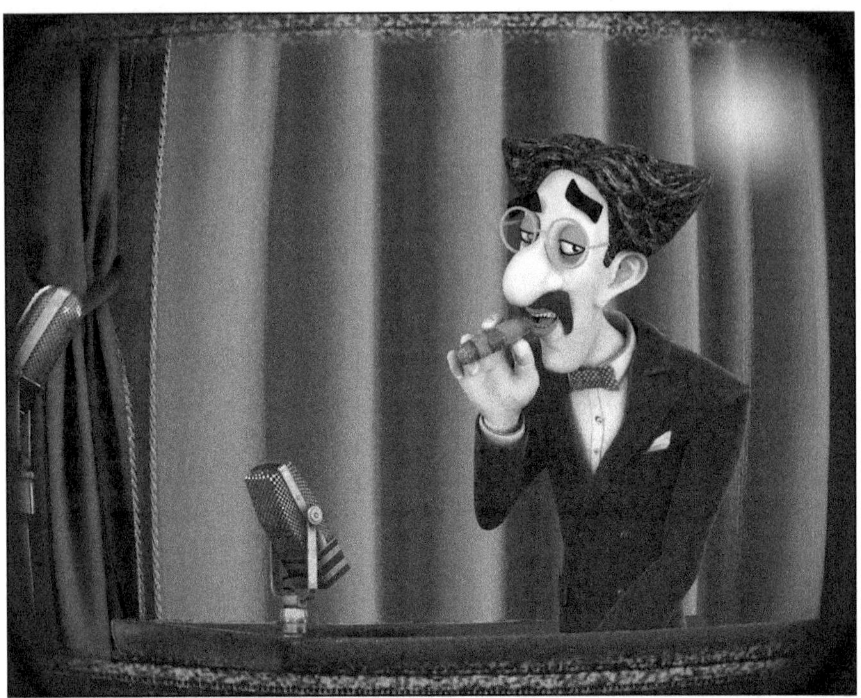

Groucho likes his cigar… From *Phil Hartman's Flat TV: You Bet Your Life* (2016). Character design by Brian Lemay. Courtesy of Paul Hartmann.

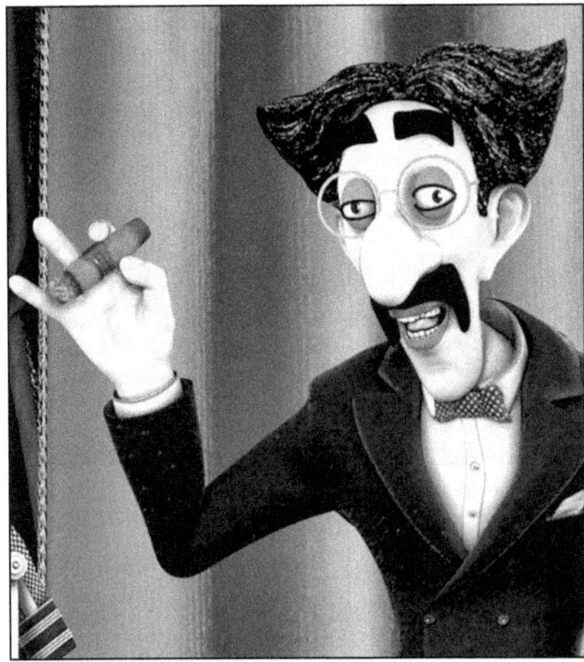

… but he takes it out once in a while. From *Phil Hartman's Flat TV: You Bet Your Life* (2016). Character design by Brian Lemay. Courtesy of Paul Hartmann.

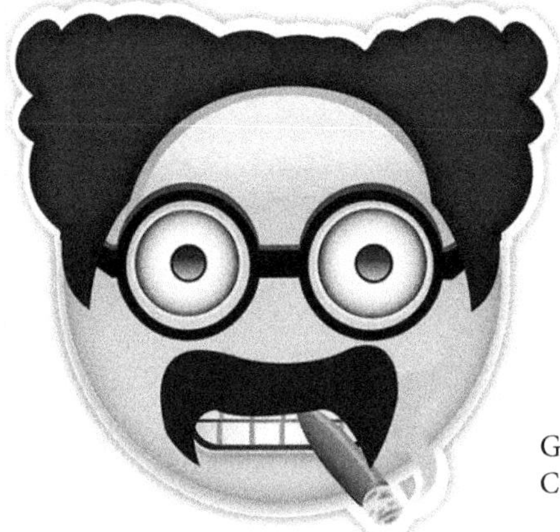

Groucho emoji.
Courtesy Terry Motley.

Harpo emoji.
Courtesy Terry Motley.

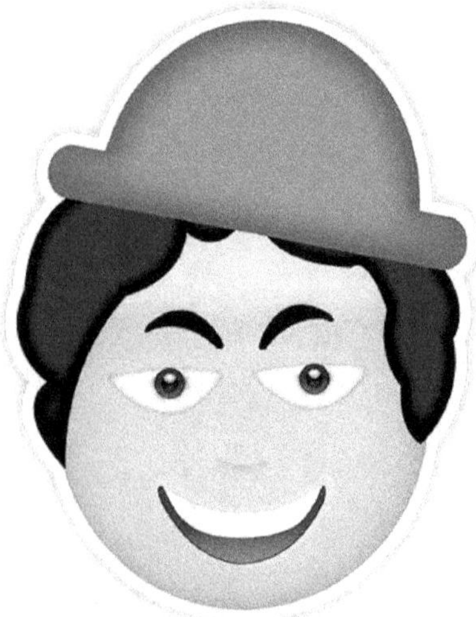

Chico emoji.
Courtesy Terry Motley.

Zeppo emoji.
Courtesy Terry Motley.

3 Animated Effects and Credits in Marx Brothers Movies

The Marx Brothers were trained in Vaudeville and honed on Broadway, and did not rely heavily on animation for gags. The gag in *Duck Soup* (1933) where a dog pops out of Harpo's doghouse tattoo is often mistakenly referred to as animation, but is in fact a process shot. The team only used animated effects once, and animated credits a few times.

Monkey Business (1931): The opening credits are animated on barrels rolling down a ship's gangplank. There is one picture per brother per barrel.

Horse Feathers (1932): This movie deals with neither horses nor birds, but the opening credits have an animated horse breaking out of a barn and running towards the camera as the title comes up.

A Night at the Opera (1935): When Harpo is in the stateroom of the three aviators, an animated butterfly flies out of one of their beards and he chases it with scissors.

In the animated credits for *Room Service* (1938), Hirschfeldian Marx Brothers peer through a transom and open and slam doors, two leitmotifs in farce. It is even fun in the colorized version. The RKO logo is also animated. It is similarly animated in Groucho's solo RKO movies *Double Dynamite* (1951) and *A Girl in Every Port* (1952).

In *Copacabana* (1947), Groucho's first solo effort, the animated neon sign on top of the club flashes all the opening credits.

Showdown at Ulcer Gulch (1956) was an industrial film made for the *Saturday Evening Post* by longtime animator Shamus Culhane featuring his then-father-in-law, Chico Marx, as well as Groucho and many other comedians. Mostly live action, it is bookended by animated segments from the magazine's popular cartoon character, Hazel. These segments were not animated by Culhane.

Groucho played a mob boss named God in his last movie, *Skidoo* (1968). It begins with animated credits of a convict, who resembles Jackie Gleason, dancing. Later in the movie, Gleason's character takes an acid trip—don't ask—and he sees Groucho's head flying around the room on a wood screw before it disappears down a sink.

FUN FACT: The latter prop, a wood screw with a model of Groucho's head on it, reportedly turned up on eBay in its early days. No word on what it sold for, if anything.

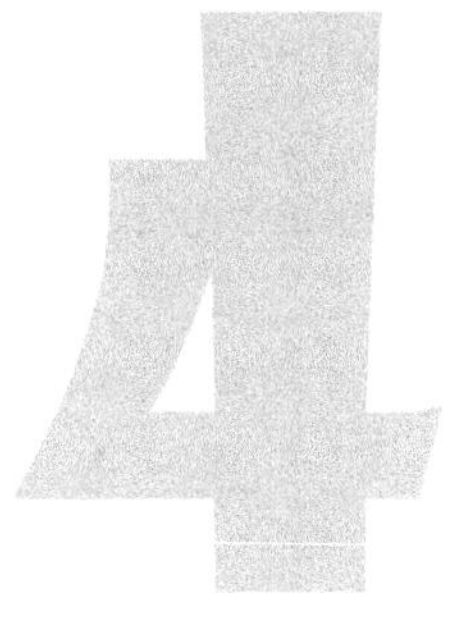

Marxtoons in *You Bet Your Life* (1950), *Groucho* (1965), and DeSoto Commercials

When *You Bet Your Life* (1950) debuted in on television, it was sponsored by DeSoto Plymouth. The opening was an animated map showing the DeSoto Plymouth dealers in all forty-eight states. This was used through the 1953–1954 season. In the 1954–1955 season, the opening was live-action footage of Groucho driving a DeSoto.

In June 1955, the now-familiar opening of the fragmentary abstract Groucho, later used in the syndicated *The Best of Groucho*, first debuted. Playhouse Pictures (PP) in Hollywood designed the spot. The owner of PP was Adrian Woolery, whose resume included being a partner at United Productions of America and a stint at Walt Disney. Founded three years previously, PP considered this to be its greatest achievement to date.

The Playhouse Pictures opening seems to have been used concurrently with a second animated opening in the 1955–1956 season. Groucho Marx drives back and forth across the background map in a DeSoto as the opening titles display. A pretty girl in a DeSoto sings, "Groucho sent me to see the new DeSoto." A handsome man and another pretty girl in DeSotos sing lines to the jingle, and then all three harmonize. Groucho drives back and forth and finishes the song.

A commercial pitching the 1955 models features an animated Groucho in a beret, a look he later adopted in real life, painting a picture of a DeSoto and singing a version of the jingle. He jumps into the canvas and drives the car and the picture crossfades to a live-action shot of the DeSoto. As announcer George Fenneman reads the commercial, animated Groucho throws in his two cents before driving off.

Another animated commercial for the 1955 models features a man and his wife singing the jingle with their friendly DeSoto dealer. Groucho is referenced, but not seen.

Ray Patin Studios did concept art for a DeSoto commercial with a Groucho caricature in a DeSoto with a pretty woman. There is a second drawing on the back of Groucho's head. No further information is available. Ray Patin was also an animator on *The Autograph Hound* (1939). Also, a non-Groucho 1959 Desoto commercial, "Spacemen" featured Daws Butler.

The fragmentary abstract opening continued to be used in the 1956–57 season. In 1957, another animated opening was also used. Groucho, dressed as a stagehand, places the stool, microphone, and podium. He crosses center and the duck flies down. Groucho hands him the script and the duck grabs it in his bill and returns to the flies, taking Groucho with him. In the closing credits, Groucho the stagehand strikes the podium. These animations were used through the 1958-1959 season.

In the 1959–1960 season, a new animated opening was used. It starts with a spinning wheel, then a shot of a hand with a cigar with the Groucho's name superimposed. The words morph into another stylized caricature of Groucho. The title appears, as does a cigar in his mouth. Groucho wiggles his eyebrows and cigar up and down. The stylized caricature was also used in the closing credits.

In the final 1960–1961 season came a title change to *The Groucho Show* and a new set of non-animated credits of Groucho posing in famous portraits.

Four years later, Groucho was asked to do an eponymous version of the show in England. In the credits, Groucho's name appears in a cigar box. A stylized caricature of him is used resembling the one in the 1959–1960 season of *You Bet Your Life* (1950), but it is fragmentary, like the earlier abstract from 1955. The pieces come together, eyebrows wiggle, eyes roll, and the cigar smokes.

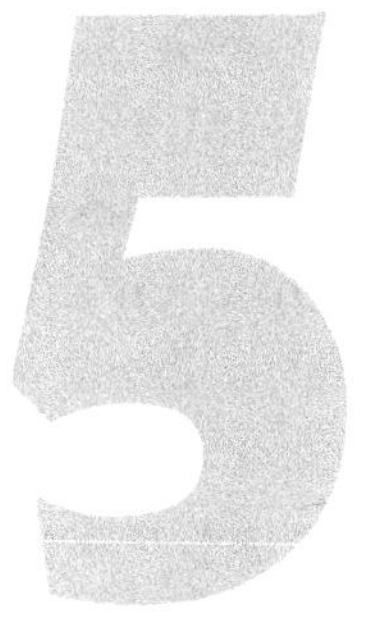

MARXTOONS TV PILOTS

The New Marx Bros. Show Pilot *"A Day at the Horse Opera"* (1966)

Filmation Associates. Director: Hal Sutherland. Producers: Norm Prescott, Lou Scheimer. Writers: Jay Burton, Mort Goode, Michael Maltese. Character Designs, Layouts: Lou Scheimer. Cast: Pat Harrington, Jr. (Groucho), Joe Besser (The Great Indian Chief), Ted Knight: (Chico, Other Voices).

In February, 1966, Filmation ran a trade ad in *Broadcasting* magazine for a Marx Brothers cartoon package, 156 seven-minute shorts. In 2009, Jerry Beck wrote, "Thank God for small favors… As far as I know this show doesn't exist."

However, in 2012, the pilot episode, rediscovered in Filmation's vaults, was shown at San Diego Comicon to a mostly appreciative audience. As Jerry Beck wrote on CartoonResearch.com, "At the Lou Scheimer/Filmation panel today they ran about four minutes of the rare 8 minute Marx Bros. cartoon pilot, and (surprise!) it WAS FUNNY!" Filmation later released it on DVD with other rarities.

Groucho was a consultant and originally was to appear in live-action segments and as a narrator/commentator. Lou Scheimer writes, "One day Groucho called. He said, 'Lou? I've got a perfect voice for you, to play me.' And I said, 'Well, who is it, Groucho?' He said, 'You're talking to him.' It was Pat Harrington [Jr.]".

The title, "A Day at the Horse Opera," is a mash up of *A Day at the Races* (1937), *Horse Feathers* (1932), and *A Night at the Opera* (1935). The characters refer to each other by their stage names. "Groucho" narrates the prologue. The credits are shown to the strains of harp music, on a background that looks like stylized harp strings. Groucho is a huckster for a medicine show in the Old West, Chico and Harpo are his musicians. The Great Indian Chief tells an Ambassador that he refuses to make peace until the Great Stone Face comes to life and marries his daughter, Minnehoho. Unfortunately for Groucho, he is the spitting image of the Great Stone Face and Minnehoho is fat. The brothers hole up in an abandoned fort and repeatedly repel the Chief's attacks (at one point, Harpo launches multiple arrows with his harp). In the end, Groucho dresses up the Ambassador as Groucho, and Minnehoho marries the Ambassador.

FUN FACT: Michael Maltese again writes Grouchoesque patter.

● ● ● ● ● ● ● ● ●

The Marx Brothers Show (2000)

Chaos Properties Corp. presents 2A Productions in association with SFP & Arte. Created by Egon Ellenberg. Developed by Steve Roberts, Bob Underwood, and Gary Kurtz with the participation of Centre National de la Cinématographie. Executive producers: Robert A. Finkelstein, Susan Marx, Mary Marx. Supervising Producers: Steve Roberts, Bob Underwood. Animation: Orange Studio Reklamy. Music: Alec Constandinos. Art Direction & Character Design: Gil Formosa. Story Editors and Written by Steve Roberts, Bob Underwood. Produced by Gary Kurtz. Casting Director/Voice Director: Doug Stone. Directed by Francis Nielsen. Cast: Frank Ferrante (Groucho), Jan Rabson (Chico), Mary Kay Bergman (Bette), and Eddie Frierson (Spike).

Night. A limo pulls up to the curb. Someone hands the driver a film reel. In the desert, revealed to be a film set, the driver throws the reel out the window. As the credits roll, The Marx Brothers escape from the reel in black and white and turn into full-colored versions. They disrupt production on a movie about ancient Egypt and a Western starring Clint Eastwood. They swim through a pirate movie set and reenact the flying bicycle scene from *E.T.* (1982). Finally, in a musical scene, they scoop up chorus girls.

The story begins with a fire in the film vaults at M Studio. In the film can of *Animal Crackers* (1930), Groucho, Harpo, and Chico are doing the scene of Captain Spaulding's entrance when they become aware of the fire. "Hey Groucho," says Chico, "you better put that cigar out." Groucho replies, "Okay, Chico, but you'll have to put out the rest of the place yourself." Chico is pronounced "cheeko" instead of "chicko." Harpo tries to douse the flames with a seltzer bottle, but it is empty. Employees work frantically to save the films, but only "the classics, the Oscar winners." *Animal Crackers* (1930) is left behind.

In the office of the studio head, Mr. Rachman, his yes men view the fire from a safe distance as he intimates he had the fire deliberately set for insurance purposes.

"Who called the fire department?" he asks.

His ex-wife, Bette, a "sexy, classy, and beautiful Barbara Stanwyck type" bursts in. "I called the fire department."

"Tragically, we are too late," he says.

She says, "You think you've won, but you haven't."

In the chaos, a fireman drops the film can containing *Animal Crackers* (1930) and The Marx Brothers escape but are caught in rising waters in the black and white film. Bette tells the firemen to save The Marx Brothers films for posterity. She has them placed in her brand-new film vault. Groucho likes her style and suggests to his brothers that she could help them make new movies.

Bette reveals that she will soon own 51% of the studio and blackmails Rachman into hiring her brother, Spike, to guard the vault. Spike is a nerdy type, but when he puts on the guard's uniform, he becomes a film Nazi, fanatical about preserving motion pictures.

The Marx Brothers escape the film can and turn into full-color versions of themselves, but Spike is hot on their trail. "What we need is air support," says Groucho, and he releases the Millennium Falcon from the *Star Wars* (1976) film can. Spike swats down the tiny Millennium Falcon and traps The Marx Brothers in a net. He captures them on Polaroid film, and leaves them there while he retrieves the film can.

The Marx Brothers spy Han Solo and Chewbacca repairing their damaged spaceship. Chewbacca frees them from their two-dimensional prison and Han Solo offers them a ride for ten thousand dollars. Groucho and Chico don't have that much money, but Harpo picking Han's pocket makes up the difference. They fly back into the *Star Wars* (1976) film can. Groucho cooks up a happy ending where Spike is tied to a tree and the brothers are getting massages from tanned beauties. "Now isn't this a much better picture?" he asks. "Stick with us, there's a lot more where this comes from."

They see two young people making out on a couch in a live-action shot. "They must've thought the show was over," says Chico. "If you ask me," says Groucho, "the show's just beginning."

Harpo gives Groucho his leg and honks his horn.

It was to be the beginning of a series, with 26 episodes budgeted at $13 million, including such installments as "A Night at the Oprah," spoofing talk shows, and "Internuts," a satire of the dot-com boom. $1.5 million was invested, and the show was sold to six European television stations. The show was the brainchild of Egon Ellenberg, an Israeli-born Frenchman and president of Chaos Properties, Inc. While trying to get the rights to Frank Sinatra's rendition of "Come Fly With Me" for a French airline commercial, Ellenberg met with Robert Finkelstein, who not only represents Sinatra's heirs but is the head of Groucho Marx Productions (GMP), which licenses the commercial use of Groucho's voice and likeness. Ellenberg soon pitched the series, which GMP accepted largely because Finkelstein believed Paris-based Chaos Properties "would be able to translate" The Marx Brothers' sensibilities to animation. The animation was done in Poland.

Casting began in January 1999. Frank Ferrante was tapped to play Groucho. The voiceover recordings probably took place between May and September of that year at Screen Music Studios. Tragically, on November 11, 1999, Mary Kay Bergman, the noted voice actress who played Bette, committed suicide.

In October 1999, a dinner was held at the MIPCOM television conference in Cannes, featuring animal crackers, duck soup, and "cocoanuts finale" for dessert. To promote the show, Ferrante did a version of his one-man stage show, *An Evening With Groucho* (1985). Legal and financial issues doomed the series. The pilot has yet to be aired on television anywhere.

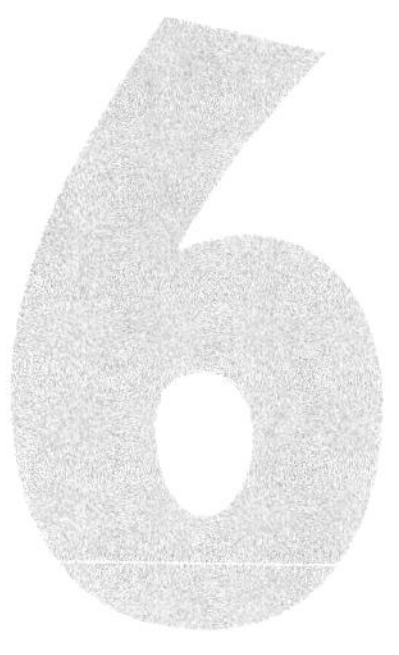

OTHER MARXTOONS

THIS CHAPTER COVERS MARXTOONS that don't fit into one of the previous categories, and as such, includes everything from one of the most primitive forms of animation—flip books—to the most modern, computer animation.

● ● ● ● ● ● ● ● ●

Flip-O-Vision Marxtoons

Flip books are one of the oldest forms of animation, dating to 1868. They are made up of a series of slightly different pictures so that when the book is flipped through, the images are animated.

In 1949, The Topps Company issued a series of sixty Flip-O-Vision books. These required some assembly: the pictures had to be cut out and put together, then a rubber band was attached to the bottom so facilitate the animation.

Two with The Marx Brothers themes were distributed during the period surrounding the release of *Love Happy* (1949). The first was called *Bubble Smoke* (1949) where Harpo does his old trick of taking a puff on a cigarette and blowing smoke out a gum bubble.

The second was *Mr. Missed Her Kisser* (1949), starring Harpo and Chico and their *Love Happy* (1949) costar, Marilyn Monroe. Chico and Marilyn play "Odds or Evens" and the winner gets to kiss the loser. The third time, Marilyn wins, but Harpo inserts himself between them and gets kissed by both. He sticks out his tongue at Chico and gives Marilyn his leg.

● ● ● ● ● ● ● ● ●

Vlasic Pickle Marxtoons

Vlasic started as a creamery before branching out into pickles. "What does a lovable stork with a Groucho Marx voice have to do with selling pickles? Some say the same thing a cheese maker has to do with pickles, but others say that—since the national birthrate was dropping at that time—concerned Vlasic managers simply offered the Stork an opportunity to deliver pickles since babies were in such short supply. You can pick the explanation you like best." That doesn't explain the Groucho part. Presumably that's because the Stork brandishes the pickle like a cigar.

In 1977, the original animation studio, Hubley, wanted Edgar Buchanan, the star of *Petticoat Junction* (1963), to play the Stork, whose name is Jovny. John Hubley designed the character to look like a station master from an old Western. The ad agency, W.B. Doner, rejected the commercial and went to Zander's Animation Parlour, which used the voice of Pat Harrington, Jr. imitating Groucho. Harrington, who was hand-picked by Groucho to play Groucho in *The New Marx Bros. Show* (1966), played the part for years. The first Stork commercial also starred Roger Bowen as the obstetrician.

Referring to the crunch, the Stork said, "Vlasic is the best tasting pickle I evah hoid!" In a 1974 commercial, people of various ages, sexes, and ethnicities imitated the Groucho Stork. This campaign was so successful, Vlasic ran it again in 1999 virtually unchanged. That year, they also had a contest to find a new Groucho imitator, and chose Bill Kaschub. Also in 1999, Vlasic came out with Sandwich Stackers, and a new commercial.

The Vlasic Pickle Stork also appeared in "Icons," a 2005 MasterCard commercial, with Mr. Peanut, Chef Boyardee, Count Chocula, Charlie the Tuna, and the Morton Salt Girl.

Vlasic apparently ran a contest for people to make their own commercials, and some used the Stork. Vlasic also mixed 3-D animation with live-action. Today, Jovny is played by Doug Preis.

• • • • • • • • •

Made-For-Video Marxtoons

Laughter is Good Medicine (1982)

Billy Budd Films. A John Canemaker Production. Directed by John Canemaker. Written by Dennis Blair, John Canemaker, and Frank Moynihan. Featuring the songs and voices of Dennis Blair. With Jane E. Brody.

Apparently made for the health care video market niche, this brief movie posits the theorem that living well and preventing problems leads to healthy life and laughter. It mentions Norman Cousins, editor of the *Saturday Review*, who famously cured himself of ankylosing spondylitis with high doses of Vitamin C and Marx Brothers movies. Caricatures of Charlie Chaplin and Laurel & Hardy appear in between the credits. Also, a large dowager says, "Doctor, I was playing my harmonica and I swallowed it." A stylized Groucho Marx dressed as a doctor comes loping in and says, "It might have been worse. You could have been playing the piano." Later, Humphrey Bogart as a doctor tells his patient, Harpo Marx, to say, "Ah." Harpo's head turns into a horn and honks in Bogie's face. Bogie grabs his lapels and says threateningly, "Say it again, Sam."

During the movie, narrating duties are shared by Jane E. Brody, health columnist for the *New York Times*, and Dennis Blair, who plays a Rodney Dangerfield-type character. Blair, a standup comedian, opened for Dangerfield for many years.

At one point, Blair, in his Dangerfield character, says to Dr. Groucho (seen here only in silhouette), "I'm worried about my weight. It's up to 230."

Groucho: "Well, put it to bed by 1:30 and you'll feel better. Did you ever have this problem before?"

"Yeah."

"Well, you got it again. Take a cold shower and a hot potato and call me in the morning."

Groovy Groucho aka Go, Disco Julius (Early-mid 1980s)

Super Vidéo Productions was a French company that mainly distributed Japanese kaiju eiga (monster movies). Its second logo showed Groucho Marx against a blue background dressed like Tony Manero in *Saturday Night Fever* (1977), walking towards the camera to disco music. He stops and looks to his left and an armchair appears. He sits and puts his feet up and a screen appears. The logo for Super Vidéo Productions appears and the camera zooms in. Then, the warning screen is shown.

Aladdin and the King of Thieves (August 13, 1996)

Walt Disney Television Animation. Directed by Tad Stones, Shinichirô Tachi, Kazuo Terada. Produced by Tad Stones, Jeannine Roussel. Animated by Masayo Matsumoto, Kazuhiro Ohmame, Kazumi Sagawa, Heihachirou Tanaka, Osamu Tanihata, Kenichi Tsuchiya, Manny Banados, Davide Benvenuti, Ty Bosco, Andrew Brooks, Simon Brown. Written by Mark McCorkle, Robert Schooley. Music: Carl Johnson, Mark Watters. Cast: Robin Williams (Genie), Scott Weinger (Aladdin), Linda Larkin (Princess Jasmine), John Rhys-Davies (The King of Thieves/ Cassim), Gilbert Gottfried (Iago the Parrot), Jerry Orbach (Sa'luk), Val Bettin (Sultan of Agrabah), Frank Welker (Abu the Monkey), Jim Cummings (Razoul the Chief Guard), CCH Pounder (The Magic Oracle), Bruce Adler (Merchant/Narrator [Singing Voice]), Brad Kane (Aladdin "Al" [Singing Voice]), Liz Callaway (Princess Jasmine [Singing Voice]).

After teasing it out for two movies and a TV series, Aladdin and Jasmine are finally to marry, except they don't, because The King of Thieves and his band disrupts the ceremony. Aladdin learns that The King of Thieves, Cassim, is his father and goes off to find him.

The Genie tries to cheer Jasmine up while Aladdin is gone by, among other things, imitating Harpo Marx.

He then imitates Chico Marx, saying, "Hey, that's no good. What the wedding needs is a theme."

Imitating Groucho Marx, he says, "It needs a groom, too, but let's work with what we have."

Jasmine scolds him, and he replies, "It's a joke. I do that."

Aladdin persuades Cassim to return for the wedding, but Cassim realizes he can't change his ways and leaves Aladdin forever.

Robin Williams returns as the Genie after missing the first sequel and the series. Genie also imitates, either vocally or through animation, Walter Cronkite, James Brown, The White Rabbit, Dustin Hoffman as Rain Man, Mrs. Doubtfire, Bing Crosby, Bob "The Road to Agrabah" Hope, Albert Einstein, Shaquille O'Neal, Marlon Brando as The Godfather, Pumbaa, Pluto, Ozzie Nelson, and Mickey Mouse as Steamboat Willie, among others.

Marxtoon Mii Avatars (2008–)

On the Nintendo console, fans can to design their own characters to play. Others can upload and use them also, via Wii Connect 24. This makes it possible to make a movie and upload it to the Internet. There are avatars of Harpo and Groucho, even Groucho without makeup. There is at least one Chico avatar, but he lacks the trademark Tyrolean hat. There is even a Zeppo avatar. At this writing, there is no Gummo.

• • • • • • • • •

Internet Marxtoons

Dubya and the Monkey in YOU BET YOUR LIFE
grouchobeer (Uploaded on May 29, 2007)

Dubya and the Monkey started as a clipart comic serial before becoming a series of movies made in various machinima engines. Machinima, a portmanteau of the words "machine," "cinema," and "animate," is defined as "the use of real-time 3D computer graphics engines, such as virtual worlds or video games, to create a cinematic production." This one was done in iClone, which allows realistic 3-D avatars to be rendered from a photograph and lip-synch to dialogue. Dubya is George W. Bush, Republican President of the United States and a lightweight. The Monkey (actually a bonobo) is Captain "Snooky" Spaulding, an officer in the Navy, an aviator, an astronaut, and Special Assistant to the President. He fights terrorism using not brawn, but brains, while Dubya often bumbles into doing the right thing. A lot of the movies involve planes or rocket ships, but this one is earthbound. Dubya and the Monkey are guests on *You Bet Your Life* (1950) with Groucho Marx, where the two writers "Manny" and "Schlomo" get Spaulding's monkey sense tingling. In fact, they are Arab terrorists who have booby-trapped the duck to blow up Dubya when he says the secret word, "Strategy." After Groucho thoroughly insults him, Dubya aces the quiz, "Nations of the Iraq Coalition," and then gambles it all on the big question, which is: Were Weapons of Mass Destruction ever found in Iraq? He says, "Yes," and loses. He explains to Spaulding that it was all part of his "strategery." He mispronounces the word several times before Schlomo yells, "No, you idiot, it's STRATEGY!" The duck flies down and blows up the terrorists. Later, over the intercom from the safety of the writers' room, Spaulding asks Dubya if he did it on purpose. "It was all part of my strategy," says Dubya, then adds, "Ah, shit." Written and directed by this author, who also provided the voices.

Strange Interregnum grouchobeer (Uploaded on September 30, 2007)

A parody of the "*Strange Interlude* [1928]" scene in *Animal Crackers* (1930), made during the campaign for the 2008 Democratic presidential nomination between Barack Obama and Hillary Clinton. "You know, you two have everything," says Groucho Marx. "You're tall and short and slim and stout and black and white and male and female and that's just the kind of president I crave." In the end, however, Groucho decides to vote for Howard Dean. Made in iClone. Written and directed by this author, who also did the voices.

Duck Soup The Rest Of Your Life grouchobeer (Uploaded on December 20, 2008)

The scene of President Firefly interviewing Chicolini for the position of Secretary of War from *Duck Soup* (1933) is intercut with eerily similar scenes of President Nixon talking with Donald Rumsfeld in 1971 about Rummy's political future. Nixon's words to Rummy are taken from actual transcripts of the White House tapes, and these scenes are animated in CrazyTalk, a machinima engine that allows still pictures to lip-synch with dialogue. Nixon tells Rummy he could do anything in the cabinet field,

"Except I wouldn't put you in Defense." We hear Rummy's thoughts: "I'll show HIM." Rummy's second tenure in the job turned out to be even more disastrous than Chicolini's. Written and directed by this author, who voiced the characters of Nixon and Rummy. Winner, 2009 Freedonia/Marxonia Film Contest.

Frost/Firefly grouchobeer (Uploaded on December 25, 2008)

Made in CrazyTalk, this is a parody of the contemporaneous movie *Frost/ Nixon* (2008). David Frost interviews retired dictator Rufus T. Firefly (Groucho Marx). Written and directed by this author, who also did the voices.

Lost Marx Bros. Movie Trailer grouchobeer (Uploaded on April 14, 2009)

Features Chico as Charles Manson, Groucho as Vincent Bugliosi, and Harpo as Squeaky, in a parody of *Helter Skelter* (1976). *Helter Skelter* was the actual New Zealand title for *Love Happy* (1949). The New Zealand poster is shown at the end. Still pictures animated in CrazyTalk, re-dubbed footage used from *A Night at the Opera* (1935). Written and directed by this author, who also did the voices.

Groucho Marx Quote John Clevesy (Uploaded on March 23, 2009)

Description: "A silent animation of a famous Groucho Marx quote." Kinetic typography is used to illustrate the saying, "Outside of a dog, a book is a man's best friend. Inside of a dog, it's too dark too read." This is frequently but probably spuriously attributed to Groucho.

Duck Soup Pose To Pose Animation Spring 2009 Rebecca Forth (Uploaded on April 2, 2009)

Description: "This is a project for my animation class. The point of the project was to create an animated clip using the technique of animating from pose to pose, and then completing the motions in between each pose. This particular clip is the infamous mirror scene from The Marx

Brothers' *Duck Soup* [1933] (a classic!). I didn't get to finish the Polished pass, but I plan to do so sometime eventually, and of course, everything is funnier when it's got the Benny Hill theme song." The figures are not fully drawn, but they have Groucho Marx mustaches and eyebrows.

Groucho Walk Pencil Test.mpg StarrynightProdsInc (Uploaded on February 26, 2010)

Description: "This is the first pencil test for the animated section of the film, 'The Babbling Banshee,' which is being produced by Starrynight Productions. 'The Babbling Banshee' is currently in post-production and began production in January of 2009. This pencil test was created at a frame rate of twelve frames a second. Only two frames had to be redrawn as there was a skip in the original footage that was modeled to create this animation. The next step will be to begin inking these frames then Adobe Photoshop will be utilized to colorize the footage. The last step will be to add in the background after the final animation has been approved." Brief, but a good caricature of Groucho and well-animated. The film is based on a play by Russell McGee set in an Irish pub. It is unclear if it was finished and how this animation was or would have been used.

Cerebus, the Aardvark: Odd Transformations Vazz Toons (Uploaded on March 3, 2010)

Cerebus the Aardvark was created by Canadian cartoonist Dave Sim, originally as a parody of sword and sorcery comics, but now difficult to summarize at over 6,000 pages.

This is an extremely short movie of Cerebus' dream with no dialogue and limited animation. There is a brief shot of Lord Julius, who is based on Groucho Marx.

"Azumanga Daioh" parody—groucho marx James Ponce (Uploaded on July 17, 2010)

A fandub of an anime of a Japanese yonkoma comedy manga series using movie dialogue from the Spaulding-Chandler scene in *Animal Crackers* (1930).

Marx Brothers Kinetic Typography—Swordfish Aphibacus192000 (Uploaded on September 7, 2011)

The theme from *A Night at the Opera* (1935) is heard before it fades out and goes into the soundtrack of the "Swordfish" scene from *Horse Feathers* (1932), rendered in kinetic typography.

Groucho animacion ClayCartoons (Uploaded on September 29, 2010)

Description (Google-translated): "A homemade animation of Groucho Marx." A brief parody of the MGM opening with Groucho as the lion done in Claymation. Groucho, Harpo, and Chico filmed a parody of the MGM opening for *A Night at the Opera* (1935), but it was not used in the movie.

Nanny 9/11 grouchobeer (Uploaded on December 12, 2010)

Nannygate, a blue-eyed goat with lipstick, haunts former Secretary of Homeland Security nominee Bernie Kerik's dreams on the eve of his day in court. The scenes with Nannygate and Kerik, as well as the still pictures, are animated in the machinima engine CrazyTalk. The cutaway scenes are animated in iClone and another machinima engine, Moviestorm. At one point, Kerik asks, "What are you gonna do? Lock me up for my crime, bigamy?" Nannygate, quoting *Animal Crackers* (1930) while wearing Groucho glasses, replies, "It's bigamy, too. It's big of all of us. One man and one woman was good enough for your grandmother, but who wants to marry your grandmother? Nobody, not even your grandfather." Written and directed by this author. Cast: Maribeth Mooney (Nannygate), Jeffrey Guyton (Bernie Kerik), Sonya (Theresa), Alex (Theresa's Child), Kedeesha Campbell (Jeanette Pinero), Richard Poshard (Thug), Stacy Lyn (Judith Regan), Christophe Schevers (First Cop), Achak Okimaw (Second Cop), Usagi (Iokiyar Kerik).

Cerebus teaser-in-progress WhatComics (Uploaded on May 11, 2011)

Cerebus—Animated Feature Film WhatComics (Uploaded on October 14, 2013)

The Third Aardvark (done for fun:) WhatComics (Uploaded on January 22, 2015)

Lord Julius enters stage left WhatComics (Uploaded on November 4, 2015)

Lord Julius enters stage left—update WhatComics (Uploaded on November 4, 2015)

Cerebus asks what does the "Secretary of the Navy" do? WhatComics (Uploaded on November 6, 2015)

The workings of Lord Julius WhatComics (Uploaded on November 14, 2015)

Lord Julius says the impossible WhatComics (Uploaded on November 16, 2015)

Lord Julius assassination WhatComics (Uploaded on February 29, 2016)

Lord Julius: "You're Fired" WhatComics (Uploaded on March 12, 2016)

Lord Julius knows WhatComics (Uploaded on March 22, 2016)

Lord Julius sequence rough puttogether WhatComics (Uploaded on March 28, 2016) ***And the Oscar goes to...*** WhatComics (Uploaded on February 25, 2017)

Snippets from a planned feature film "based on the legendary alternative comic *Cerebus* that basically started alternative comics." There are several clips of Lord Julius (John Di Crosta). Director Oliver Simonsen says a release is planned for late 2017.

Marx Brothers Bank Crisis an animated spoof part 1,
Marx Brothers Bank Crisis an animated spoof part 2,
Marx Brothers Bank Crisis an animated spoof part 3,
Marx Brothers Bank Crisis an animated spoof part 4;
Animated Marx Bros spoof, Bank Crisis part 5;
Marx Brothers in Bank Crisis animated spoof part 5b,
Marx Brothers in Bank Crisis animated spoof part 6,
Marx Brothers in Bank Crisis animated spoof part 7,
Marx Brothers in Bank Crisis animated spoof part 8
animatedProfessor (Uploaded on January 5, 2012)

Description (Part 1): "The wacky Marx brothers are running a saving and loan bank in this animated cartoon, and you can guess what antics may ensue when you trust people's money to such a crazy bunch. Not unlike what really happened. [sic]" Groucho is Mr. Pennypucker, Chico is Marconi, and Harpo is Slovanovich. There is a character named Jamison, but he does not look or sound like Zeppo.

"Part four of our Marx Brothers spoof shows the harm that uncaring bankers can do when they get your money and think they can anything they want, like it's their money already. Bankers have to be good public servants, or they will just causing economic havoc [sic]."

(Part 5): "Those crazy Marx brothers can't run a bank, they are just screwing things up. Much like the real bankers that caused the credit crunch and housing slump recently."

(Part 6): "In this part the depositors at the Saving and Loan want their money but as Mr. Pennypucker (Groucho) explains, the money isn't in the bank. They refer to the Jimmy Steward movie, *It's A Wonderful Life* [1946], where he explains that money invested by savers is lent out to others so they can buy homes, so in effect the depositor's money is in other people's houses [sic]."

(Part 8) "In part 8 of Bank Crisis, starring the zany comedy team of the Animated Marx Brothers, they decide that running a bank isn't a good way to make money, the real way to make money is to get elected to congress, then you can divert some of the billions, even trillions of dollars that congress controls into your own pocket [sic]."

Made in Flash MX with digital cutout animation "using the Flash program to cut part of the image (the arm for instance) and rotating it a bit then pasting back on the image [sic]." All voices, including Margaret Dumont's, are apparently done by the same person. The videos are supposed to be promoting cybersuccessuniversity.org, but no such website seems to exist anymore. The ending teases a sequel, *Going to Washington*, which does not appear to have been finished. Although YouTube had long allowed videos of more than ten minutes at the time this was made, it was uploaded in nine parts. "Part 5b (we had to break up number five cause it was too long). One way to make video load faster is to make it in smaller sized segments. We like to keep them 3 to 5 minutes long. Another advantage of shorter clips is that they add up quickly, giving the image of greater production. Also, people often prefer shorter clips as they don't want to commit to a long upload or viewing time. So use shorter clips to make videos load faster." Okay.

West Coast Caws WWE 12 The Three Stooges vs The Marx Brothers WestCoastCaws (Uploaded April 15, 2012)

Machinima made on an Xbox 360 with the game *WWE 12*. Caws is an acronym for "Create a WWE Superstar."

The intro is in black and white. The Three Stooges enter and both of their theme songs are played. The Marx Brothers enter to generic music. The Three Stooges and Groucho are fairly good likenesses, but Harpo's and Chico's wigs are wrong, as is Chico's hat. None of the characters behave as the movie characters did. We switch to color for the actual match. The Stooges win, if you care about that sort of thing.

Chico Marx cameo voiced by Daniel Geduld! WhatComics (Uploaded on June 4, 2012)

Still picture of a pencil test of Duke Leonardi (based on Chico) from *Cerberus* with a brief Chico vocal impersonation.

Groucho Marx skull TwigaArts (Uploaded on March 6, 2014)

Extremely brief animation in Maya, a computer modeling and animation software, of a skull wearing a Groucho disguise. Its eyeballs dart back and forth, the mouth opens, and the eyebrows wiggle.

HISTORY DRINK—Groucho e Karl Marx Rogério Batista Ayres (Uploaded on July 9, 2014)

Description (Google-translated from Portuguese): "Marxists are a pain in the ass to the cool cartoon." Karl Marx and his "cousin" Groucho share a drink. In Portuguese.

"Halloween Marx" BOW TIE (ep 91) Bow Tie (Uploaded on September 30, 2014)

Description: "Halloween Month begins on BOO TIE. Get ready for spills, chills, thrills, and four original spook-tacular songs!" I guess this is one of the spook-tacular songs, spoke-sung by a woman dressed as Groucho Marx while a woman dressed as Harpo accompanies her on the guitar.

Marx Brothers Jack Urbs (Uploaded on December 6, 2014)

Extremely short movie using Legos and stop motion animation. The Four Marx Brothers sit on a couch. Chico pushes Harpo off. Harpo decks Chico, then Zeppo. Groucho hides behind the couch.

Animated GROUCHO MARX Promo For RAISED EYEBROWS By Steve Stoliar rialtos1 (Uploaded on June 30, 2015)

Description: "This is an animated promotional video about *Raised Eyebrows: My Years Inside Groucho's House*, a bittersweet memoir written by Steve Stoliar, who worked for Groucho as his secretary and archivist in the comedian's final years. The book is being made into a film to be directed by Rob Zombie. (Animation for this ad by Terry Motley at motleypr.com

[Motley PR Designs and Marketing].)" The book cover is shown, with its caricature of Groucho by Drew Friedman. Animated Groucho's eyes roll and brows waggle as cigar smoke wafts upward.

Whiteboard Animation GROUCHO Promo For RAISED EYEBROWS by Steve Stoliar rialtos1 (Uploaded on July 3, 2015)

Description: "This is a whiteboard animation promotional video about *Raised Eyebrows: My Years Inside Groucho's House*, a bittersweet memoir written by Steve Stoliar, who worked for Groucho as his secretary and archivist in the comedian's final years. The book is being made into a film to be directed by Rob Zombie. (Animation for this ad by Terry Motley at motleypr.com [Motley PR Designs and Marketing].)"

The animator (Terry Motley) draws, and the pictures are then filled in with photographs of the same thing. The animator first draws the book, then a picture of Groucho Marx with the author, then Groucho's house, and finally the book again. Titles give a brief synopsis of the book.

REMEMBERING GROUCHO Marx Promo For Steve Stoliar's Live Show rialtos1 (Uploaded on September 18, 2015)

Description: "Promo for *Remembering Groucho* [2015], a one-man touring show featuring Steve Stoliar, Groucho's former secretary and the author of *Raised Eyebrows: My Years Inside Groucho's House.*"

The animator (Terry Motley) draws on a whiteboard and the drawing turns into a photograph of Groucho and Stoliar. Stoliar narrates. Made by Motley PR Designs and Marketing.

What is Marxism? (Karl Marx + Super Mario Bros.) Legendado Leonardo Bardini (Uploaded on September 27, 2015)

Description: "The ideology of Karl Marx explained in Mario Brothers." Sprites ripped out from games were downloaded and then made into a movie using the program After Effects. This gets into the book for its opening title pun alone, "Karl Marxio Brothers".

Going Down, Mr. Trump?! (1936)—Marx Brothers RonJammin (Uploaded on October 19, 2015)

Made with the machinima engine Plotagon. Harpo asks Donald Trump (here called "Donald Chump") to throw a Halloween party, and Chump refuses. For the rest of the movie, the gang tries to help Harpo get revenge. Of The Marx Brothers, only Groucho and Harpo appear. There is no dialogue, and only occasional sound effects, but there is a musical score all the way through.

A Day at the Airport grouchobeer (Uploaded on January 20, 2016)

Made in Plotagon, this short movie parodies the silverware-dropping scene in *Animal Crackers* (1930) and is a satire on airport security. Hennessey Henderson, an Irish-accented TSA agent decides not to arrest Harpo Marx. As he obliviously lets him off with a warning, knives drop out of Harpo's coat, followed by a dirty bomb. Featuring Groucho, Harpo, Chico, and Henderson as themselves, and Zeppo Marx as "Escalator." Written and directed by this author, who actually did all the voices.

Marx Bros. Meets Tigger Actors for Autism (Uploaded on January 29, 2016)

Done with cutout animation, The Marx Brothers meet Tigger, who is about ten feet tall here. He bites Groucho on the leg. This is followed by The Marx Brothers and Tigger doing a CBS identification. This is "From the Actors for Autism archives." Apparently made for or by people with autism.

Groucho Marx: El Humor es Cosa Seria (5) (Humor is a Serious Thing) Roy Smart (Uploaded on February 22, 2016)

Description (Google-translated): "Best humor's the clever one. That's what we find in The Marx Brothers' classical filmography: the best moments of humor ever in a film. Today you're invited to remember them and to subscribe to my Youtube channel."

"Groucho quotes" in Spanish, one from *Duck Soup* (1933), the others of dubious attribution, are displayed against mostly static backdrops. At one point, the screen turns into a stage curtain and opens, the only real animation in this short. Apparently, there were ten of these at some point, but only one is on YouTube.

Karl Marx no mundo de Super Mario (Karl Marx in the World of Super Mario) Filosofia Hoje (Uploaded on February 29, 2016)

This is *What is Marxism? (Karl Marx + Super Mario Bros.) 8-Bit Philosophy* in Portuguese.

Video Marketing terry motley (Uploaded April 18, 2016)

A promotional video by and for motleypr.com. Photos of Edgar Allan Poe and Groucho are shown. "See what happens when great minds collide. Welcome to *You Bet Your Life*!" Edgar Allan Poe, with a greasepaint mustache and eyebrows and a cigar, hosts. "You bet your life your life your marketing works. Say the secret word and win! What's the word? Here's Ducky."

A raven flies down with the secret word, "Necrophilia."

"Now you know why I've been ravin' about this duck. They're dying to see that."

The word changes to "Incest."

"This is a family show. Enough about my marriage."

The sign changes to "Video Marketing."

"That's the secret word!"

Phil Hartman's Flat TV: You Bet Your Life (Uploaded August 10, 2016)

Phil Hartman made this recording in the late 1970s or early 1980s as a sort of audition in the lean years before he became a star on *Saturday Night Live* (1975). The tapes were lost for years and only found after his murder in 1998. *Phil Hartman's Flat TV* is about a dysfunctional nuclear family and the radio and TV shows they listen to. Hartman does most of the voices, including the woman in this sketch. His brother, John Hartmann (Phil changed the spelling of his surname for show business purposes) released it as a CD in 2002. In 2013, Worker Studios teamed up with Paul Hartmann, another brother, to develop it as an animated film.

This segment is more loving homage than gentle parody, with the remarks not uncharacteristic of the actual Groucho Marx, although some of them would have been censored for broadcast. Groucho wears his signature 1950s quizmaster bow tie, but his suit is dark and his hair and makeup is from the 1930s. The actual opening credits are used, as are the opening and closing musical themes, and there are cutaways to an actual live audience. The contestants are Bonita Rayez and her fiancé, Bruno. Bonita is drawn as a hideous woman with several of her own teeth. "You'd be a fine catch for any man," says Groucho, playing on her name. Bonita works at a cannery as "de file clerk." "De file clerk? Well, you're one clerk a lot of fellas would like to defile." Bonita is engaged. "Whose clutch are you engaged in?" Bruno's. What does he do for a living? "I fish." "Another fish? I don't know how you two stay out of the water so long." Character Design: Brian Lemay. Character 3D Modeling: Tayler Edwards, Miru Kim. Technical Direction: Evgenni Zlochevskii, Miguel Ramirez. 3D Set Build: Miru Kim. Textures, Lighting & Render Farm Manager: Miru Kim. Character & Effects Animation: Brian Lemay. Directed by Brian Lemay. Produced by Paul Hartmann. Filmed in Mississauga by The Animated Cartoon Factory. A Wooden Meatloaf Production.

Private Parks—A Jimmy Giraffe Cartoon
StanLeesKidsUniverse (Uploaded on January 9, 2017)

Jimmy Giraffe is a character created by Zachary Strobel, and this is Jimmy's seventh cartoon appearance. "The overall goal of the cartoon was to not only have Jimmy go on another adventure, but to also pay homage to the comedies made by MGM during the '20s, '30s, and '40s. This of course includes the Marx Brothers. My strongest influence [is] my favorite director, Tex Avery, who made the best cartoons there from 1942 to [1954.]" Strobel sent the storyboards to Nancy Avery-Arkley, Tex's daughter, and her son Avery, who commended them. Production began at WiDesource Global, which went out of business in late 2015, and the files were held on an animator's computer until he was paid. Strobel met George Zakk, Executive Producer of *xXx* (2002), who now works at Stan Lee's Kids Universe in Century City, CA. Zakk paid the animator to get the files back and Strobel spent eight weeks in-house at Stan Lee's Kids Universe finishing the cartoon.

Strobel writes, "What I like about the Marx Brothers is that they have to freedom to say and do whatever they want to anyone's face yet get away scot-free and still remain likable."

Jimmy Giraffe, a heroic cartoon comedian in the mold of Bugs Bunny and Woody Woodpecker, is frolicking in a park. A crooked cop, Putz Panther, decides to charge $5 admission fee to the park and ejects Jimmy when he can't pay. Putz decides to raise the admission to $10. Jimmy decides to take care of Putz himself.

Jimmy pushes a hot dog cart, wearing a green hat and talking like Chico Marx. A wheel of the hot dog cart falls on Putz's foot. Jimmy, now made up like Groucho, says, "Ya know pal, you don't look so good. So what else is new? [Rimshot.]" Dressed again as Chico, Jimmy offers Putz one of his $10 hot dogs in exchange for admission and Putz reluctantly agrees. The "hot dog" is a stick of dynamite, which blows up in Putz's face. Dressed as Harpo, Jimmy honks at Putz and launches a boxing glove from his horn and runs into the park, with Putz in hot pursuit.

Jimmy makes Putz play hopscotch until Putz falls off a cliff into a river, ending up in a wishing well. Instead of money, Jimmy tosses an anvil down the well, hitting Putz in the head. Jimmy continues to pummel Putz in varying ways until people start throwing money, thinking it is street theater. Jimmy gathers up the money and gives it to Putz, who is arrested by the real police officer, a pig.

You Bet Your Life [1950] Slot Machine (2006)

Yes, Virginia, there is a Groucho Marx slot machine. It was originally made by WMS Gaming, licensed by Groucho Marx Productions, and features the vocal stylings of Frank Ferrante.

The symbols in the payline include a caricature of Groucho against a Looney Tunes-style backdrop, Groucho glasses, George Washington wearing Groucho glasses, a stylized version of the easel from the credits of *You Bet Your Life* (1950), the Duck on a coin, the Duck against a Looney Tunes-style backdrop, a cigar, a microphone, a camera, and a television. A smaller Duck, the Secret Duck, is next to some of the versions of the symbols.

Gameplay description is from Arcade History, with my interpolations in brackets, because I didn't have a box. "The Groucho Bonus is triggered when 3 Groucho symbols land on an active payline. An animated Groucho wheels out a pick board. The board has 16 selectable [tiles] from which the player reveals awards. Starting off with 3 picks, the possible awards behind each of the [tiles] are credit awards, credit awards +1 extra pick, extra pick or a Duck. The player continues selecting spaces until there are no more picks left. [Groucho hits the tiles with items such as a wand, a mallet, and a board.] At that point, Groucho throws any ducks that have been collected up to the top screen. On the top screen are a combination of large credits amounts and extra picks. The player wins one of these awards for each Duck earned. If the player is awarded extra picks, then after all Ducks have been used, the player returns to the lower screen, and continues picking. The bonus ends when there are no picks or collected Ducks remaining." [Groucho caricatures appear on the "Extra Picks" tiles. Groucho throws in comments, such as "Good job!"]

"In the Duck Bonus, three Duck symbols on reels 3, 4, and 5 on an active payline trigger the bonus. On the top screen, 13 ducks appear. Each worth a credit amount… [Groucho says, "…just press the button to roll the dice…." He calls out the number, then points upward.] On the top screen, the arrow in the center of the duck circle moves the amount of spaces indicated by the dice and points to a duck. Credits are awarded for the duck and the multiplier moves up one level. The dice roll again to move the arrow to a new duck for more bonus credits. The ducks turn into bombs whenever they are awarded. When the arrow lands on a bomb, the bonus ends and the multiplier level reached multiplies all bonus credits." [Groucho says, "This is amazing! Stop the presses! Stop the blackjack dealers! Stop the showgirls! Stop the showgirls? Sorry, I lost myself for a while." On the lower screen, the Duck against the Looney Tunes-style backdrop becomes animated. On the upper screen, the Duck juggles balls with his picture, one-handed.]

"...[O]n the third reel... [i]f a symbol with a Secret Duck is part of a winning combination, additional credits, The Groucho Bonus or The Duck Bonus are awarded."

Marx Emoji (2015)

Emoji, the "smileys" used in electronic messages and web pages, originated in Japan in the late 1990s and have since spread worldwide. The word "emoji" comes from the Japanese words "e" (picture) + "moji" (character). Although they are used similarly to emoticons, the name is coincidental.

In 2016, Terry Motley, former owner of motleypr.com, designed emojis based on The Four Marx Brothers. At this writing, he plans to animate them soon.

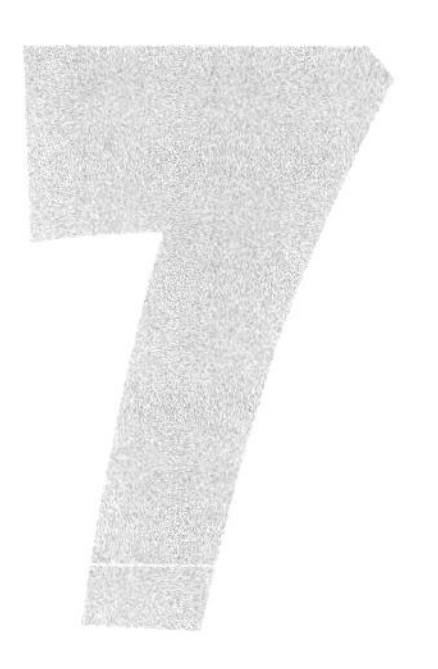

MARXTOONS TRIVIA

Shamus, also known as Jimmy, Jimmie, James, James H., or Seamus Culhane worked on many Marxtoons. He married Chico's daughter, Maxine; and directed his father-in-law and Groucho in *Showdown at Ulcer Gulch* (1956). Née James, he changed his name at the behest of Maxine, who said it would bring him more business. It did.

In the break-in scene of *Duck Soup* (1933), Harpo, after being warned to be quiet, knocks over a duck music box that starts playing "Who's Afraid of the Big, Bad Wolf?" from the Walt Disney cartoon, *Three Little Pigs* (1933). This was apparently part of a planned larger sequence that may or may not have been filmed. It is not in the movie and not known to exist.

The Fleischers' Screen Song *The Peanut Vendor* (1933) contains not only the title song, which is sung by Chico in *Duck Soup* (1933), but "Everyone Says I Love You" from *Horse Feathers* (1932).

In *Betty in Blunderland* (1933), Betty Boop sings "Everyone, How Do You Do" to the tune of "Everyone Says I Love You" from *Horse Feathers* (1932).

I Yam What I Yam (1933), the second cartoon starring Popeye, uses "Whatever It Is, I'm Against It" from *Horse Feathers* (1932).

Porky's Road Race (1937) was reissued in retraced color versions where Charlie Chaplin's hair is tinted blonde to resemble Harpo. The cartoon was originally directed by Frank Tashlin.

Harpo is said to have been the model for Dopey in *Snow White and the Seven Dwarfs* (1937). Sneezy was played by Billy Gilbert, who appears in *A Night at the Opera* (1935). Gideon in *Pinocchio* (1940) was also modeled on Harpo. All of the villainous character's lines were deleted, making him mute. Three hiccoughs, voiced by Mel Blanc, were left in, making them, joked Blanc, the most expensive sounds ever recorded.

In the Warner Bros. Merrie Melodies cartoon, *Curious Puppy* (1939), a boxer dog pursues the title character into a funhouse, where, according to Jerry Beck, "… they do the Marx Brothers (*Duck Soup* [1933]) mirror routine."

Daws Butler appeared as a guest on *You Bet Your Life* on May 26, 1960.

In 1961, Screen Gems announced plans for a Marx Brothers cartoon show, which would have presumably been produced by Hanna-Barbera.

The 1966 Filmation pilot of *The New Marx Bros. Show* was called "A Day at the Horse Opera." According to a gossip column item, the working title of *A Day at the Races* (1937) was *A Night at the Horse Opera*, although this might have been a joke or a bogus plant by a publicity agent.

Bob Kane, creator of Batman, discussed an animated Marx Brothers series with Groucho. The project fell through when Groucho's business manager, Erin Fleming, demanded $100,000 up front.

In 1979, Filmation, which produced *The New Marx Bros. Show*, announced plans for a different animated Marxtoon series. They secured the rights to Groucho, Harpo, and Chico for primetime-only, with an expiration date of June 1, 1980, to make a sale. There was a minimum of 13 episodes, budgeted around $500,000 per episode. S. J. Perelman, a screenwriter on *Monkey Business* (1931) and *Horse Feathers* (1932), was in talks to write the scripts before he died on October 17, 1979. Apparently, Earl Kress wrote a script. The show was never sold, and the rights expired.

Mark Evanier says he was approached by a producer who wanted to make a cartoon series with Chico, Harpo, and Zeppo, but not Groucho. Evanier says he knows at least four other writers who were approached to do Marxtoon series. Another time, Evanier was approached by a producer who had or thought he could get rights to Groucho, Chico, and Harpo. Evanier suggested Dayton Allen for Groucho and Paul Frees for Chico. The producer asked, "Who could do Harpo?" Kidding, Evanier replied, "Marcel Marceau," and the producer dutifully wrote it down.

Animated TV pilots rejected by Groucho Marx Productions included a Saturday morning cartoon called *The Little Marx Brothers* and a 3-D project by comedian Morey Amsterdam. Concepts from Disney and Bill Melendez also failed to come to fruition.

In *The Simpsons* (1989) Season 5, Episode 6, "Marge on the Lam" (November 4, 1993), George Fenneman, Groucho's longtime announcer on *You Bet Your Life* (1950), parodied his own role as the Narrator on *Dragnet* (1951).

Animaniacs, Season 1, Episode 10 "King Yakko" (September 24, 1993) is a pastiche of *Duck Soup* (1933) with Yakko becoming King of a mythical country and going to war with a rival nation. There are Margaret Dumont and Louis Calhern stand-ins, but the Animaniacs stay in their own characters and do not imitate The Marx Brothers, so I do not consider this a proper Marxtoon, but part of the Apocrypha.

In *Wandering Warners We*, an unproduced feature film based on *Animaniacs* (1993), there is a fourth Warner sibling, Lakko, who is fired from the team because he is short on talent (cf. Gummo and Zeppo Marx).

In *Sam & Max: Freelance Police* Season 1, Episode 1, "The Thing That Wouldn't Stop It" (October 4, 1997), the title characters knock on a door. A voice inside says, "What's the password? And if you say 'swordfish' I'm gonna lose it!"

In the Kirby Nintendo franchise, there is a Jester named Marx, but he has nothing to do with any of the brothers, despite his apt occupation. The Japanese name is "Maruku," and a better translation might actually be "Mark." A video on YouTube called *Let's Play Kirby Superstar | (Ep.7) Groucho Marx* (2013) was reviewed for this book, but it has nothing to do with Groucho or The Marx Brothers.

In the Animal Crossing Nintendo franchise, there are characters named Chico and Groucho. They appear to have nothing to do with the Marxes. Chico is pronounced "cheeko" and is a word for "boy" in some languages, and in Japanese, his name refers to the color of his fur. Groucho is just a grouchy character and has different names in different languages.

In the Nintendo game *Purple Koopa Bro.*, there is a "Big Boo Boss" named Marx, who apparently has nothing to do with The Marx Brothers, or Kirby or Animal Crossing for that matter.

Similarly, Gus Groucho in the cartoon *Sick Bricks* (2015) and video game franchise has nothing to do with Groucho Marx.

In *Family Guy* (1999), Season 7, Episode 3, "Road to Germany" (October 19, 2008), Stewie parodies the *Duck Soup* (1933) mirror scene with Hitler.

In *Family Guy* (1999) Season 14, Episode 6, "Peter's Sister" (November 15, 2015), there is a cutaway gag with a commercial for "Chico's Monkey Farm." Chico, pronounced "cheeko," wears a pith helmet and a Grouchoesque mustache, but no glasses.

There are several animated logos for Oprah Winfrey's studio, Harpo Productions, but the name has nothing to do with Harpo Marx. "Harpo" is "Oprah" spelled backwards.

In 2009, Andrew T. Smith wrote that in researching his book *Marx and Re-Marx – Creating and Recreating the Lost Marx Brothers Radio Series*, "… I was informed of an animated series from Japan that was based on the Marx Brothers' radio series *Flywheel, Shyster and Flywheel* [1932]. I have no idea as to the style or content of the show but one of my contacts apparently has an episode. It's one I'd love to see just as reassurance it actually exists!" In 2016, he wrote, "... if I recall correctly my Japanese contact was never able to turn up any concrete evidence of the production."

In the video game *Batman: Arkham Asylum* (2009), The Joker (Mark Hamill) says, "Batman may look like an idiot, and sound like an idiot, but don't let that fool you. He really is an idiot." This is a paraphrase of Groucho Marx's line in *Duck Soup* (1933): "Gentlemen, Chicolini here may talk like an idiot, and look like an idiot, but don't let that fool you. He really is an idiot." Mark Hamill (@HamillHimself) said on Twitter of The Marx Brothers: "I worship these guys! I actually met Groucho when I was ten years old and nearly burst into tears of joy #MarkLovesMarx".

In the interest of completeness, I must mention that this author has made many movies under the nom de plume "grouchobeer" that reference The Marx Brothers in addition to those above where the Marxes actually appear, and other Dubya and the Monkey movies featuring Captain Spaulding. *Lame Duck Soup* (2007), and the remake, *Lame Duck Soup Reducks* (2013), are pastiches of the trial scene in *Duck Soup* (1933) with George W. Bush prosecuting Saddam Hussein. *Welcome Back, Carter* (2007) features this author as Joe Lieberman as Robert Hegyes as Chico Marx as Epstein. Many other movies have lines that are quotes or paraphrases from Marx Brothers films. All of the episodes of the webseries *Sugar Babes* (2008) have titles that are phrases associated with The Marx Brothers.

In terms of the total revenue generated by films he has participated in, the actor listed in 2011 as the number one in the "All Time Top 100 Stars at the Box Office" was Frank Welker.

WHERE TO BUY MARXTOONS

In the following collections, only the Marxtoons are listed.

Chapter 1: Theatrical Marxtoons

The following DVD are available from the Cartoon Research Garage Sale:

Columbia Cartoons #2: Hollywood Goes Krazy (1932)

Columbia Cartoons #3: Seeing Stars (1932)

Columbia Cartoons #4: Scrappy's Party (1933), *Movie Struck* (1933)

Columbia Cartoons #5: Hollywood Babies (1933), *Scrappy's Auto Show* (1933), *The Autograph Hunter* (1934)

Columbia Cartoons #8: Doctor Bluebird (1936)

Columbia Cartoons #9: The Novelty Shop (1936), *Merry Mutineers* (1936)

Columbia Cartoons #11: Scrappy's News Flashes (1937), *Hollywood Picnic* (1937)

Columbia Cartoons #14: Hollywood Sweepstakes (1939)

Columbia Cartoons #17: Red Riding Hood Rides Again (1941), *A Hollywood Detour* (1942)

50s PARAMOUNT #3: Forest Fantasy (1952), *The Case of the Cockeyed Canary* (1952)

FAMOUS 1940s #4: The Baby Sitter (1947), *The Golden State* (1948)

FAMOUS 1940s #6: Toys Will Be Toys (1949), *Strolling Thru the Park* (1949), *Blue Hawaii* (1950)

LANTZ #5: The Lumber Champ (1933), *Pin Feathers* (1933)

LANTZ #6: The Merry Old Soul (1933), *Wax Works* (1934)

LANTZ #10: Duck Hunt (1936)

LANTZ #12: Hollywood Bowl (1938)

LANTZ #13: Nellie of the Circus (1939)

LOST FLEISCHER #2: The Wizard of Arts (1941)

LOST FLEISCHER #9: Springtime in the Rockage (1940)

MGM #5: Art Gallery (1939)

MGM #6: Abdul the Bulbul-Ameer (1941)

TERRYTOONS Vol. 11—1938–9: String Bean Jack (1938), *The Glass Slipper* (1938)

TERRYTOONS Vol. 23: Felix the Fox (1948)

TERRYTOONS Vol. 24: Out Again, In Again (1948)

TERRYTOONS Vol. 28: Movie Madness (1951)

UB IWERKS #3: Soda Squirt (1933), *The Brave Tin Soldier* (1934)

VAN BEUREN #9: Cubby's World Flight (1933)

The following are available on Amazon and/or Amazon Video:

Aladdin (1992)

Cartoons that Time Forgot: The Ub Iwerks Collection, Volume 1: The Brave Tin Soldier (1934)

Cartoons that Time Forgot: The Ub Iwerks Collection, Volume 2: Stratos Fear (1933), *Soda Squirt* (1933)

Classic Cartoon Favorites, Vol. 5—Extreme Sports Fun: Mickey's Polo Team (1936)

The Complete Adventures of Cubby Bear: Cubby's World Flight (1933)

Dot Goes to Hollywood (1987)

Grease (1978)

The Great Animation Studios: Famous Studios: The Golden State (1948)

Looney Tunes: Golden Collection, Vol. 2: Hollywood Steps Out (1941)

Looney Tunes: Golden Collection, Vol. 3: The CooCoo Nut Grove (1936), *Porky's Road Race* (1937 version, not colorized), *Wideo Wabbit* (1956)

The Looney, Looney, Looney Bugs Bunny Movie (1981)

The Mayor of Hell (1933): Contains *The Organ Grinder* (1933) as an extra.

Popeye The Sailor: 1933-1938: The Complete First Volume: I Yam What I Yam (1933), *Sock-a-Bye Baby* (1934)

Popeye the Sailor: 1938-1940: The Complete Second Volume: Puttin on the Act (1940), *Popeye Meets William Tell* (1940)

Popeye the Sailor: 1941-1943: The Complete Third Volume: Popeye Meets Rip Van Winkle (1941)

Sausage Party (2016)

Uncensored Bosko #2: Bosko's Dog Race (1932)

Walt Disney Treasures—The Chronological Donald, Volume One (1934-1941): The Autograph Hound (1939)

Walt Disney Treasures—Mickey Mouse in Black and White: Mickey's Gala Premier (1933)

Walt Disney Treasures—Mickey Mouse in Living Color: Mickey's Polo Team (1936)

Walt Disney Treasures—Silly Symphonies: Who Killed Cock Robin? (1935)

Walt Disney Treasures: More Silly Symphonies (1929–1938), Volume 2: Mother Goose Goes Hollywood (1938)

World's Greatest Animation: A Sundae in New York (1983)

Chapter 2: Television Marxtoons

The Mad, Mad, Mad Comedians (1970): http://www.premiereopera.com/dvd9495themadmadmadcomedians.aspx

Available on Amazon and/or Amazon Video:

"Remember the Daze": *The Yogi Bear Show—The Complete Series*

"So What and the Seven Whatnots" (1962): *Bob Clampett's Beany and Cecil (Special Edition)*

The Kwicky Koala Show (Crazy Claws) (1981).

Alice Through the Looking Glass (1987)

"The Joke's on Ray" (1988): *The Real Ghostbusters, Vols. 1–5*

"Out of Scale" (1990): *Chip 'n Dale: Rescue Rangers Complete Series—Volume 1 & 2*

"Fields of Honey" (1990): *Tiny Toon Adventures*

"Hercule Yakko" (1993), "You Risk Your Life" (1993), "Wakko's New Gookie" (1995), "The

Warners' 65th Anniversary Special" (1994): *Steven Spielberg Presents Animaniacs, Volumes 1-3.*

Snow White and the Magic Mirror (1994)

"The Perfect Match" (1994): *Garfield and Friends*

"Homie the Clown" (1995): *The Simpsons: Season 6*

"Middle Aged Felix" (1995): *The Twisted Tales of Felix the Cat*

"A Trophied Duck" (1997): *Duckman: Seasons Three and Four*

"Pinky and the Brain… and Larry" (1997): *Steven Spielberg Presents Pinky and The Brain: Vol. 3*

"Communuts" (1999): *Histeria! The Complete Series*

"The Wacky Watcher" (2000): *Pokémon: Adventures in the Orange Islands—The Complete Collection*

"Homecoming: A Shot in the Dark" (2002): *Clone High: Complete First Season*

"Tachikoma Runaway/The Movie Director's Dream" aka "Escape from" (20003): *Ghost in the Shell SAC Complete 1st Season Collection Box Set*

"Coffins and Cradles" (2003): *Home Movies–Season Three*

"Abra Catastrophe!" (2003): *Fairly OddParents: Season 3*

"Peterotica" (2006), "420" (2009): *Family Guy, Volume Four*

"Grumpy Old Man (2011)": *Family Guy: Volume Eleven/Season 10*

"Honk," *Clarence* (2014)

"The Executive Treatment" (2015): *SpongeBob SquarePants* (1999)

The following episodes of *The Simpsons* (1989) mentioned herein are not on DVD, they are only available through pay services. "O Brother, Where Bart Thou?" (2009), "How Munched Is That Birdie in the Window?" (2010), "Clown in the Dumps" (2014).

Chapter 3: Animated Credits and Effects in Live-Action Marx Brothers Movies

Available on Amazon and/or Amazon Video: *Monkey Business* (1931), *Horse Feathers* (1932), *A Night at the Opera* (1935), *Room Service* (1938), *Copacabana* (1947), *Double Dynamite* (1951), *Skidoo* (1968).

Showdown at Ulcer Gulch can be found on *The Marx Brothers TV Collection.*

Chapter 4: Marxtoons in *You Bet Your Life* (1950), *Groucho* (1965), and Desoto Commercials

Numerous *You Bet Your Life* (1950) collections are available at Amazon, some with original commercials and credits. *Groucho* (1965) is on *The Marx Brothers TV Collection.*

Chapter 5: Marxtoon TV Pilots

"A Day at the Horse Opera": *Filmation Presents—Rarely Seen History*
http://www.ontherunvideo.com/store/product63.html

BIBLIOGRAPHY

Articles: Print and Web

"Animaniacs Tribute" http://thatguywiththeglasses.wikia.com/wiki/Animaniacs_Tribute

Amidi, Amid. "*About Face* [1978] by Chris James" *Cartoon Brew*, February 21, 2011. http://www.cartoonbrew.com/shorts/about-face-by-chris-james-37032.html

———. "Interview with John Canemaker About *Two Guys Named Joe*" *Cartoon Brew*, July 12, 2010. http://www.cartoonbrew.com/books/interview-with-john-canemaker-about-two-guys-named-joe-25219.html

Barat, Christopher E. "Bonkers Episode Guide," http://tooncop.info/archive/trailmix.nm.ru/GuideCEBarat.htm

Beck, Jerry. "Filmation's Marx Brothers?" *Cartoon Brew*, July 22, 2009. http://www.cartoonbrew.com/tv/filmations-marx-brothers- 15252.html

Boyes, Emma. "UK paper names top game franchises" *GameSpot*, January 10, 2007.

Bradshaw, Peter. "Frank Welker: the most successful Hollywood actor you've never heard of" *The Guardian*, August 9, 2011 https://www.theguardian.com/film/2011/aug/09/frank-welker

Closs, Larry. "Spielberg Toons In" *TV Guide*, October 28, 1995. http://www.platypuscomix.net/people/berg951.html

Drinnon, Benny. "*Mickey's Gala Premier* [1930]." http://benny-drinnon.blogspot.com/2012/03/mickeys-gala-premeir.html

Evanier, Mark. "Daffy Duck Soup" News from Me, October 25, 2007. http://www.newsfromme.com/2007/10/25/daffy-duck-soup/

———. "P.S." News from Me, December 19, 2011. http://www.newsfromme.com/2011/12/19/p-s-11/

———. "Today's Video Link" News from Me, October 25, 2007. http://www.newsfromme.com/2007/10/25/todays-video-link-1158/

Evans, Bradford. "Phil Hartman's Comedy Album Is Being Turned Into an Animated Movie" Splitsider, May 7, 2013. http://splitsider.com/2013/05/phil-hartmans-comedy-album-is-being-turned-into-an-animated-movie/

"*Dot and the Kangaroo.*" http://www.loyalbooks.com/book/dot-and-the-kangaroo-by-ethel-c-pedley

Friedman, Drew. "Topps FLIP•O•VISION." http://drewfriedman.blogspot.com/2012/03/topps-flipovision.html

"Garbo's Famous Feet." Garbo Forever, http://www.garboforever.com/Garbos_Beauty-07.htm

Goldsmith, Charles. "Marx Brothers' Heirs Square Off In Lawsuit About Licensing Fee" *Wall Street Journal*, updated December 2, 1999. http://www.wsj.com/articles/SB944084208240055257

"Groucho Marx." Wikiquote, https://en.wikiquote.org/wiki/Groucho_Marx

"Groucho." Animal Crossing Wiki, http://animalcrossing.wikia.com/wiki/Groucho

Haendiges, Jerry. "*The Mickey Mouse Theater of the Air* [1938]" Jerry Haendiges Vintage Radio Logs, http://www.otrsite.com/logs/logm1032.htm

Hahn, Matthew. "Comics" http://www.stripcreator.com/comics/CHUBBY/

"Isambard Kingdom Brunel." http://www.ssgreatbritain.org/story/isambard-kingdom-brunel

Kazaleh, Mike. "Celebrity Voices Impersonated" Cartoon Research, May 17, 2014. http://cartoonresearch.com/index.php/celebrity-voices-impersonated/

———. "Groucho Marx for DeSoto" Cartoon Research, September 28, 2013. http://cartoonresearch.com/index.php/groucho-marx-for-desoto/

Lammle, Rob. "Way More Than You Ever Wanted to Know About Animaniacs" Mental Floss, http://mentalfloss.com/article/30629/way-more-you-ever-wanted-know-about-animaniacs

"Machinima," http://www.avatarrepertorytheater.org/machinima.php

Maltin, Leonard. "A Harpo Marx Flip Book… And More" IndieWire, Mar 7, 2012. http://www.indiewire.com/2012/03/a-harpo-marx-flip-bookand-more-255666/

"Marx." Kirby Wiki http://kirby.wikia.com/wiki/Marx

"Marx (PKB)." Fantendo http://fantendo.wikia.com/wiki/Marx_(PKB)

"Norman Cousins: A Laughter/Pain Case Study." http://www.laughteronlineuniversity.com/norman-cousins-a-laughterpain-case-study/

Rayner, Karly. "These 11 Celebrities Who Inspired Your Favorite Disney Characters Might Just Surprise You" Moviepilot, August 5, 2015. http://moviepilot.com/posts/3438712

Skolsky, Sidney. "Hollywood" Milwaukee Sentinel, May 28, 1936.

Sporn, Michael. "Vlasic Business at the Hubley's," Michael Sporn Animation, Inc. Splog http://www.michaelspornanimation.com/splog/?p=3131

"Super Productions Vidéo." http://www.closinglogos.com

Sutton, Ellis Anthony Andy, Jr. "Buddy: The Most Boring Looney Toons Character Ever" https://ellisanthonyandysuttonjr.wordpress.com/tag/hugh-harman/

Welkos, Robert W. "Is the Monkey Business Over At Last?" *Los Angeles Times*, April 23, 2000. http://articles.latimes.com/2000/apr/23/entertainment/ca-22416

Books

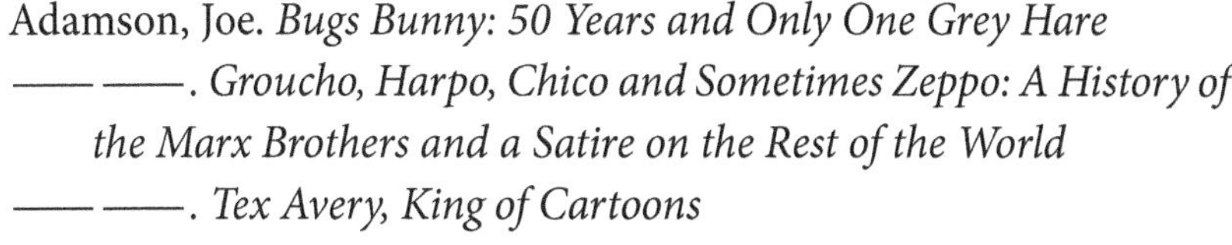

Adamson, Joe. *Bugs Bunny: 50 Years and Only One Grey Hare*

———. *Groucho, Harpo, Chico and Sometimes Zeppo: A History of the Marx Brothers and a Satire on the Rest of the World*

———. *Tex Avery, King of Cartoons*

———. *The Walter Lantz Story*
Barrier, Michael. *Hollywood Cartoons: American Animation in its Golden Age*
Beck, Jerry. *Looney Tunes and Merrie Melodies*
Coniam, Matthew. *The Annotated Marx Brothers*
Culhane, Shamus. *Talking Animals and Other People*
Canemaker, John. *Two Guys Named Joe*
Kane, Bob. *Batman and Me*
Kenworthy, John. *The Hand Behind the Mouse*
Lenburg, Jeff. *The Encyclopedia of Animated Cartoons*
———. *The Great Cartoon Directors*
Maltin, Leonard. *Of Mice and Magic*
Marx, Groucho. *The Groucho Phile*
Merritt, Russell and J.B. Kaufman. *Walt Disney's Silly Symphonies, A Companion to the Classic Cartoon Series*
Mitchell, Glenn. *The Marx Brothers Encyclopedia*
Mitchell-Waite, Antony and Joanne. *Laurel & Hardy's Animated Antics A–Z 3rd Edition*
Scheimer, Lou. *Creating the Filmation Generation*
Smith, Andrew T. *Marx & Re-Marx: Creating And Re-Creating The Lost Marx Brothers Radio Series*
Yahn, Michael. *The Music Of The Marx Brothers, A Bio-Discography of the Works of Groucho, Harpo, Chico, Gummo, and Zeppo Marx*

DVD

Behind the Tunes: Looney Tunes—A Cast of Thousands (2006).
The CooCoo Nut Grove (1936). Audio commentary by Michael Barrier.
The Marx Brothers in a Nutshell (1982)
Popeye Meets William Tell (1940). Audio commentary by Shamus Culhane.

Websites

Arcade-History.com
BCdB.com
BehindTheVoiceActors.com
ClosingLogos.com
IMdB.com
Ebay.com
Intanibase.com
Jet.com
MarxBrothers.nu
NewsFromMe.com
SickBricks.com
Toonopedia.com
Vlasic.com
YouTube.com

EPILOGUE

AT AGE 85, Groucho Marx was enjoying his career revival, but he had never seen a Marxtoon, although Walt Disney had personally presented him with a signed cel from *Mother Goose Goes Hollywood* (1938), which was proudly displayed in his home. On February 13, 1975, Groucho went to Disney Studios along with his companion, Erin Fleming, and his assistant, Henry J. Golas, at the invitation of Dave Smith, Head Archivist to The Walt Disney Studios. At Disney, they were met by "Groucho groupies" before walking to one of the screening rooms on the third floor of the Animation Building to watch *Mickey's Polo Team* (1936), *Mother Goose Goes Hollywood* (1938), and *The Autograph Hound* (1939).

Groucho enjoyed the Marxtoons, and later borrowed screeners from Disney to show at his house. Smith says, "Groucho was quite spry, and still had his sense of humor. As we walked back to the parking lot, he kept making jokes—some funny, some not so funny. One I remember. We had been talking about a famous star who just died, and he said, 'More and more people are dying recently; people who have never died before.'"

NOTES

Acknowledgements

"Over thirty years ago": The 1986 *Freedonia Gazette* Annual Open House Program of Film and Video Clips.

"'Examples are discovered'": Mitchell.

Introduction

"Felix the Cat": Mitchell-Waite.

"'I wonder'": 24 FPS on the Animation Show Forum, quoted in Mitchell-Waite.

"Michael Barrier says": Audio commentary to the DVD of *The CooCoo Nut Grove*.

"Animators such as Joe Grant": ibid.

"Keith Scott says": In the documentary *Behind the Tunes: Looney Tunes—A Cast of Thousands* (2006).

"big feet": In real life, Garbo's shoe size was a Women's 7AA, but her preference for men's footwear and house slippers on film sets gave rise to the legend that she had big feet. http://www.garboforever.com/Garbos_Beauty-07.htm)

Chapter 1

Casts and crews compiled from IMdB.com and BCdB.com unless stated otherwise. Discrepancies are noted. Some details of Silly Symphonies come from Merritt. Synopses and reviews are my own, unless specified otherwise.

"Walt Disney": Lenburg, *The Great Cartoon Directors.*

"Bosko": Barrier, Maltin.

"Isadore 'Friz' Freleng": Lenburg, *The Great Cartoon Directors.*

"*Celebrity Chase*": Title from Ira Dolnick, personal correspondence.

"Scrappy": Maltin, *Of Mice and Magic.*

"his little brother": Scrappyland.com. He is not referred to by name in any of the movies I've seen. Various sources call him Oopie or Poopsie or Vonsey or Vontzy, but we will refer to him in this book as Oopy.

"Walter Lantz was": Lenburg, *The Great Cartoon Directors.*

"Walt Disney asked Iwerks": Kenworthy.

"Joe Grant": Canemaker.

"Jasmine Bligh": Drinnon.

"*Movie Star Mickey* (1933)": BCdB.com.

"*Lessons for Birds*": Title from personal correspondence with Ira Dolnick.

"After Harman and Ising": Toonopedia.

"*Cubby's World Flight* (1933)": Synopsis from IMdB.com, written by this author.

"Ub Iwerks": Lenburg, *The Great Cartoon Directors.*

BCdB.com speculates that other Flip shorts originally may have been in color.

"Willie Whopper": Lenburg, *The Great Cartoon Directors.*

"*Cleopatra* (1917)": IMdB.com.

"George Winkler": Lenburg, *The Great Cartoon Directors.*

"Dave Fleischer": ibid.

"Popeye": op. cit.

"ComiColor": supra.

"*The Steadfast Tin Soldier*": Mitchell-Waite.

"Buddy": Sutton.

"'But the court scene'": Merritt.

Merritt says Legs is based on Edward G. Robinson, but he seems to be more of a composite of contemporaneous tough-guy actors.

"Episode 17": Haendiges.

"First Buddy color short": Sutton.

"*Mickey's Polo Team* (1936)": Cast: BCdB.com credits Pinto Colvig and does not credit Ned Norton.

"Animator Dick Huemer": Canemaker.

"His original sketches": See them online at http://npgportraits.si.edu/emuseumnpg/code/emuseum.asp?style=text¤trecord=81&page=seealso&profile=CAP&searchdesc=Related%20to%20Joseph%20Grant.......&searchstring=constituentid/,/is/,/67578/,/false/,/true&newvalues=1&newcurrentrecord=1

"A Columbia Color Rhapsody": https://jet.com/product/Doctor-Bluebird-Movie-Poster-Print-27-x-40/e04b1572456a4411834a4fce5e2af991.

"Freleng was put": Lenburg, *The Great Cartoon Directors.*

"Terrytoons": Maltin, *Of Mice and Magic.*

"*Mother Goose Goes Hollywood* (1938)": IMdB.com credits Dave Barry for Groucho and the other voices, BCdB.com credits Pinto Colvig. "Joe Penner" sure sounds like Colvig to me. Groucho doesn't have any actual lines, unless singing in the chorus counts.

"*The Hollywoods*": Merritt.

"Nominated": BCdB.com.

"Mickey Mouse became": Maltin, *Of Mice and Magic.*

"The Nellie series": IMdB.com.

"Woody Woodpecker": "In a May 5, 1981, interview with Lowell Elliott, a Lantz studio staffer, Joe Adamson discovered that the Woody Woodpecker of *Knock Knock* (1940) started life as a caricature of Harpo Marx, before further development of the storyboard effected his evolution into a very wacky but noisy woodpecker bearing only a passing resemblance to Harpo." (Joe Adamson, personal correspondence.)

"*Busy Bakers* (1940)": BCBD.com says Pinto Colvig also did voices on this movie.

"One of a series": Maltin, *Of Mice and Magic.*

"*Puttin on the Act* (1940)": Sammy Timberg info from TimbergAlley.com.

"Shamus Culhane agrees." DVD commentary, *Popeye the Sailor, Volume 2, 1938–40.*

"*Mississippi Swing*": IMdB.com says this came out February 7, 1939. The *Gone With the Wind* (1939) references would seem to put it after the release of that film, which came out at the end of the year. Also, February 7, 1939 was a Tuesday, and February 7, 1941 was a Friday, which seems a more likely day to release a movie. The BCdB says February 7, 1941, and the credits appear to read "MCMXLI".

"'Abdul the Bulbul-Ameer'": Song history from IMdB.com. Cast from YouTube.

"Harry Stanton": IMdB.com

"painting backgrounds for Oswald": Lenburg, *The Great Cartoon Directors.*

"Sally Strand": IMdB.com.

"Gable kisses him": IMdB.com.

"Celebrity caricatures": IMdB.com.

"Comedy Store": BCdB.com.

"Animated Antics": Maltin, *Of Mice and Magic*; BCdB.com, and Lenburg, *The Encyclopedia of Animated Cartoons.*

"*Who's Zoo In Hollywood* (1940)": Info from BCdB.com and IMdB.com.

"*Red Riding Hood Rides Again* (1941)": Some sources give the release date as December 25, 1941. The IMdB does not credit Michael Maltese. If he did write it, this would be his first known Marxtoon.

"Academy Award Nominee": BCdB.com.

"In 1944": Maltin, *Of Mice and Magic.*

"Friz Freleng": Unpublished memoirs.

"'Groucho adopts'": Mitchell.

"Katherine Allamong Jacob": Jacob.

"Dayton Allen": https://www.youtube.com/watch?v=VVCfepf-L3c.

"Song Car-Tunes": Maltin, *Of Mice and Magic.*

"*Out Again, In Again* (1948)": Dayton Allen is credited here according to IMdB.com and BCdB.com, but this was the era Ned Sparks voiced Heckle and Jeckle. Perhaps Dayton Allen did the Groucho imitation? Roy Halee would also play Heckle and Jeckle later in the series, but before the Dayton Allen era. It is unclear what he did here.

"'were basically antagonistic'": Maltin.

"*Movie Madness* (1951)": IMdB again credits Dayton Allen for Heckle and Jeckle, but this was the Roy Halee era. BCdB credits both actors as playing Heckle and Jeckle. Again, it seems likely that Dayton Allen at least did the Groucho imitation.

"Kartunes": BCdB.com.

"Little Audrey": Maltin, *Of Mice and Magic.*

"Robert McKimson started": Lenburg, *The Great Cartoon Directors.*

"The last executive": Maltin, *Of Mice and Magic.*

"The last of the Merrie Melodies": IMdB.com.

"Robert McKimson": Lenburg, *The Great Cartoon Directors.*

"political incorrectness": IMdB.com.

"Isambard Kingdom Brunel": http://www.ssgreatbritain.org/story/isambard-kingdom-brunel.

"*About Face* (1978)": Description and credits: Amidi, "*About Face* [1978] by Chris James," Youtube.

"Winner": BCdB.com.

"Partners David DePatie and Friz Freleng": Lenburg, *The Great Cartoon Directors.*

"*The Looney, Looney, Looney Bugs Bunny Movie*": IMdB.com.

"*Dot and the Kangaroo*": http://www.loyalbooks.com/book/dot-and-the-kangaroo-by-ethel-c-pedley.

"An animated film": IMdB.com.

"Technically the last": IMdB.com.

"The movie's failure": IMdB.com.

"*Aladdin* (1992)": Beck, *The Animated Movie Guide.*

"Joe Grant": Canemaker.

Chapter 2

"William Hanna": Lenburg, *The Great Cartoon Directors.*

"Snagglepuss": Toonopedia. Snaggletooth is sometimes considered a different character.

"'So What and the Seven Whatnots'" Airdate from BCdB.com.

"Groucho Marx wrote": Lenburg, *The Great Cartoon Directors.*

"*The Mad, Mad, Mad Comedians*": BCdB.com also credits Frees with playing Harpo Marx, who has no lines, only whistles and honks.

"later performed in Vaudeville": Bader.

"heavily edited": The Vaudeville script appears in *The Groucho Phile.*

Magic Shadows (1974) cancellation date: Email from tvo.org.

"*Electric Company*": Sources vary on episode number. Show info from IMdB.com

"*The Robonic Stooges* [1978]": Lenburg, *The Encyclopedia of Animated Cartoons.*

Title: "When *Skatebirds* was cancelled and CBS spun the Robonic [Stooges] off into their own half hour series in early 1978, some sources reflect that the series was in TV listings, by CBS, as *The Three Robonic Stooges…* but, to the best of my knowledge:
[1.] Hanna-Barbera never generated a new title card or revised the toons to reflect the network's name-tweak. The toons always said *The Robonic Stooges.*
[2.] The spinoff aired the two alternate openings carried over from *Skatebirds*, and both show onscreen and are heard in John

Stephenson's voiceover as *The Robonic Stooges*." (Brent Seguine, personal correspondence.)

"After leaving": Lenburg, *The Great Cartoon Directors.*

Crazy Claws (1981) quotes from IMdB.com.

"*Alice Through the Looking Glass* (1987)": Release date estimated in BCdB.com.

"*Muppet Babies* [1984]": Lenburg, *The Encyclopedia of Animated Cartoons.*

"*The Real Ghostbusters* (1986)": ibid.

"Chip 'n Dale": op. cit."*Tiny Toon Adventures* (1990)": supra.

"Sherri Stoner once said": "Animaniacs Tribute."

"*Bonkers (1993)*": Barat.

"*Animaniacs* (1993)": Lammle.

"Tom Ruegger": IMdB.com.

"Spielberg said": Closs.

"Michelangelo": Michelangelo looks and sounds like Kirk Douglas. He previously appeared in the episode "Hooked on a Ceiling" (1993). Why Douglas instead of Charlton Heston, who played Michelangelo in *The Agony and the Ecstasy* (1965)? Tom Ruegger explains, sort of: "You know, here's my guess: We had this great caricature of Kirk Douglas. We didn't have such a great drawing of Charlton Heston. Also, the voice for Kirk is so much funnier than Charlton, at least what we were doing Charlton." From: http://thatguywiththeglasses.wikia.com/wiki/Animaniacs_Tribute

"good, marketable character": Davis in a 1982 interview with *The Washington Post.*

"*Bump in the Night* (1994)": Lenburg, *The Encyclopedia of Animated Cartoons.*

"*The Simpsons* (1989)": BCdB.com.

"Felix the Cat": Lenburg, *The Encyclopedia of Animated Cartoons.*

"*Duckman: Private Dick/Family Man* (1994)": Lenburg, *The Encyclopedia of Animated Cartoons.*

"*Celebrity Deathmatch* (1998)": BCdB.com.

""[I]t was cancelled"": TV.com.

"*Pokémon* (1997)": Airdate is English dub in the United States.

"Pokémon is": Boyes.

"*Clone High* (2001)": Lenburg, *The Encyclopedia of Animated Cartoons.*

"An anime series": Lenburg, *The Encyclopedia of Animated Cartoons.*

"*Home Movies* (1999)": IMdB.com.

"*The Fairly Oddparents* (2001)": IMdB.com.

"*Family Guy* (1999)": IMdB.com.

"Dipper and Mabel": BCdb.com.

"*The Garfield Show* [2008]": Airdate from TVGuide.com.

"*Pluto's Judgement Day* (1935)": IMdB.com.

"*Little Charley Bear* (2011)": IMdB.com.

"Ferrante recalls": Personal correspondence.

"'I was given'": Personal correspondence.

Chapter 4

Details of credits and commercials extrapolated from repeated viewings and from Kazaleh, "Groucho Marx for Desoto," which includes a reprint of the article "Abstract Animation for a Desoto Commercial" from *Broadcasting* magazine, June 6, 1955.

PP also did some concept art that seems to have never been used: https://comics.ha.com/itm/animation-art/groucho-marx-you-bet-your-life-title-concept-drawing-group-playhouse-pictures-c-late-1950s-total-3-items-/a/121516-13183.s.

"Ray Patin Studios": http://www.ebay.com/itm/1950s-GROUCHO-MARX-Animation-Drawing-commercial-cartoon-modern-/311653218365?hash=item488ffab83d:g:fbcAAOSw7NNT6lWs.

Chapter 5

"*The New Marx Bros. Show*": In the DVD of the pilot, the credits simply state, "The Marx Bros. in *A Day at the Horse Opera*." Title of the series is from the ad in *Broadcasting* magazine, February 14, 1966.

"In 2009": Beck, *Filmation's Marx Brothers?*

Credits from the DVD and Scheimer.

"Lou Scheimer": Scheimer.

"*The Marx Brothers Show*": Credits assembled from the recording and correspondence with Frank Ferrante and Doug Stone. Stone also supplied details of the production.

"It was to be": Goldsmith.

Chapter 6

Flip Books

"Flip-O-Vision": Friedman; Maltin, "A Harpo Marx Flip Book… And More"

Vlasic Pickle Marxtoons

"What does a lovable stork": http://www.vlasic.com/meet-the-stork.

"In 1977": Sporn.

"Pat Harrington": Kazaleh, "Celebrity Voices Impersonated".

"1982": A commenter on YouTube claims the Stork here is Ron Masak.

Made-For-Video Marxtoons

"*Laughter is Good Medicine* (1982)": Credits are from video.

"Norman Cousins": http://www.laughteronlineuniversity.com/norman-cousins-a-laughterpain-case-study/.

"Super Vidéo Productions": www.closinglogos.com.

"two movies and a TV series": IMdB.com.

Marxtoon Mii Avatars

"Mii Avatars": Mitchell-Waite.

Internet Marxtoons

Unless noted otherwise, titles, usernames, dates, and descriptions (where in quotes) are verbatim from YouTube, with minor changes in punctuation and formatting in some cases. This is the wild and woolly world of the web.

"Dubya and the Monkey": Hahn.

"Machinima": http://www.avatarrepertorytheater.org/machinima.php.

"actually a bonobo": Hahn.

"spuriously attributed": Wikiquote.

"It is unclear": Private messages to StarryNightProdsInc went unanswered.

"Oliver Simonsen": Personal correspondence with Oliver Simonsen.

"Stoliar narrates.": Personal correspondence with Steve Stoliar.

"Sprites": Personal correspondence with Josh Udvig.

"Harpo asks": Synopsis from personal correspondence with RonJammin.

"*Phil Hartman's Flat TV: You Bet Your Life*" (2016): Evans.

You Bet Your Life [1950] Slot Machine (2006)

"Arcade History": http://www.arcade-history.com/?n=you-bet-your-life&page=detail&id=6151.

Marx Emoji (2006)

Personal correspondence with Terry Motley.

Chapter 7

"'Who's Afraid of the Big, Bad Wolf'": Coniam.

"*Betty in Blunderland* (1933)": Personal correspondence with Ira Dolnick.

"Popeye": Mitchell.

"gossip column": Skolsky.

"*Porky's Road Race* (1937)": Mitchell.

"Dopey": Mitchell.

"*Pinocchio*": Rayner.

"Jerry Beck": Beck, *Looney Tunes and Merrie Melodies.*

"Daws Butler": https://www.youtube.com/watch?v=EPPaFZclOTk

"In 1961": Evanier, October 25, 2007.

"Bob Kane": Kane.

"In 1979": Scheimer.

"Mark Evanier": Evanier, October 25, 2007 and December 19, 2011.

"Animated TV pilots rejected": WSJ. Morey Amsterdam was discussing his proposed pilot as late as 1976: https://news.google.com/newspapers?nid=1356&dat=19760716&id=nAYkAAAAIBAJ&sjid=jwUEAAAAIBAJ&pg=5508,3627228&hl=en.

"*Animaniacs*": IMdB.com.

"*Wandering Warners We*": Lammle.

"*Sam & Max*": https://www.youtube.com/watch?v=fc6998pK1ak&list=PL29CA9B765F78EDDBv=fc6998pK1ak&list=PL6F5E9FD99326F98C.

"Kirby": http://kirby.wikia.com/wiki/Marx.

"*Let's Play Kirby Superstar | (Ep.7) Groucho Marx* (2013)": https://www.youtube.com/watch?v=3DNApbFo82s&t=1199s

"Animal Crossing": http://animalcrossing.wikia.com/wiki/Groucho.

"Purple Koopa Bro.": http://fantendo.wikia.com/wiki/Marx_(PKB).

"*Sick Bricks*": SickBricks.com

"Hitler": https://www.youtube.com/watch?v=dDnmZrZQNzo

"Chico's Monkey Farm": https://www.youtube.com/watch?v=s8kAXeYQzbE

"In 2009": Beck, "Filmation's Marx Brothers?"

"In 2016": Personal correspondence.

"Frank Welker": Bradshaw.

Epilogue

"February 13, 1975": Date from personal correspondence with Henry Golas and Dave Smith, confirmed by Groucho's calendar on eBay and an actual program from the event, in the Groucho Marx Archives at the Smithsonian Institution National Museum of American History Archives Center.

"Dave Smith": Personal correspondence with Dave Smith.

INDEX

Numbers in **bold** indicate photographs

ABOUT THE AUTHOR

MATTHEW HAHN is an award-winning filmmaker, a published cartoonist, and a pioneering Maryland craft brewer. He endowed Freedonia/Marxonia, an annual Marx Brothers festival held at State University of New York-Fredonia, with his wife Cheri. They live outside Washington, DC, with Thelma Todd and ZaSu Pitts.

www.ingramcontent.com/pod-product-compliance
Lightning Source LLC
LaVergne TN
LVHW050630100826
845148LV00011B/1812

* 9 7 8 1 6 2 9 3 3 2 2 4 6 *